A WHOLE NEW MIND

S "AUDACIOUS AND POWERFUL."

—*The Miami Herald*

"MASTERFUL."

—*Fort Worth Star-Telegram*

ly favorite business book."

–Thomas L. Friedman,

uthor of *The World Is Flat*

"ORIGINAL."

—Tom Peters

ROFOUND."

—*Booklist*

"THOUGHT-PROVOKING."

—*International Herald Tribune*

WOW! A WHOLE NEW MIND IS ONE OF THOSE RARE BOOKS THAT MARKS A TURNING POINT."

—Seth Godin

PRAISE FOR

A Whole New Mind

"This book is a miracle. On the one hand, it provides a completely original and profound analysis of the most pressing personal and economic issue of the days ahead—how the gargantuan changes wrought by technology and globalization are going to impact the way we live and work and imagine our world. Then, Dan Pink provides an equally original and profound and practical guidebook for survival—and joy—in this topsy-turvy environment. I was moved and disturbed and exhilarated all at once. A few years ago, Peter Drucker wondered whether the modern economy would ever find its Copernicus. With this remarkable book, we just may have discovered our Copernicus for the brave new age that's accelerating into being." —Tom Peters

"[Pink's] ideas and approaches are wise, compassionate, and supportive of a variety of personal and professional endeavors. It's a pleasant and surprisingly entertaining little trip as he explores the workings of the brain, celebrates the proliferation and democratization of Target's designer products, and learns to draw and play games, all as a means of illustrating ways we can think and live in a better, more meaningful and productive manner. What surprised me about this book is how Pink realized that to empower individuals, it's necessary to really understand and act upon the powerful socioeconomic forces that shape the world economy. Unlike many of the recent xenophobic screeds that rail against the evils of outsourcing, Pink has figured out several paths that individuals and society can pursue that play to our strengths. So if Pink is correct, we're almost there. All it may take is for individuals and institutions to recognize this reality by using the tools we already possess. And that may well require *A Whole New Mind*." —*The Miami Herald*.

"Since Pink's . . . *Free Agent Nation* has become a cornerstone of employee-management relations, expect just as much buzz around his latest theory."

—*Publishers Weekly*

continued . . .

"A breezy, good-humored read . . . For those wishing to give their own creative muscles a workout, the book is full of exercises and resources."

—*Harvard Business Review*

"Former White House speechwriter Daniel H. Pink, an informed and insightful commentator on social, economic, and cultural trends, has questioned the conventional wisdom from which most Americans draw their thinking on the way the world works. The author of this well-researched and delightfully well-written treatise delivers that assertion after transporting the reader through a consciousness-awakening examination of how the information age, characterized predominantly by L-Directed (left brain) Thinking is being superseded by an age of high concept and touch, which brings R-Directed (right brain) Thinking more into play. The L-Directed Thinking is particularly in evidence in the guidance he provides to readers in what to read, where to go, and what to do to learn how to more fully engage their right hemispheres."

—*Fort Worth Star-Telegram*

"Will give you a new way to look at your work, your talent, your future."

—*Worthwhile*

"Read this book. Even more important, give this book to your children."

—Alan Webber, founding editor of *Fast Company*

"'Abundance, Asia, and automation.' Try saying that phrase five times quickly, because if you don't take these words into serious consideration, there is a good chance that sooner or later your career will suffer because of one of those forces. Pink, bestselling author of *Free Agent Nation* and also former chief speechwriter for former vice president Al Gore, has crafted a profound read packed with an abundance of references to books, seminars, websites, and such to guide your adjustment to expanding your right brain if you plan to survive and prosper in the Western world."

—*Booklist*

A WHOLE NEW MIND

WHY RIGHT-BRAINERS WILL RULE THE FUTURE

Daniel H. Pink

RIVERHEAD BOOKS

New York

RIVERHEAD BOOKS
Published by the Penguin Group
Penguin Group (USA) LLC
375 Hudson Street, New York, New York 10014, USA

USA • Canada • UK • Ireland • Australia • New Zealand • India • South Africa • China

penguin.com

A Penguin Random House Company

The Library of Congress has catalogued the Riverhead hardcover edition as follows:

Pink, Daniel H.
A whole new mind: moving from the Information Age to the Conceptual Age / Daniel H. Pink.
p. cm.
Includes bibliographical references and index.
ISBN 1-57322-308-5
1. Creative thinking. 2. Success—Psychological aspects. I. Title.
BF408.P49 2005 2004056948
158—dc22

First Riverhead hardcover edition: March 2005
First Riverhead trade paperback edition: March 2006
Riverhead trade paperback ISBN: 978-1-59448-171-0

PRINTED IN THE UNITED STATES OF AMERICA

35 34 33 32 31 30

Cover and stepback design by Benjamin Gibson
Cover and stepback art by CSA Images
Book design by Amanda Dewey

In memory of

MOLLIE LAVIN

CONTENTS

Introduction 1

PART ONE

The Conceptual Age

One Right Brain Rising 7

Two Abundance, Asia, and Automation 28

Three High Concept, High Touch 48

PART TWO

The Six Senses

Introducing the Six Senses 65

Four Design 68

Five Story 100

Six Symphony 129

Seven Empathy 158

Eight Play 185

Nine Meaning 216

Afterword 245

Notes 248

Acknowledgments 265

Index 268

"I have known strong minds, with imposing, undoubting, Cobbett-like manners; but I have never met a great mind of this sort. The truth is, a great mind must be androgynous."

—SAMUEL TAYLOR COLERIDGE

INTRODUCTION

The last few decades have belonged to a certain kind of person with a certain kind of mind—computer programmers who could crank code, lawyers who could craft contracts, MBAs who could crunch numbers. But the keys to the kingdom are changing hands. The future belongs to a very different kind of person with a very different kind of mind—creators and empathizers, pattern recognizers, and meaning makers. These people—artists, inventors, designers, storytellers, caregivers, consolers, big picture thinkers—will now reap society's richest rewards and share its greatest joys.

This book describes a seismic—though as yet undetected—shift now under way in much of the advanced world. We are moving from an economy and a society built on the logical, linear, computerlike capabilities of the Information Age to an economy and a society built on the inventive, empathic, big-picture capabilities of what's rising in its place, the Conceptual Age. *A Whole New Mind* is for anyone who wants to survive and thrive in this emerging world—people uneasy in their careers or dissatisfied with their lives, entrepreneurs and business leaders eager to stay ahead of the next wave, parents who want to equip their children for the future, and the legions of emotionally astute and creatively adroit people whose distinctive abilities the Information Age has often overlooked and undervalued.

In this book, you will learn the six essential aptitudes—what I call "the six senses"—on which professional success and personal satisfaction increasingly will depend. Design. Story. Symphony. Empathy. Play. Meaning. These are fundamentally human abilities that everyone can master—and helping you do that is my goal.

A CHANGE of such magnitude is complex. But the argument at the heart of this book is simple. For nearly a century, Western society in general, and American society in particular, has been dominated by a form of thinking and an approach to life that is narrowly reductive and deeply analytical. Ours has been the age of the "knowledge worker," the well-educated manipulator of information and deployer of expertise. But that is changing. Thanks to an array of forces—material abundance that is deepening our nonmaterial yearnings, globalization that is shipping white-collar work overseas, and powerful technologies that are eliminating certain kinds of work altogether—we are entering a new age. It is an age animated by a different form of thinking and a new approach to life—one that prizes aptitudes that I call "high concept" and "high touch."[1] High concept involves the capacity to detect patterns and opportunities, to create artistic and emotional beauty, to craft a satisfying narrative, and to combine seemingly unrelated ideas into something new. High touch involves the ability to empathize with others, to understand the subtleties of human interaction, to find joy in one's self and to elicit it in others, and to stretch beyond the quotidian in pursuit of purpose and meaning.

As it happens, there's something that encapsulates the change I'm describing—and it's right inside your head. Our brains are divided into two hemispheres. The left hemisphere is sequential, logical, and analytical. The right hemisphere is nonlinear, intuitive, and holistic. These distinctions have often been caricatured. And, of course, we enlist both halves of our brains for even the simplest tasks. But the well-established differences between the two hemispheres of the brain yield a powerful metaphor for interpreting our present and guiding our future. Today, the defining skills of the previous era—the "left brain" capabilities that powered the Information Age—are necessary but no longer sufficient. And the capabilities we once disdained or thought frivolous—the "right-brain" qualities of inventiveness, empathy, joyfulness, and meaning—increasingly will determine who flourishes and who flounders. For individuals, families, and organizations, professional success and personal fulfillment now require a whole new mind.

A FEW WORDS about the organization of this book. Perhaps not surprisingly, *A Whole New Mind* is itself high concept and high touch. Part One—the Conceptual Age—lays out the broad animating idea. Chapter 1 provides an overview of the key differences between our left and right hemispheres and explains why the structure of our brains offers such a powerful metaphor for the contours of our times. In Chapter 2, I make a resolutely hardheaded case, designed to appeal to the most left-brained among you, for why three huge social and economic forces—Abundance, Asia, and Automation—are nudging us into the Conceptual Age. Chapter 3 explains high concept and high touch and illustrates why people who master these abilities will set the tempo of modern life.

Part Two—the Six Senses—is high touch. It covers the six essential abilities you'll need to make your way across this emerging landscape. Design. Story. Symphony. Empathy. Play. Meaning. I devote one chapter to each of these six senses, describing how it is being put to use in business and everyday life. Then, at the end of each of these chapters, marked off by shaded pages, is a Portfolio—a collection of tools, exercises, and further reading culled from my research and travels that can help you surface and sharpen that sense.

In the course of the nine chapters of this book, we'll cover a lot of ground. We'll visit a laughter club in Bombay, tour an inner-city American high school devoted to design, and learn how to detect an insincere smile anywhere in the world. But we need to start our journey in the brain itself—to learn how it works before we learn how to work it. So the place to begin is the National Institutes of Health in Bethesda, Maryland, where I'm strapped down, flat on my back, and stuffed inside a garage-size machine that is pulsing electromagnetic waves through my skull.

PART ONE

The Conceptual Age

One

RIGHT BRAIN RISING

The first thing they do is attach electrodes to my fingers to see how much I sweat. If my mind attempts deception, my perspiration will rat me out. Then they lead me to the stretcher. It's swaddled in crinkly blue paper, the kind that rustles under your legs when you climb onto a doctor's examination table. I lie down, the back of my head resting in the recessed portion of the stretcher. Over my face, they swing a cagelike mask similar to the one used to muzzle Hannibal Lecter. I squirm. Big mistake. A technician reaches for a roll of thick adhesive. "You can't move," she says. "We're going to need to tape your head down."

Outside this gargantuan government building, a light May rain is falling. Inside—smack in the center of a chilly room in the subbasement—I'm getting my brain scanned.

I've lived with my brain for forty years now, but I've never actually seen it. I've looked at drawings and images of other people's brains. But I don't have a clue as to what my own brain looks like or how it works. Now's my chance.

For a while now, I've been wondering what direction our lives will take in these outsourced, automated, upside-down times—and I've begun to suspect that the clues might be found in the way the brain is organized. So I've volunteered to be part of the control group—what researchers call "healthy volunteers"—for a project at the National Institute of Mental Health, outside Washington, D.C. The study involves capturing images of brains at rest and at work, which means I'll soon get to see the organ that's been leading me around these past four decades—and, in the process, perhaps gain a clearer view of how all of us will navigate the future.

The stretcher I'm on juts from the middle of a GE Signa 3T, one of the world's most advanced magnetic resonance imaging (MRI) machines. This $2.5 million baby uses a powerful magnetic field to generate high-quality images of the inside of the human body. It's a huge piece of equipment, spanning nearly eight feet on each side and weighing more than 35,000 pounds.

At the center of the machine is a circular opening, about two feet in diameter. The technicians slide my stretcher through the opening and into the hollowed-out core that forms the belly of this beast. With my arms pinned by my side and the ceiling about two inches above my nose, I feel like I've been crammed into a torpedo tube and forgotten.

TCHKK! TCHKK! TCHKK! goes the machine. *TCHKK! TCHKK! TCHKK!* It sounds and feels like I'm wearing a helmet that somebody is tapping from the outside. Then I hear a vibrating

ZZZHHHH! followed by silence, followed by another *ZZZHHHH!* and then more silence.

After a half hour, they've got a picture of my brain. To my slight dismay, it looks pretty much like every other brain I've seen in textbooks. Running down the center is a thin vertical ridge that cleaves the brain into two seemingly equal sections. This feature is so prominent that it's the first thing a neurologist notes when he inspects the images of my oh-so-unexceptional brain. "[The] cerebral hemispheres," he reports, "are grossly symmetric." That is, the three-pound clump inside my skull, like the three-pound clump inside yours, is divided into two connected halves. One half is called the left hemisphere, the other the right hemisphere. The two halves look the same, but in form and function they are quite different, as the next phase of my stint as a neurological guinea pig was about to demonstrate.

That initial brain scan was like sitting for a portrait. I reclined, my brain posed, and the machine painted the picture. While science can learn a great deal from these brain portraits, a newer technique—called *functional* magnetic resonance imaging (fMRI)—can capture pictures of the brain in action. Researchers ask subjects to do something inside the machine—hum a tune, listen to a joke, solve a puzzle—and then track the parts of the brain to which blood flows. What results is a picture of the brain spotted with colored blotches in the regions that were active—a satellite weather map showing where the brain clouds were gathering. This technique is revolutionizing science and medicine, yielding a deeper understanding of a range of human experience—from dyslexia in children to the mechanisms of Alzheimer's disease to how parents respond to babies' cries.

The technicians slide me back inside the high-tech Pringles can. This time, they've set up a periscopelike contraption that allows me to see a slide screen outside the machine. In my right hand is a small clicker, its cord attached to their computers. They're about to put my brain to work—and provide me with a metaphor for what it will take to thrive in the twenty-first century.

My first task is simple. They display on the screen a black-and-white photo of a face fixed in an extreme expression. (A woman who looks as if Yao Ming just stepped on her toe. Or a fellow who apparently has just remembered that he left home without putting on pants.) Then they remove that face, and flash on the screen two photos of a different person. Using the buttons on my clicker, I'm supposed to indicate which of those two faces expresses the same emotion as the initial face.

For example, the researchers show me this face:

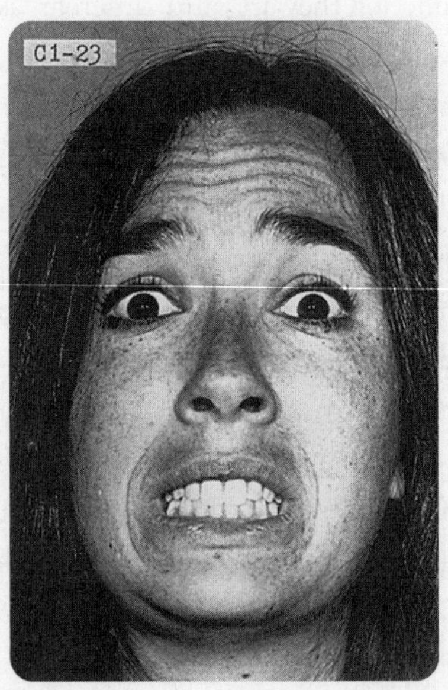

Then they remove it and show me these two faces:

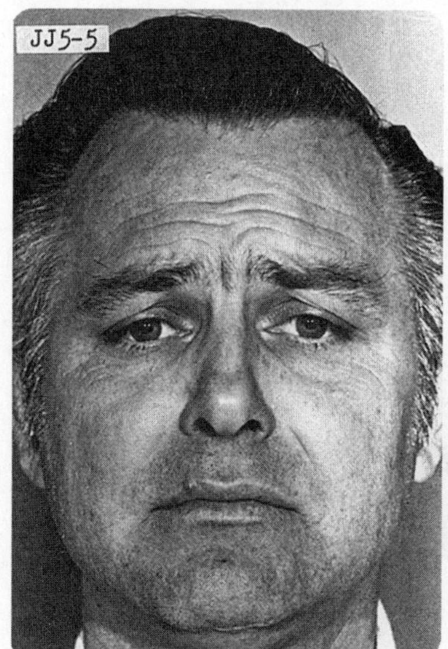

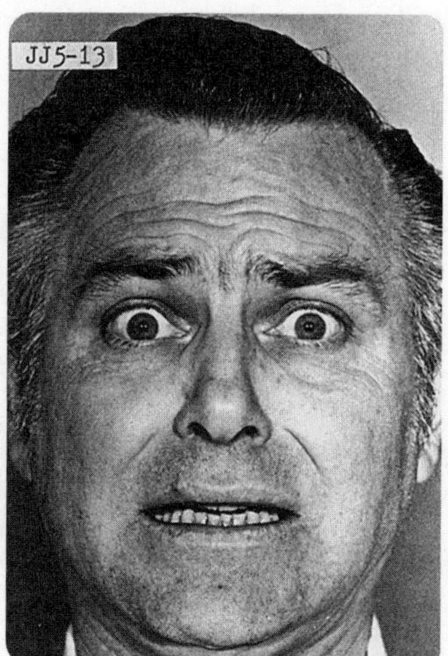

I click the button on the right because the face on the right expresses the same emotion as the earlier face. The task, if you'll pardon the expression, is a no-brainer.

When the facial matching exercise is over, we move to another test of perception. The researchers show me forty-eight color photos, one after another, in the manner of a slide show. I click the appropriate button to indicate whether the scene takes place indoors or outdoors. These photos occupy two extremes. Some are bizarre and disturbing; others are banal and inoffensive. The photos include a coffee mug sitting on a counter, several people brandishing guns, a toilet overflowing with waste, a lamp, and a few explosions.

For instance, the researchers display an image like this:*

So I click the button that indicates that this scene takes place inside. The task requires that I concentrate, but I don't much strain. The exercise feels about the same as the previous one.

What happens inside my brain, however, tells a different story. When the brain scans appear on the computers, they show that when I looked at the grim facial expressions, the right side of my brain sprang into action and enlisted other parts of that hemisphere. When I looked at the scary scenes, my brain instead called in greater sup-

*The photos I saw during this phase of the research came from a standard set of images called the International Affective Picture System (IAPS). The creator and owner of the IAPS, Professor Peter J. Lang of the University of Florida, requested that I not reproduce any of these images in this book. "Making these materials familiar to the general public can seriously compromise their value as stimuli in many research projects," he explained. The image I've reprinted, therefore, is not from the actual IAPS collection. But it is similar in subject, tone, and composition to the photos in this experiment.

port from the left hemisphere.[1] Of course, parts of both sides worked on each task. And I felt precisely the same during each exercise. But the fMRI clearly showed that for faces, my right hemisphere responded more than my left—and for gun-wielding bad guys and similar predicaments, my left hemisphere took the lead.

Why?

The Right (and Left) Stuff

Our brains are extraordinary. The typical brain consists of some 100 billion cells, each of which connects and communicates with up to 10,000 of its colleagues. Together they forge an elaborate network of some one *quadrillion* (1,000,000,000,000,000) connections that guides how we talk, eat, breathe, and move. James Watson, who won the Nobel Prize for helping discover DNA, described the human brain as "the most complex thing we have yet discovered in our universe."[2] (Woody Allen, meanwhile, called it "my second favorite organ.")

Yet for all the brain's complexity, its broad topography is simple and symmetrical. Scientists have long known that a neurological Mason-Dixon Line divides the brain into two regions. And until surprisingly recently, the scientific establishment considered the two regions separate but unequal. The left side, the theory went, was the crucial half, the half that made us human. The right side was subsidiary—the remnant, some argued, of an earlier stage of development. The left hemisphere was rational, analytic, and logical—everything we expect in a brain. The right hemisphere was mute, nonlinear, and instinctive—a vestige that nature had designed for a purpose that humans had outgrown.

As far back as the age of Hippocrates, physicians believed that the left side, the same side that housed the heart, was the essential half.

And by the 1800s, scientists began to accumulate evidence to support that view. In the 1860s, French neurologist Paul Broca discovered that a portion of the left hemisphere controlled the ability to speak language. A decade later, a German neurologist named Carl Wernicke made a similar discovery about the ability to *understand* language. These discoveries helped produce a convenient and compelling syllogism. Language is what separates man from beast. Language resides on the left side of the brain. Therefore the left side of the brain is what makes us human.

This view prevailed for much of the next century—until a soft-spoken Caltech professor named Roger W. Sperry reshaped our understanding of our brains and ourselves. In the 1950s, Sperry studied patients who had epileptic seizures that had required removal of the corpus callosum, the thick bundle of some 300 million nerve fibers that connects the brain's two hemispheres. In a set of experiments on these "split-brain" patients, Sperry discovered that the established view was flawed. Yes, our brains were divided into two halves. But as he put it, "The so-called subordinate or minor hemisphere, which we had formerly supposed to be illiterate and mentally retarded and thought by some authorities to not even be conscious, was found to be in fact the superior cerebral member when it came to performing certain kinds of mental tasks." In other words, the right wasn't inferior to the left. It was just different. "There appear to be two modes of thinking," Sperry wrote, "represented rather separately in the left and right hemispheres, respectively." The left hemisphere reasoned sequentially, excelled at analysis, and handled words. The right hemisphere reasoned holistically, recognized patterns, and interpreted emotions and nonverbal expressions. Human beings were literally of two minds.

This research helped earn Sperry a Nobel Prize in medicine, and forever altered the fields of psychology and neuroscience. When

Sperry died in 1994, *The New York Times* memorialized him as the man who "overturned the prevailing orthodoxy that the left hemisphere was the dominant part of the brain." He was the rare scientist, said the *Times,* whose "experiments passed into folklore."[3]

Sperry, though, had some help transporting his ideas from the laboratory to the living room—in particular, a California State University art instructor named Betty Edwards. In 1979, Edwards published a wonderful book titled *Drawing on the Right Side of the Brain.* Edwards rejected the notion that some people just aren't artistic. "Drawing is not really very difficult," she said. "Seeing is the problem."[4] And the secret to seeing—really seeing—was quieting the bossy know-it-all left brain so the mellower right brain could do its magic. Although some accused Edwards of oversimplifying the science, her book became a bestseller and a staple of art classes. (We'll learn about Edwards's techniques in Chapter 6.)

Thanks to Sperry's pioneering research, Edwards's skillful popularization, and the advent of technologies like the fMRI that allow researchers to watch the brain in action, the right hemisphere today has achieved a measure of legitimacy. It's real. It's important. It helps make us human. No neuroscientist worth her PhD ever disputes that. Yet beyond the neuroscience labs and brain-imaging clinics, two misconceptions about the right side of the brain persist.

The Wrong Stuff

These two misconceptions are opposite in spirit but similar in silliness. The first considers the right brain a savior; the second considers it a saboteur.

Adherents of the savior view have climbed aboard the scientific evidence on the right hemisphere and raced from legitimacy to reverence. They believe that the right brain is the repository of all that is good and just and noble in the human condition. As neuroscientist Robert Ornstein puts it in *The Right Mind*, one of the better books on this subject:

> Many popular writers have written that the right hemisphere is the key to expanding human thought, surviving trauma, healing autism, and more. It's going to save us. It's the seat of creativity, of the soul, and even great casserole ideas.[5]

Oh, my. Over the years, peddlers of the savior theory have tried to convince us of the virtues of right-brain cooking and right-brain dieting, right-brain investing and right-brain accounting, right-brain jogging and right-brain horseback riding—not to mention right-brain numerology, right-brain astrology, and right-brain lovemaking, the last of which may well lead to babies who'll eventually achieve greatness by eating right-brain breakfast cereal, playing with right-brain blocks, and watching right-brain videos. These books, products, and seminars often contain a valid nugget or two—but in general they are positively foolish. Even worse, this cascade of baseless, New Age gobbledygook has often served to degrade, rather than enhance, public understanding of the right hemisphere's singular outlook.

Partly in response to the tide of inane things that have been said about the right brain, a second, contrary bias has also taken hold. This view grudgingly acknowledges the right hemisphere's legitimacy, but believes that emphasizing so-called right-brain thinking risks sabotaging the economic and social progress we've made by applying the force of logic to our lives. All that stuff that the right hemisphere does—interpreting emotional content, intuiting answers, perceiving things holistically—is lovely. But it's a side dish to the main course of true intelligence. What distinguishes us from other animals is our ability to reason analytically. We are humans, hear us calculate. That's what makes us unique. Anything else isn't simply different; it's *less.* And paying too much attention to those artsy-fartsy, touchy-feely elements will eventually dumb us down and screw us up. "What it comes down to," Sperry said shortly before he died, "is that modern society [still] discriminates against the right hemisphere." Within the saboteur position is the residual belief that although the right side of our brains is real, it's still somehow inferior.

Alas, the right hemisphere will neither save us nor sabotage us. The reality, as is so often the case with reality, is more nuanced.

The Real Stuff

The two hemispheres of our brains don't operate as on-off switches—one powering down as soon as the other starts lighting up. Both halves play a role in nearly everything we do. "We can say that certain regions of the brain are more active than others when it comes to certain functions," explains one medical primer, "but we can't say those functions are confined to particular areas."[6] Still, neuroscientists agree that the two hemispheres take significantly different approaches to guiding our actions, understanding the world, and reacting to events. (And those differences, it turns out, offer considerable guidance for piloting our personal and professional lives.) With more than three decades of research on the brain's hemispheres, it's possible to distill the findings to four key differences.

1. The left hemisphere controls the right side of the body; the right hemisphere controls the left side of the body.

Raise your right hand. Seriously, if you can, hold your right hand high in the air. Your left hemisphere (or, more accurately, a region of your left hemisphere) did that. Now, if you're able, tap your left foot. A region of your right hemisphere did that. Our brains are "contralateral"—that is, each half of the brain controls the opposite half of the body. That's why a stroke on the right side of someone's brain will make it difficult for that person to move the left side of her body and a stroke on the left side will impair the functioning of the right. Since roughly 90 percent of the population is right-handed, that means that in roughly 90 percent of the population, the left hemisphere is controlling important movements such as handwriting, eating, and maneuvering a computer mouse.

Contralateralization comes into play, not only when we sign our name or kick a ball, but also when we move our heads and our eyes. Here's another exercise. Turn your head slowly to the left. Once again, the opposite hemisphere—the right side of your brain—largely guided that maneuver. Now turn your head slowly to the right. This time, the left hemisphere did the steering. Now, using whichever part of your brain you'd like, think of an activity that involves the latter movement—that is, slowly moving your head and eyes from left to right. Here's a hint: you're doing it now. In Western languages, reading and writing involve turning from left to right, and therefore exercise the brain's left hemisphere. Written language, invented by the Greeks around 550 B.C.E., has helped reinforce left hemisphere dominance (at least in the West) and created what Harvard classicist Eric Havelock called "the alphabetic mind."[7] So perhaps it's no surprise, then, that the left hemisphere has dominated the game. It's the only side that knows how to write the rules.

2. The left hemisphere is sequential; the right hemisphere is simultaneous.

Consider another dimension of the alphabetic mind: it processes sounds and symbols in sequence. When you read this sentence, you begin with the "when," move to the "you," and decode every letter, every syllable, every word in progression. This, too, is an ability at which your brain's left hemisphere excels. In the sequential words of one neuroscience textbook:

> [T]he left hemisphere [is] particularly good at recognizing *serial events*—events whose elements occur one after the other—and controlling sequences of behavior. The left hemisphere is also involved in controlling serial behaviors. The serial functions performed by the left hemisphere include verbal activities, such as talking, understanding the speech of other people, reading, and writing.[8]

By contrast, the right hemisphere doesn't march in the single-file formation of A-B-C-D-E. Its special talent is the ability to interpret things simultaneously. This side of our brains is "specialized in seeing many things at once: in seeing all the parts of a geometric shape and grasping its form, or in seeing all the elements of a situation and understanding what they mean."[9] This makes the right hemisphere particularly useful in interpreting faces. And it confers on human beings a comparative advantage over computers. For instance, the iMac computer on which I'm typing this sentence can perform a million calculations per second, far more than the fastest left hemisphere on the planet. But even the most powerful computers in the world can't recognize a face with anywhere close to the speed and accuracy of my toddler son. Think of the sequential/simultaneous difference like this: the right hemisphere is the picture; the left hemisphere is the thousand words.

3. The left hemisphere specializes in text;
the right hemisphere specializes in context.

In most people, language originates in the left hemisphere. (This is true of about 95 percent of right-handers and 70 percent of left-handers. In the rest—about 8 percent of the population—the division of linguistic labor is more complicated.) But the right hemisphere doesn't cede full responsibility to the left. Instead, the two sides carry out complementary functions.

Suppose that one night you and your spouse are preparing dinner. Suppose, too, that midway through the preparations, your spouse discovers that you forgot to buy the dinner's most important ingredient. Suppose then that your spouse grabs the car keys, curls a lip, glares at you, and hisses, "I'm going to the store." Nearly everyone with an intact brain would understand two things about the words just uttered. First, your spouse is heading to Safeway. Second, your spouse is pissed. Your left hemisphere figured out the first part—that is, it deciphered the sounds and syntax of your spouse's words and arrived at their literal meaning. But your right hemisphere understood the second aspect of this exchange—that the ordinarily neutral words "I'm going to the store" weren't neutral at all. The glare of the eyes and the hiss of the voice signal that your spouse is angry.

Individuals with damage to one hemisphere can't reach this dual conclusion. A person with an impaired right hemisphere, and thus only a functioning *left* hemisphere, would hear such comments and understand that the spouse is driving to the store—but would remain oblivious to the anger and annoyance fueling the trip. A person with an impaired left hemisphere, and thus only a functioning *right* hemisphere, would understand that the spouse is miffed—but might not know where the spouse just went.

This distinction applies not only to understanding language but also to speaking it. Patients with damage to certain regions of their right hemisphere can talk coherently—abiding the rules of grammar and deploying a standard vocabulary. But as British psychologist Chris McManus notes in his prizewinning book *Right Hand Left Hand*:

> Their language . . . is not normal, lacking the musical quality of speech, prosody, whereby the tone goes up and down, and the words accelerate and decelerate or get louder and softer, providing emotion and emphasis. Speech without prosody is like those computer-synthesized voices one hears on telephones.[10]

To oversimplify just a bit, the left hemisphere handles *what* is said; the right hemisphere focuses on *how* it's said—the nonverbal, often emotional cues delivered through gaze, facial expression, and intonation.

But the distinction between left and right comprises more than the difference between verbal and nonverbal. The text/context distinction, originally put forward by Robert Ornstein, applies more broadly. For instance, certain written languages depend heavily on context. Languages such as Arabic and Hebrew are often written only in consonants, which means the reader must figure out what the vowel is by the surrounding concepts and ideas. In those languages, if you read the equivalent of "stmp n th bg," you'd fill in different vowels depending on whether the phrase appeared in a pest control manual ("stomp on the bug") or a short story about a trip to the post office ("stamp in the bag"). Unlike English, languages that require the reader to supply the vowels by discerning the context are usually written from right to left.[11] And as we learned a few pages ago, moving one's eyes in that direction depends on the brain's right hemisphere.

Context is also important in other dimensions of language. For example, many studies have shown that the right hemisphere is responsible for our ability to comprehend metaphors. If you tell me that José has "a heart the size of Montana," my left hemisphere quickly assesses who José is, what a heart is, and how big Montana is. But when the literal meaning of the sentence doesn't compute—how can a 147,000-square-mile heart fit inside José's modest chest cavity?—it calls in the right hemisphere to resolve the incongruity. The right hemisphere explains to the left that José doesn't have some bizarre cardiac condition but instead is a generous and loving person. "Neither side of the brain . . . can do the job without the other," Ornstein writes. "We need the text of our lives to be in context."[12]

4. The left hemisphere analyzes the details; the right hemisphere synthesizes the big picture.

In 1951, Isaiah Berlin wrote an essay about *War and Peace* and gave it a room-emptying title: "Leo Tolstoy's Historical Skepticism." Berlin's publisher loved the essay but hated the headline, so he changed the title to something catchier: "The Hedgehog and the Fox," after an ancient Greek adage, "The fox knows many things; the hedgehog knows one big thing." The retitled essay helped make Berlin famous. And the concept provides a useful way of illuminating a fourth difference between the two sides of our brain. The left side is a fox; the right side is a hedgehog.

"In general the left hemisphere participates in the *analysis* of information," says a neuroscience primer. "In contrast, the right hemisphere is specialized for *synthesis*; it is particularly good at putting isolated elements together to perceive things as a whole."[13] Analysis and synthesis are perhaps the two most fundamental ways of interpreting information. You can break the whole into its components. Or you can weave the components into a whole. Both are essential to human reasoning. But they are guided by different parts of the brain. Roger Sperry noted this key difference in a paper he wrote (with Jerre Levy-Agresti) in 1968:

> The data indicate that the mute, minor [right] hemisphere is specialized for Gestalt perception, being primarily a synthesist in dealing with information input. The speaking, major hemisphere, in contrast, seems to operate in a more logical, analytic computer-like fashion. Its language is inadequate for the rapid complex syntheses achieved by the minor hemisphere.[14]

The left converges on a single answer; the right diverges into a Gestalt. The left focuses on categories, the right on relationships. The left can grasp the details. But only the right hemisphere can see the big picture.

All of which leads back to those brain scans.

Fear and Loathing in My Amygdalas

Toward the base of the brain sit two almond-shaped structures that serve as the brain's Department of Homeland Security.[15] They're called the amygdalas—and they play a crucial role in processing emotions, especially fear. With one located in the left hemisphere and the other in the right, the amygdalas are ever on the lookout for threats in our midst. Not surprisingly, when I was inside the MRI machine looking at pictures of upset people and unsettling scenes, my amygdalas issued alerts. But which amygdala—left or right—sounded the warning differed considerably depending on which images I was viewing.

As the brain scans later revealed, when I looked at the faces, both of my amygdalas activated—but the right was much more active than the left. When I looked at the scenes, the left was more active than the right. This turns out to be consistent with what we know about the two sides of the brain.

Why did the left side respond more actively to scenes than to faces? Because accurately assessing each scene depended on the rapid-fire sequential reasoning at which the left hemisphere excels. Consider the photo on page 12 and the chain of logic it unfurled: *This is a gun. Guns are dangerous. He's pointing a gun at me. This is a scary situation.* So my left amygdala leaps from its chair, breaks the glass, and pulls the alarm. By contrast, the left amygdala was relatively quiet (though not entirely inactive) when I viewed the faces. That's because the right hemisphere, as countless studies have shown, is specialized both for recognizing faces and for interpreting expressions. Those skills depend not on sequential, analytic reasoning—we don't look at the eyes, then the nose, then the teeth—but on the ability to interpret the parts of the face simultaneously and to synthesize those details into a larger conclusion.

There are also other reasons for my differing responses. Understanding that a man pointing a pistol represents a threat is something we've *learned.* According to Ahmad Hariri, the neuroscientist who headed this portion of the NIH project I participated in, the response to such images is "likely learned through experience and social transmission and, thus, may be derived from, if not dependent on, responses in the left hemisphere brain regions."[16] If I were to show that image to someone who'd never seen a gun, and therefore had never learned that they were dangerous, the reaction might be bewilderment rather than fear. But if I showed the face on page 10 to someone who'd never seen a Caucasian woman, or perhaps had never encountered anyone outside of his own village, he'd still likely be able to identify the expression. In fact, that is precisely what University of California, San Francisco, professor Paul Ekman, who developed this set of images (called the Facial Action Coding System) and whom we'll meet in Chapter 7, has found in thirty-five years of research testing these expressions with subjects ranging from college students to remote tribes in New Guinea: "There has never been an instance in which the majority in two cultures ascribes a different emotion to the same expression."[17]

My brain, then, is not merely ordinary in its looks. It is also ordinary in its actions. Both sides work together—but they have different specialties. The left hemisphere handles logic, sequence, literalness, and analysis. The right takes care of synthesis, emotional expression, context, and the big picture.

A Whole New Mind

There are two kinds of people in the world, an old joke goes: those who believe that everything can be divided into two categories—and the rest of you. Human beings somehow seem naturally inclined to see life in contrasting pairs. East versus West. Mars versus Venus. Logic versus emotion. Left versus right. Yet, in most realms we usually don't have to pick sides—and it's often dangerous if we do. For instance, logic without emotion is a chilly, Spock-like existence. Emotion without logic is a weepy, hysterical world where the clocks are never right and the buses always late. In the end, yin always needs yang.

This is especially true when it comes to our brains. The two sides work in concert—two sections of an orchestra that sounds awful if one side packs up its instruments and goes home. As McManus puts it:

> However tempting it is to talk of right and left hemispheres in isolation, they are actually two half-brains, designed to work together as a smooth, single, integrated whole in one entire, complete brain. The left hemisphere knows how to handle logic and the right hemisphere knows about the world. Put

> the two together and one gets a powerful thinking machine. Use either on its own and the result can be bizarre or absurd.[18]

In other words, leading a healthy, happy, successful life depends on both hemispheres of your brain.

But the contrast in how our cerebral hemispheres operate does yield a powerful *metaphor* for how individuals and organizations navigate their lives. Some people seem more comfortable with logical, sequential, computer-like reasoning. They tend to become lawyers, accountants, and engineers. Other people are more comfortable with holistic, intuitive, and nonlinear reasoning. They tend to become inventors, entertainers, and counselors. And these individual inclinations go on to shape families, institutions, and societies.

Call the first approach *L-Directed Thinking.* It is a form of thinking and an attitude to life that is characteristic of the left hemisphere of the brain—sequential, literal, functional, textual, and analytic. Ascendant in the Information Age, exemplified by computer programmers, prized by hardheaded organizations, and emphasized in schools, this approach is directed *by* left-brain attributes, *toward* left-brain results. Call the other approach *R-Directed Thinking.* It is a form of thinking and an attitude to life that is characteristic of the right hemisphere of the brain—simultaneous, metaphorical, aesthetic, contextual, and synthetic. Underemphasized in the Information Age, exemplified by creators and caregivers, shortchanged by organizations, and neglected in schools, this approach is directed *by* right-brain attributes, *toward* right-brain results.*

*Because very few things human beings do are governed exclusively by one hemisphere or the other, I've chosen the terms "L-Directed" and "R-Directed" instead of the more convenient "left-brain thinking" and "right-brain thinking." This is not a book about neuroscience, of course. It's a book that uses neuroscience to create a metaphor. But even (perhaps especially) in the realm of metaphor, it's important to be true to the science.

Of course, we need both approaches in order to craft fulfilling lives and build productive, just societies. But the mere fact that I feel obliged to underscore that obvious point is perhaps further indication of how much we've been in the thrall of reductionist, binary thinking. Despite those who have deified the right brain beyond all scientific evidence, there remains a strong tilt toward the left. Our broader culture tends to prize L-Directed Thinking more highly than its counterpart, taking this approach more seriously and viewing the alternative as useful but secondary.

But this is changing—and it will dramatically reshape our lives. Left-brain-style thinking used to be the driver and right-brain-style thinking the passenger. Now, R-Directed Thinking is suddenly grabbing the wheel, stepping on the gas, and determining where we're going and how we'll get there. L-Directed aptitudes—the sorts of things measured by the SAT and deployed by CPAs—are still necessary. But they're no longer sufficient. Instead, the R-Directed aptitudes so often disdained and dismissed—artistry, empathy, taking the long view, pursuing the transcendent—will increasingly determine who soars and who stumbles. It's a dizzying—but ultimately inspiring—change. And in the next chapter, I'll explore the reasons why it's happening.

Two

ABUNDANCE, ASIA, AND AUTOMATION

Return with me to the thrilling days of yesteryear—the 1970s, the decade of my childhood. When I was a kid, middle-class parents in the United States typically dished out the same plate of advice to their children: Get good grades, go to college, and pursue a profession that will deliver a decent standard of living and perhaps a dollop of prestige. If you were good at math and science, you should become a doctor. If you were better at English and history, become a lawyer. If blood grossed you out and your verbal skills needed work, become an accountant. A bit later, as computers appeared on desktops and CEOs on magazine covers, the youngsters who were *really* good at math and science chose high tech, while many others flocked to business school, thinking that success was spelled MBA.

Lawyers, doctors, accountants, engineers, and executives. The great Peter Drucker gave this cadre of professionals an enduring, if somewhat wonky, name: "knowledge workers." Knowledge workers are "people who get paid for putting to work what one learns in school rather than for their physical strength or manual skill," Drucker wrote. What distinguished this group from the rest of the workforce was their "ability to acquire and to apply theoretical and analytic knowledge." (In other words, they excelled at L-Directed Thinking.) They might never become a majority, said Drucker, but they nonetheless "will give the emerging knowledge society its character, its leadership, its social profile."[1]

Drucker, as always, was spot-on. Knowledge workers and their thinking style have indeed shaped the character, leadership, and social profile of the modern age. Consider the tollbooths that any middle-class American must pass on his way to the land of knowledge work. Here are some examples: the PSAT, the SAT, the GMAT, the LSAT, the MCAT. Notice any similarity beyond the final two initials? These instruments all measure what is essentially undiluted L-Directed Thinking. They require logic and analysis—and reward test-takers for zeroing-in, computerlike, on a single correct answer. The exercise is linear, sequential, and bounded by time. You answer one question with one right answer. Then you move to the next question and the next and the next until time runs out. These tests have become important gatekeepers for entry into meritocratic, middle-class society. They've created an SAT-ocracy—a regime in which access to the good life depends on the ability to reason logically, sequentially, and speedily. And this is not just an American phenomenon. From entrance exams in the United Kingdom to cram schools in Japan, most developed nations have devoted considerable time and treasure to producing left-brained knowledge workers.

This arrangement has been a rousing success. It has broken the stranglehold of aristocratic privilege and opened educational and professional opportunities to a diverse set of people. It has propelled the world economy and lifted living standards. But the SAT-ocracy is now in its dying days. The L-Directed Thinking it nurtures and rewards still matters, of course. But it's no longer enough. Today, we're moving into an era in which *R-Directed Thinking* will increasingly determine who gets ahead.

To some of you, this is delightful news. To others, it sounds like a crock. This chapter is mainly for the latter group of readers—those who followed your parents' advice and scored well on those aptitude tests. To persuade you that what I'm saying is sound, let me explain the reasons for this shift using the left-brain, mechanistic language of cause and effect. The effect: the diminished relative importance of L-Directed Thinking and the corresponding increased importance of R-Directed Thinking. The causes: Abundance, Asia, and Automation.

Abundance

Another vignette from the 1970s: every August my mother would take my brother, sister, and me to buy clothes for the new school year. That inevitably meant a trip to Eastland Mall, one of three big shopping centers in central Ohio. Inside the mall we'd visit a national department store such as Sears or JCPenney or a local one such as Lazarus, where the children's departments featured maybe a dozen racks of clothing from which to choose. The rest of the mall consisted of about thirty other stores, smaller in size and selection, lined up between the department store anchors. Like most Americans of the time, we considered Eastland and those other climate-controlled enclosed shopping centers the very zenith of modern plenty.

My own kids would consider it underwhelming. Within a twenty-minute drive of our home in Washington, D.C., are about forty different mega-shopping sites—the size, selection, and scope of which didn't exist thirty years ago. Take Potomac Yards, which sits on Route 1 in northern Virginia. One Saturday morning in August, my wife and I and our three children drove there for our own back-to-school shopping excursion. We began at the giant store on the far end of the site. In the women's section of that store, we chose from Mossimo designer tops and sweaters, Merona blazers, Isaac Mizrahi jackets, and Liz Lange designer maternity wear. The kids' clothing section was equally vast and almost as hip. The Italian designer Mossimo had a full line of children's wear—including a velour pants and jacket set for our two girls. The choices were preposterously more interesting, more attractive, and more bountiful than the clothing I chose from back in the seventies. But there was something even more noteworthy about this stylish kiddie garb when I compared it to the more pedestrian fashions of my youth: the clothes cost less. Because we weren't at some swank boutique. My family and I were shopping at Target. That velour Mossimo ensemble? $14.99. Those women's designer tops? $9.99. My wife's new suede Isaac Mizrahi jacket? Forty-nine bucks. A few aisles away were home furnishings, created by designer Todd Oldham and less expensive than what my parents used to pick up at Sears. Throughout the store were acres of good-looking, low-cost merchandise.

And Target was just one of an array of Potomac Yards stores catering to a mostly middle-class clientele. Next door we could visit Staples, a 20,000-square-foot box selling 7,500 different school and office supplies. (There are more than 1,500 Staples stores like it in the United States and Europe.) Next to Staples was the equally cavernous PetSmart, one of more than six hundred such pet supply stores in the United States and Canada, each one of which, on an average day, sells $15,000 worth of merchandise for nonhumans.[2] This particular outlet even had its own pet-grooming studio. Next to PetSmart was Best Buy, an electronics emporium with a retail floor that's larger than the entire block on which my family lives. One section was devoted to home theater equipment, which displayed an arms race of televisions—plasma, high-definition, flat panel—that began with a 42-inch screen and escalated to 47-inch, 50-inch, 54-inch, 56-inch, and 65-inch versions. In the telephone section were, by my count, 39 different varieties of cordless phones. And these four stores constituted only about one-third of the entire shopping facility.

But what's so remarkable about Potomac Yards is how utterly unremarkable it is. You can find a similar swath of consumer bounty just about anyplace in the United States—and, increasingly, in Europe and sections of Asia as well. These shopping meccas are but one visible example of an extraordinary change in modern life. For most of history, our lives were defined by scarcity. Today, the defining feature of social, economic, and cultural life in much of the world is *abundance.*

Our left brains have made us rich. Powered by armies of Drucker's knowledge workers, the information economy has produced a standard of living in much of the developed world that would have been unfathomable to our great-grandparents.

A few examples of our abundant era:

- During much of the twentieth century, the aspiration of most middle-class Americans was to own a home and a car. Now more than two out of three Americans own the homes in which they live. (In fact, some 13 percent of homes purchased today are *second* homes.[3]) As for autos, today the United States has more cars than licensed drivers—which means that, on average, everybody who can drive has a car of his own.[4]

- Self-storage—a business devoted to providing people a place to house their extra stuff—has become a $17 billion annual industry in the United States, larger than the motion picture business. What's more, the industry is growing at an even faster rate in other countries.[5]
- When we can't store our many things, we just throw them away. As business writer Polly LaBarre notes, "The United States spends more on trash bags than ninety other countries spend on *everything.* In other words, the receptacles of our *waste* cost more than all of the goods consumed by nearly half of the world's nations."[6]

But abundance has produced an ironic result: the very triumph of L-Directed Thinking has lessened its significance. The prosperity it has unleashed has placed a premium on less rational, more R-Directed sensibilities—beauty, spirituality, emotion. For businesses, it's no longer enough to create a product that's reasonably priced and adequately functional. It must also be beautiful, unique, and meaningful, abiding what author Virginia Postrel calls "the aesthetic imperative."[7] Perhaps the most telling example of this change, as our family outing to Target demonstrated, is the new middle-class obsession with design. World-famous designers such as the ones I mentioned earlier, as well as titans such as Karim Rashid and Philippe Starck, now design all manner of goods for this quintessentially middle-class, middle-brow, middle-American store. Target and other retailers have sold nearly three million units of Rashid's Garbo molded polypropylene wastebasket. A designer wastebasket! Try explaining that one to your left brain.

Or how about this item, which I purchased during that same Target trip?

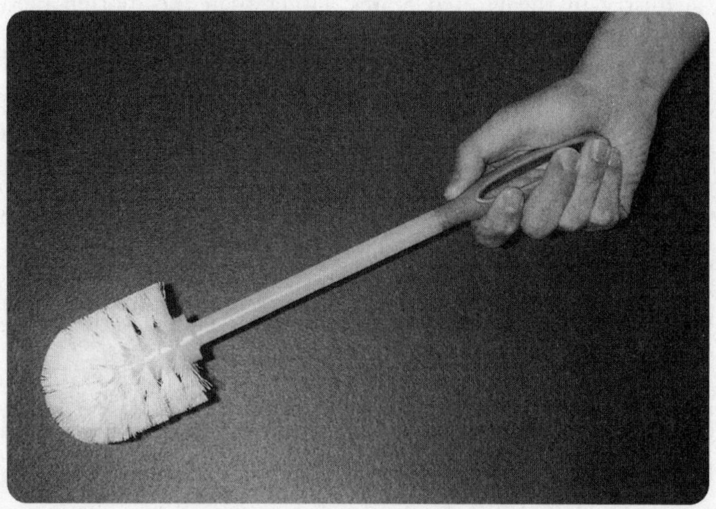

It's a toilet brush—a toilet brush designed by Michael Graves, a Princeton University architecture professor and one of the most renowned architects and product designers in the world. The cost: $5.99. Only against a backdrop of abundance could so many people seek beautiful trash cans and toilet brushes—converting mundane, utilitarian products into objects of desire.

In an age of abundance, appealing only to rational, logical, and functional needs is woefully insufficient. Engineers must figure out how to get things to work. But if those things are not also pleasing to the eye or compelling to the soul, few will buy them. There are too many other options. Mastery of design, empathy, play, and other seemingly "soft" aptitudes is now the main way for individuals and firms to stand out in a crowded marketplace.

Abundance elevates R-Directed Thinking another important way as well. When I'm on my deathbed, it's unlikely that I'll look back on my life and say, "Well, I've made some mistakes. But at least I snagged one of those Michael Graves toilet brushes back in 2004." Abundance has brought beautiful things to our lives, but that bevy of material goods has not necessarily made us much happier. The paradox of prosperity is that while living standards have risen steadily decade after decade, personal, family, and life satisfaction haven't budged. That's why more people—liberated by prosperity but not fulfilled by it—are resolving the paradox by searching for meaning. As Columbia University's Andrew Delbanco puts it, "The most striking feature of contemporary culture is the unslaked craving for transcendence."[8]

Visit any moderately prosperous community in the advanced world and along with the plenteous shopping opportunities, you can glimpse this quest for transcendence in action. From the mainstream embrace of once-exotic practices such as yoga and meditation to the rise of spirituality in the workplace and evangelical themes in books and movies, the pursuit of purpose and meaning has become an integral part of our lives. People everywhere have moved from focusing on the day-to-day text of their lives to the broader context. Of course, material wealth hasn't reached everyone in the developed world, not to mention vast numbers in the less developed world. But abundance has freed literally hundreds of millions of people from the struggle for survival and, as Nobel Prize–winning economist Robert William Fogel writes, "made it possible to extend the quest for self-realization from a minute fraction of the population to almost the whole of it."[9]

On the off chance that you're still not convinced, let me offer one last—and illuminating—statistic. Electric lighting was rare a century ago, but today it's commonplace. Lightbulbs are cheap. Electricity is ubiquitous. Candles? Who needs them? Apparently, lots of people. In the United States, candles are a $2.4-billion-a-year business[10]—for reasons that stretch beyond the logical need for luminosity to a prosperous country's more inchoate desire for beauty and transcendence.

Asia

Here are four people I met while researching this book:

They are the very embodiment of the knowledge worker ethic I described at the outset of this chapter. Like many bright middle-class kids, they followed their parents' advice. They did well in high school, went on to earn either an engineering or computer science degree from a good university, and now work at a large software company, helping to write computer code for North American banks and airlines. For their high-tech work, none of these four people earns more than about $15,000 a year.

Knowledge workers, meet your new competition: Srividya, Lalit, Kavita, and Kamal of Mumbai, India.

In recent years, few issues have generated more controversy or stoked more anxiety than outsourcing. These four programmers and their counterparts throughout India, the Philippines, and China are scaring the bejeezus out of software engineers and other left-brain professionals in North America and Europe, triggering protests, boycotts, and plenty of political posturing. The computer programming they do, while not the most sophisticated that multinational companies need, is the sort of work that until recently was done almost exclusively in the United States—and that provided comfortable white-collar salaries of upward of $70,000 a year. Now twenty-five-year-old Indians are doing it—just as well, if not better; just as fast, if not faster—for the wages of a Taco Bell counter jockey. Yet, their pay, while paltry by Western standards, is roughly twenty-five times what the typical Indian earns—and affords them an upper-middle-class lifestyle with vacations and their own apartments.

The programmers I met in Mumbai are but four well-educated drops in a global tsunami. Each year, India's colleges and universities produce about 350,000 engineering graduates.[11] That's one reason that more than half of the Fortune 500 companies now outsource software work to India.[12] For instance, about 48 percent of GE's software is developed in India. The company employs a whopping twenty thousand people there (and has even posted signs in its Indian offices reading, "Trespassers will be recruited"). Hewlett-Packard employs several thousand software engineers in India. Siemens employs three thousand computer programmers in India and is moving another fifteen thousand such jobs overseas. Oracle has a five-thousand-person Indian staff. The large Indian IT consultancy Wipro employs some seventeen thousand engineers who do work for Home Depot, Nokia, and Sony. And the list goes on. As the chief executive of GE India told London's *Financial Times*: "Any job that is English-based in markets such as the U.S., the U.K. and Australia can be done in India.

The only limit is your imagination."[13] Indeed, active imaginations have already expanded India's professional ranks well beyond computer programmers. Financial services firms such as Lehman Brothers, Bear Stearns, Morgan Stanley, and JPMorgan Chase have contracted out number crunching and financial analysis to Indian MBAs.[14] The financial news service Reuters has offshored low-level editorial jobs. And throughout India, you'll find chartered accountants who prepare American tax returns, lawyers who do legal research for American lawsuits, and radiologists who read CAT scans for American hospitals.

But it's not just India. L-Directed white-collar work of all sorts is migrating to other parts of the world as well. Motorola, Nortel, and Intel operate software development centers in Russia, where Boeing has also sent a large portion of its aerospace engineering work. The computer services giant Electronic Data Systems has software developers in Egypt, Brazil, and Poland. Meantime, Hungarian architects are drawing basic blueprints for California design firms. Philippine accountants are performing audits for CapGemini Ernst & Young. And the Dutch firm Philips employs some seven hundred engineers in China, a nation that is now producing nearly as many engineering graduates each year as the United States.[15]

The main reason is money. In the United States, a typical chip designer earns about $7,000 per month; in India, she earns about $1,000. In the United States, a typical aerospace engineer earns about $6,000 each month; in Russia, his monthly salary is closer to $650. And while an accountant in the United States can earn $5,000 a month, an accountant in the Philippines brings in about $300 a month, no small sum in a country where the *annual* per capita income is $500.[16]

For these battalions of international knowledge workers, this new world order is a dream. But for white-collar, left-brain workers in Europe and North America, the implications are more nightmarish. For example:

- One out of ten jobs in the U.S. computer, software, and information technology industry will move overseas in the next two years. One in four IT jobs will be offshored by 2010.[17]
- According to Forrester Research, "at least 3.3 million white-collar jobs and $136 billion in wages will shift from the U.S. to low-cost countries like India, China, and Russia" by 2015.[18]
- Nations such as Japan, Germany, and the United Kingdom will see similar job loss. The United Kingdom alone will lose some 25,000 IT jobs and upwards of 30,000 finance positions to India and other developing nations in the next few years. By 2015, Europe will lose 1.2 million jobs to offshore locales.[19]

Much of the anxiety over this issue outstrips the reality. We are not all going to lose our jobs tomorrow. Outsourcing is overhyped in the short term. But it's underhyped in the long term. As the cost of communicating with the other side of the globe falls essentially to zero, and as developing nations continue to mint millions of extremely capable knowledge workers, the working lives of North Americans, Europeans, and Japanese people will change dramatically. If standardized, routine L-Directed work such as many kinds of financial analysis, radiology, and computer programming can be done for a lot less overseas and delivered to clients instantly via fiber optic links, that's where the work will go. This upheaval will be difficult for many, but it's ultimately not much different from transitions we've weathered before. This is precisely what happened to routine mass production jobs, which moved across the oceans in the second half of the twentieth century. And just as those factory workers had to master a new set of skills and learn how to bend pixels instead of steel, many of today's knowledge workers will likewise have to command a new set of aptitudes. They'll need to do what workers abroad cannot do equally well for much less money—using R-Directed abilities such as forging relationships rather than executing transactions, tackling novel challenges instead of solving routine problems, and synthesizing the big picture rather than analyzing a single component.

Automation

Meet two more people. One is an iconic figure who may have been real. The other is a real human being who, perhaps to his regret, may become iconic.

The first is this fellow, immortalized here on a U.S. postage stamp:

As most American schoolchildren could tell you, John Henry was a steel-driving man. Born with a hammer in his hand, he was a figure of immense strength and integrity. (Alas, nobody is certain whether he was an actual person. Many historians believe he was a former slave who worked on the railroads after the Civil War, though none have been able to verify his existence.) He was part of a team of workers who smashed through mountains to clear tunnels for laying railroad tracks. But John Henry was no ordinary laborer. He could drive steel faster and more powerfully than any man alive, and his prowess soon became the stuff of legend.

One day, the tale goes, a salesman arrived at the workers' camp bearing a new steam-powered drill that he claimed could outperform even the strongest man. John Henry scoffed at the notion that gears and grease were any match for human muscle. So he proposed a contest—man vs. machine—to see which could blast through a mountainside the fastest.

The next afternoon, the race began—the steam drill on the right, John Henry on the left. The machine took the lead, but John Henry quickly rallied. Chunks of rocks fell as the duo bored through their tunnels. Before long, John Henry had closed in on his competitor. And in an instant before the end of the race, he surged past the steam drill and broke through the other side of the mountain first. His fellow workers cheered. But John Henry, exhausted by the superhuman effort, collapsed. Then he died. The story spread. In ballads and books, John Henry's demise became a parable of the Industrial Age: machines could now do some things better than human beings, and as a result a measure of human dignity had been sacrificed.

Now meet our second figure:

Mario Tanna, Getty Images

Garry Kasparov is a chess grand master—the finest chess player of his generation and perhaps the greatest of all time. He's also the John Henry of our new age—a person whose seemingly superhuman prowess has been surpassed by a machine.

Kasparov won his first chess world championship in 1985, around the same time that several research teams began developing computer programs that could play chess. Over the next decade, Kasparov never lost a match. And in 1996, he defeated what was then the world's most powerful chess computer.

But in 1997, Kasparov took on an even more powerful machine, a 1.4-ton IBM supercomputer called Deep Blue, in a six-game match that some dubbed "the brain's last stand."[20] To the surprise of many, Deep Blue defeated Kasparov, the consequences of which the cover of *Inside Chess* magazine reduced to a single word: "ARMAGEDDON!"[21] Seeking vengeance—for himself and for all flesh-and-blood L-Directed thinkers—Kasparov then arranged a rematch against another computer, Deep Junior, a still more potent Israeli computer that had thrice won the world computer chess championship.

Chess is in many ways the quintessential left-brain activity. It leaves relatively little room for emotion—and depends heavily on memory, rational thinking, and brute calculation, two things at which computers excel. Kasparov says that when he looks at the board, he can examine between one and three moves per second. Deep Junior is, uh, slightly more impressive. Each second, it analyzes between two and three *million* possible moves. Yet, Kasparov believed that human beings had other advantages that would level the sixty-four-square playing field.

On Super Bowl Sunday 2003, Kasparov strutted into the posh New York Downtown Athletic Club to begin another epic contest between man and machine—a six-game match with a million-dollar purse. Hundreds of fans watched in person. Millions more followed the action on the Internet. Kasparov won game one and settled for a draw in game two. In game three, he started strong, but on the edge of victory, he fell into one of Junior's traps and lost. In game four, Kasparov played haltingly and eked out another draw, still so distraught over blowing game three that he admitted that he "couldn't sleep and lost confidence."[22] Game five was another draw, leaving the outcome of the match to the sixth and final game.

Kasparov quickly took the lead. As *Newsweek* later reported, "Against any human player, he would have moved aggressively and gone for the win. But he wasn't playing against a human." In his tentativeness, he made a slight mistake and that left him

> devastated in a way that an unfeeling machine would never be. Worse, having yielded the advantage he had no hope—as he would have against a human—that his well-programmed opponent might make its own mistake and let him back in the game. The realization paralyzed even the great Kasparov, and it haunted him for the rest of the match.[23]

In the end, he settled for a draw—in this game and the entire match.[24]

Human beings have much to recommend, but when it comes to chess—and increasingly other endeavors that depend heavily on rule-based logic, calculation, and sequential thinking—computers are simply better, faster, and stronger. What's more, computers don't fatigue. They don't get headaches. They don't choke under pressure or sulk over losses. They don't worry what the audience thinks or care what the press will say. They don't space out. They don't slip up. And that has humbled even the notoriously egomaniacal grand master. In 1987, Kasparov, then the chess world's enfant terrible, boasted: "No computer can ever beat me."[25] Today, Kasparov, now our modern John Henry, says: "I give us only a few years. Then they'll win every match, and we may have to struggle to win even a single game."[26]

Last century, machines proved they could replace human backs. This century, new technologies are proving they can replace human left brains. Management meta-guru Tom Peters puts it nicely, saying that for white-collar workers "software is a forklift for the mind." It won't eliminate every left-brain job. But it will destroy many and reshape the rest. Any job that depends on routines—that can be reduced to a set of rules, or broken down into a set of repeatable steps—is at risk. If a $500-a-month Indian chartered accountant doesn't swipe your comfortable accounting job, TurboTax will.

Consider three heavily L-Directed professions: computer programmers, physicians, and lawyers. "In the old days," says computer scientist Vernor Vinge, "anybody with even routine skills could get a job as a programmer. That isn't true anymore. The routine functions are increasingly being turned over to machines."[27] Indeed, a small British company called Appligenics has created software that can write software. Where a typical human being—whether the Indians I met or their higher-paid counterparts in the United States—can write about four hundred lines of computer code per day, Appligenics applications can do the same work in *less than a second.*[28] The result: as the scut work gets off-loaded, engineers and programmers will have to master different aptitudes, relying more on creativity than competence, more on tacit knowledge than technical manuals, and more on fashioning the big picture than sweating the details.

Automation is also changing the work of many doctors. Much of medical diagnosis amounts to following a series of decision trees—Is it a dry cough or a productive one? Is the T-cell count above or below a certain level?—and honing in on the answer. Computers can process the binary logic of decision trees with a swiftness and accuracy humans can't begin to approach. So an array of software and online programs has emerged that allow patients to answer a series of questions on their computer screens and arrive at a preliminary diagnosis without the assistance of a physician. Health care consumers have begun to use such tools both to "figure out their risk of serious diseases—such as heart failure, coronary artery disease and some of the most common cancers—[and] to make life-and-death treatment decisions once they are diagnosed," reports the *Wall Street Journal.*[29] At the same time, there's been an explosion of electronic databases of medical and health information. In a typical year, about 100 million people worldwide go online for health and medical information and visit more than 23,000 medical Web sites.[30] As patients self-diagnose and tap the same reservoir of information available to physicians, these tools are transforming the doctor's role from omniscient purveyor of solutions to empathic advisor on options. Of course, the day-to-day work of physicians often involves challenges too complex for software alone—and we'll still rely on experienced doctors to diagnose unusual diseases. But, as I'll show later in this book, these developments are changing the emphasis of many medical practices—away from routine, analytical, and information-based work and toward empathy, narrative medicine, and holistic care.

A similar pattern is unfolding in the legal profession. Dozens of inexpensive information and advice services are reshaping law practice. For example, CompleteCase.com, which calls itself "the premier online uncontested divorce service center," will handle your divorce for a mere $249. At the same time, the Web is cracking the information monopoly that has long been the source of many lawyers' high incomes and professional mystique. Attorneys charge an average of $180 per hour. But many Web sites—for instance, Lawvantage.com and USLegalforms.com—now offer basic legal forms and other documents for as little as $14.95. As *The New York Times* reports, "Instead of asking lawyers to draft contracts at a cost of several thousand dollars," clients now find the proper forms online—and then take "the generic documents to lawyers, who customize them at a cost of several hundred dollars apiece." The result, says the *Times*, is that the legal industry "may be on the verge of fundamental changes . . . [that] could reduce the demand for traditional services and force lawyers to lower fees."[31] The attorneys who remain will be those who can tackle far more complex problems and those who can provide something that databases and software cannot—counseling, mediation, courtroom storytelling, and other services that depend on R-Directed Thinking.

TO RECAP, three forces are tilting the scales in favor of R-Directed Thinking. Abundance has satisfied, and even oversatisfied, the material needs of millions—boosting the significance of beauty and emotion and accelerating individuals' search for meaning. Asia is now performing large amounts of routine, white-collar, L-Directed work at significantly lower costs, thereby forcing knowledge workers in the advanced world to master abilities that can't be shipped overseas. And automation has begun to affect this generation's white-collar workers in much the same way it did last generation's blue-collar workers, requiring L-Directed professionals to develop aptitudes that computers can't do better, faster, or cheaper.

So what happens next? What happens to us as our lives get clipped by automation and Asia—and reconfigured by abundance? I'll examine that in the next chapter.

Three

HIGH CONCEPT, HIGH TOUCH

Think of the last 150 years as a three-act drama.

In Act I, the Industrial Age, massive factories and efficient assembly lines powered the economy. The lead character in this act was the mass production worker, whose cardinal traits were physical strength and personal fortitude.

In Act II, the Information Age, the United States and other nations began to evolve. Mass production faded into the background, while information and knowledge fueled the economies of the developed world. The central figure in this act was the knowledge worker, whose defining characteristic was proficiency in L-Directed Thinking.

Now, as the forces of Abundance, Asia, and Automation deepen and intensify, the curtain is rising on Act III. Call this act the

Conceptual Age. The main characters now are the *creator* and the *empathizer*, whose distinctive ability is mastery of R-Directed Thinking.

I've depicted this progression in Figure 3.1, broadening the story to include the Industrial Age's predecessor, the Agriculture Age. The horizontal axis shows time. The vertical axis shows a combination of affluence, technological progress, and globalization (what I've short-handed ATG). As individuals grow richer, as technologies become more powerful, and as the world grows more connected, these three forces eventually gather enough collective momentum to nudge us into a new era. That is how, over time, we moved from the Agriculture Age to the Industrial Age to the Information Age. The latest instance of this pattern is today's transition from the Information Age to the Conceptual Age once again fed by affluence (the abundance that

Figure 3.1

FROM THE AGRICULTURE AGE TO THE CONCEPTUAL AGE

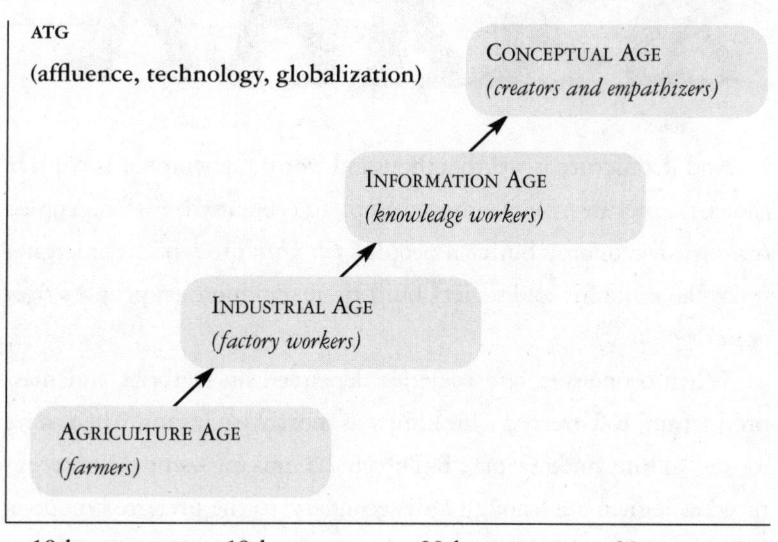

characterizes Western life), technological progress (the automation of several kinds of white-collar work), and globalization (certain types of knowledge work moving to Asia).

In short, we've progressed from a society of farmers to a society of factory workers to a society of knowledge workers. And now we're progressing yet again—to a society of creators and empathizers, of pattern recognizers and meaning makers.

Figure 3.2 depicts this same evolution, but in a way that might speak more to the right side of your brain.

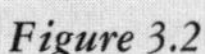

Figure 3.2

And if a picture is worth a thousand words, a metaphor is worth a thousand pictures. We've moved from an economy built on people's *backs* to an economy built on people's *left brains* to what is emerging today: an economy and society built more and more on people's *right brains.*

When economies and societies depended on factories and mass production, R-Directed Thinking was mostly irrelevant. Then as we moved to knowledge work, R-Directed Thinking came to be recognized as legitimate, though still secondary, to the preferred mode of L-Directed Thinking. Now, as North America, Western Europe,

Australia, and Japan evolve once again, R-Directed Thinking is beginning to achieve social and economic parity—and, in many cases, primacy. In the twenty-first century, it has become the first among equals, the key to professional achievement and personal satisfaction.

But let me be clear: the future is not some Manichean world in which individuals are either left-brained and extinct or right-brained and ecstatic—a land in which millionaire potters drive BMWs and computer programmers scrub counters at Chick-fil-A. L-Directed Thinking remains indispensable. It's just no longer sufficient. In the Conceptual Age, what we need instead is a *whole* new mind.

High Concept and High Touch

To survive in this age, individuals and organizations must examine what they're doing to earn a living and ask themselves three questions:

1. Can someone overseas do it cheaper?
2. Can a computer do it faster?
3. Is what I'm offering in demand in an age of abundance?

If your answer to question 1 or 2 is yes, or if your answer to question 3 is no, you're in deep trouble. Mere survival today depends on being able to do something that overseas knowledge workers can't do cheaper, that powerful computers can't do faster, and that satisfies one of the nonmaterial, transcendent desires of an abundant age.

That is why high tech is no longer enough. We'll need to supplement our well-developed high-tech abilities with abilities that are high concept and high touch. (As I mentioned in the Introduction, high concept involves the ability to create artistic and emotional beauty, to detect patterns and opportunities, to craft a satisfying narrative, and to combine seemingly unrelated ideas into a novel invention. High touch involves the ability to empathize, to understand the subtleties of human interaction, to find joy in one's self and to elicit it in others, and to stretch beyond the quotidian, in pursuit of purpose and meaning.)[1]

High concept and high touch are on the rise throughout the world economy and society. But for the most persuasive evidence, it helps to look in the most unlikely places. Take medical schools, long a bastion for those with the best grades, highest test scores, and the keenest powers of analytical thinking. Today, the curriculum at American medical schools is undergoing its greatest change in a generation. Students at Columbia University Medical School and elsewhere are being trained in "narrative medicine," because research has revealed that despite the power of computer diagnostics, an important part of a diagnosis is contained in a patient's story. At the Yale School of Medicine, students are honing their powers of observation at the Yale Center for British Art, because students who study paintings excel at noticing subtle details about a patient's condition. Meantime, more than fifty medical schools across the United States have incorporated spirituality into their coursework. UCLA Medical School has established a Hospital Overnight Program, in which second-year students are admitted to the hospital overnight with fictitious ailments. The purpose of this playacting? "To develop medical students' empathy for patients," says the school. Jefferson Medical School in Philadelphia has even developed a new measure of physician effectiveness—an empathy index.[2]

Or leave American teaching hospitals and head for the world's second largest economy. Japan, which rose from the ashes of World War II thanks to its intense emphasis on L-Directed Thinking, is now reconsidering the source of its national strength. Although Japanese students lead the world in math and science scores, many in Japan suspect that the nation's unrelenting focus on schoolbook academics might be an outdated approach. So the country is remaking its vaunted education system to foster greater creativity, artistry, and play. Little wonder. Japan's most lucrative export these days isn't autos or electronics. It's pop culture.[3] Meanwhile, in response to the mind-melting academic pressures on Japanese youth, the Education Ministry has been pushing students to reflect on the meaning and mission of their lives, encouraging what it calls "education of the heart."

Then, when you've returned from Japan, check out a third unlikely setting—the mammoth multinational General Motors. A few years ago, GM hired a man named Robert Lutz to help turn around the ailing automaker. Bob Lutz is not exactly a touchy-feely, artsy-fartsy kind of guy. He's a craggy, white-haired white man in his seventies. During his career, he's been an executive at each of the big three American automakers. He looks and acts like a marine, which he once was. He smokes cigars. He flies his own plane. He believes global warming is a myth peddled by the environmental movement. But when Lutz took over his post at beleaguered GM, and *The New York Times* asked him how his approach would differ from that of his predecessors, here's how he responded: "It's more right brain. . . . I see us being in the art business. Art, entertainment and mobile sculpture, which, coincidentally, also happens to provide transportation."[4]

Let that comment settle in for a moment. General Motors—an exemplar not even of the Information Age but of the *Industrial* Age—says it's in the art business. The *art* business. And the person leading GM into this right-brain world isn't some beret-topped artiste but a seventy-something piss-and-vinegar former marine. To paraphrase Buffalo Springfield, there's something happening here—and what it is is becoming more clear. High-concept and high-touch aptitudes are moving from the periphery of our lives to the center.

MBAs and MFAs

Getting admitted to Harvard Business School is a cinch. At least that's what several hundred people must think each year after they apply to the graduate program of the UCLA Department of Art—and don't get in. While Harvard's MBA program admits about 10 percent of its applicants, UCLA's fine arts graduate school admits only 3 percent. Why? A master of fine arts, an MFA, is now one of the hottest credentials in a world where even General Motors is in the art business. Corporate recruiters have begun visiting the top arts grad schools—places such as the Rhode Island School of Design, the School of the Art Institute of Chicago, Michigan's Cranbrook Academy of Art—in search of talent. And this broadened approach has often come at the expense of more traditional business graduates. For instance, in 1993, 61 percent of management consultancy McKinsey's recruits had MBA degrees. Less than a decade later, it was down to 43 percent, because McKinsey says other disciplines are just as valuable in helping new hires perform well at the firm. With applications climbing and ever more arts grads occupying key corporate positions, the rules have changed: the MFA is the new MBA.

The reasons for this go back to two of the forces I explained in the previous chapter. Because of Asia, many MBA graduates are becoming this century's blue-collar workers—people who entered a workforce full of promise, only to see their jobs move overseas. Investment banks, as we learned, are hiring MBAs in India to handle financial analysis. A. T. Kearney estimates that in the next five years, U.S. financial services companies will transfer a half-million jobs to low-cost locales such as India. As the *Economist* put it, the sorts of entry-level MBA tasks that "would once have been foisted on ambitious but inexperienced young recruits, working long hours to earn their spurs in Wall Street or the City of London, are, thanks to the miracle of fibre-optic cable, foisted on their lower-paid Indian counterparts." At the same time, because of Abundance, businesses are realizing that the only way to differentiate their goods and services in today's overstocked marketplace is to make their offerings physically beautiful and emotionally compelling. Thus the high-concept abilities of an artist are often more valuable than the easily replicated L-Directed skills of an entry-level business graduate.

In the middle of the last century, Charlie Wilson, a GM executive who became U.S. defense secretary, famously remarked that what was good for General Motors was good for America. It's time to update Wilson's maxim for a new century. What is happening to General Motors is happening to America—and what is happening to America is happening in many other countries. Today we're all in the art business.

In the United States, the number of graphic designers has increased tenfold in a decade; graphic designers outnumber chemical engineers by four to one. Since 1970, the United States has 30 percent more people earning a living as writers and 50 percent more earning a living by composing or performing music. Some 240 U.S. universities have established creative writing MFA programs, up from fewer than twenty two decades ago.[5] More Americans today work in arts, entertainment, and design than work as lawyers, accountants, and auditors.[6] (A sign of these new times is a young venture in Alexandria, Virginia. When routine legal research goes overseas and basic legal information is available online, what's left for the litigious? High-concept work like that done by Animators at Law, a graphic design firm staffed by law graduates that prepares exhibits, videos, and visual aids to help top trial attorneys persuade juries.)

In 2002, Carnegie Mellon University urban planner Richard

Florida identified a group of 38 million Americans that he labeled the "creative class" and claimed were the key to economic development. Although Florida's definition of "creative" was bizarrely expansive—he includes accountants, insurance adjusters, and tax attorneys as "creatives"—the growth of this class's ranks is hard to ignore. Its share of the U.S. workforce has doubled since 1980 and is ten times what it was a century ago.[7] A similar trend toward high-concept work is afoot elsewhere in the world. Using a more sensible definition of "creative"—to include fifteen industries from design to performing arts to research and development to video games—British analyst John Howkins estimates that the creative sector in the United Kingdom is producing nearly $200 billion of goods and services each year. Howkins calculates that within fifteen years, this sector will be worth about $6.1 trillion internationally, making High Concept Nation one of the largest economies in the world.[8] Meantime, British organizations such as the London Business School and the Yorkshire Water Company have established artist-in-residence programs. Unilever UK employs painters, poets, and comic book creators to inspire the rest of its staff. One North London football club even has its own poet in residence.

But art in the traditional sense is neither the only, nor the most important, component of these emerging whole-minded aptitudes. Go back to those Information Age rock stars, computer programmers. The outsourcing of routine software work is putting a new premium on software engineers with high-concept abilities. As the Lalits and Kavitas of the world take over the routine work of software fabrication, maintenance, testing, and upgrading, Conceptual Age software types will concentrate on novelty and nuance. After all, before the Indian programmers have something to fabricate, maintain, test, or upgrade, that something first must be imagined or invented. And these creations must then be explained and tailored to customers and entered into the swirl of commerce, all of which require aptitudes that can't be reduced to a set of rules on a spec sheet—ingenuity, personal rapport, and gut instinct.

IQ and EQ

When museum curators of the future assemble an exhibit on American schooling in the twentieth century, they'll have many artifacts to choose from—chunky textbooks, dusty blackboards, one-piece injection-molded desks with wraparound writing surfaces. But one item deserves special consideration. I recommend that in the center of the exhibition, enclosed in a sparkling glass case, the curators display a well-sharpened No. 2 pencil.

If the global supply chain ever confronted a shortage of No. 2 pencils, the American education system might collapse. From the time children are able even to grasp one of these wooden writing sticks, they use them to take an endless battery of tests that purport to measure their current ability and future potential. In elementary school, we assess children's IQs. Later on, we measure their skill in reading and math—then plot their scores against children from the rest of the state, the country, and the world. By the time kids arrive in high school, they're preparing for the SAT, the desert they must cross to reach the promised land of a good job and a happy life. As I've noted, this SAT-ocracy has its virtues. But America's test-happy system also has several weaknesses that are only recently being acknowledged.

For example, Daniel Goleman, author of the groundbreaking book *Emotional Intelligence*, has examined an array of academic studies that have attempted to measure how much IQ (which, like the SAT, measures pure L-Directed Thinking prowess) accounts for career success. What do you think these studies found? Grab a No. 2 pencil and take a guess.

According to the latest research, IQ accounts for what portion of career success?

a. 50 to 60 percent
b. 35 to 45 percent
c. 23 to 29 percent
d. 15 to 20 percent

The answer: between 4 and 10 percent. (Confining oneself only to the answers presented is a symptom of excessive L-Directed Thinking.) According to Goleman, IQ can influence the profession one enters. My IQ, for instance, is way too low for a career in astrophysics. But within a profession, mastery of L-Directed Thinking matters relatively little. More important are qualities that are tougher to quantify, the very kinds of high-concept and high-touch abilities I've been mentioning—imagination, joyfulness, and social dexterity. For instance, research by Goleman and the Hay Group has found that within organizations, the most effective leaders were funny (that is, *funny ha-ha,* not *funny strange*). These leaders had their charges laughing three times more often than their managerial counterparts.[9] (And humor, as I'll discuss in Chapter 8, depends heavily on the brain's right hemisphere.) But where have you seen a standardized test that measures comedic aptitude?

Actually, you could find one in New Haven, Connecticut, where a Yale University psychology professor is developing an alternative SAT. Professor Robert Sternberg calls his test the Rainbow Project—and it certainly sounds like a lot more fun than the pressure-packed exam many of us endured as teenagers. In Sternberg's test, students are given five blank *New Yorker* cartoons—and must craft humorous captions for each one. They must also write or narrate a story, using as their guide only a title supplied by the test givers (sample title: "The Octopus's Sneakers"). And students are presented with various real-life challenges—arriving at a party where they don't know anybody, or trying to convince friends to help move furniture—and asked how they'd respond. Although still in its experimental stages, the Rainbow Project has been twice as successful as the SAT in predicting how well students perform in college. What's more, the persistent gap in performance between white students and racial minorities evident on the SAT narrows considerably on this test.

Sternberg's test doesn't aim to replace the SAT—only to augment it. (In fact, one of its funders is the College Board, which sponsors the SAT.) And the SAT itself recently has been revised to include a writing component. But the Rainbow Project's very existence is revealing. "If you don't do well on [the SAT]," Sternberg says, "everywhere you turn the access routes to success in our society are blocked." But as more educators are recognizing, those roadblocks can exclude people with aptitudes that the SAT doesn't measure.[10]

This is especially true for high-touch abilities—that is, the capacity for compassion, care, and uplift—which are becoming a key component of many occupations in the Conceptual Age. The number of jobs in the "caring professions"—counseling, nursing, and hands-on health assistance—is surging. For example, while advanced nations are exporting high-tech computer programming jobs, they are importing nurses from the Philippines and other Asian countries. As a result of this shortage, nursing salaries are climbing and the number of male registered nurses has doubled since the mid-1980s.[11] We'll learn more about this in Chapter 7.

Money and Meaning

While work is going high concept and high touch, the most significant change of the Conceptual Age might be occurring outside the office—and inside our hearts and souls. Pursuits devoted to meaning and transcendence, for instance, are now as mainstream as a double tall latte. In the United States, ten million adults now engage in some form of regular meditation, double the number a decade ago. Fifteen million practice yoga, twice the number in 1999. American popular entertainment is so awash in spiritual themes that *TV Guide* heralds the rise of "transcendental television."[12]

The aging of U.S. baby boomers—as well as the even more notable aging of the populations of Japan and the European Union—is also accelerating this shift. "As people mature," writes psychologist David Wolfe, "their cognitive patterns become less abstract (left-brain orientation) and more concrete (right-brain orientation) which results in a sharpened sense of reality, increased capacity for emotion, and enhancement of their sense of connectedness" (parentheses in the original).[13] In other words, as individuals age, they place greater emphasis in their own lives on qualities they might have neglected in the rush to build careers and raise families: purpose, intrinsic motivation, and meaning.

Indeed, two researchers have argued that this fleet of empathic, meaning-seeking boomers has already started wading ashore. In 2000, Paul Ray and Sherry Ruth Anderson identified a subculture of fifty million Americans that they dubbed "Cultural Creatives." Cultural Creatives, they claim, account for one-fourth of U.S adults, a population roughly the size of France. And the attributes of this cohort echo many of the elements of an R-Directed approach to life. For instance,

Cultural Creatives "insist on seeing the big picture," the authors write. "They are good at synthesizing." And they "see women's ways of knowing as valid: feeling empathy and sympathy for others, taking the viewpoint of the one who speaks, seeing personal experiences and first-person stories as important ways of learning, and embracing an ethic of caring."[14]

Baby boomers are entering the Conceptual Age with an eye on their own chronological age. They recognize that they now have more of their lives behind them than ahead of them. And such indisputable arithmetic can concentrate the mind. After decades of pursuing riches, wealth seems less alluring. For them, and for many others in this new era, meaning is the new money.

WHAT DOES all this mean for you and me? How can we prepare ourselves for the Conceptual Age? On one level, the answer is straightforward. In a world tossed by Abundance, Asia, and Automation, in which L-Directed Thinking remains necessary but no longer sufficient, we must become proficient in R-Directed Thinking and master aptitudes that are high concept and high touch. We must perform work that overseas knowledge workers can't do cheaper, that computers can't do faster, and that satisfies the aesthetic, emotional, and spiritual demands of a prosperous time. But on another level, that answer is inadequate. What exactly are we supposed to do?

I've spent the last few years investigating that question. And I've distilled the answer to six specific high-concept and high-touch aptitudes that have become essential in this new era. I call these aptitudes "the six senses." Design. Story. Symphony. Empathy. Play. Meaning. And it is to helping you understand and master these six aptitudes that I devote the second part of this book.

PART **TWO**

The Six Senses

INTRODUCING THE SIX SENSES

In the Conceptual Age, we will need to complement our L-Directed reasoning by mastering six essential R-Directed aptitudes. Together these six high-concept, high-touch senses can help develop the whole new mind this new era demands.

1. ***Not just function but also DESIGN.*** It's no longer sufficient to create a product, a service, an experience, or a lifestyle that's merely functional. Today it's economically crucial and personally rewarding to create something that is also beautiful, whimsical, or emotionally engaging.

2. ***Not just argument but also STORY.*** When our lives are brimming with information and data, it's not enough to mar-

shal an effective argument. Someone somewhere will inevitably track down a counterpoint to rebut your point. The essence of persuasion, communication, and self-understanding has become the ability also to fashion a compelling narrative.

3. ***Not just focus but also SYMPHONY.*** Much of the Industrial and Information Ages required focus and specialization. But as white-collar work gets routed to Asia and reduced to software, there's a new premium on the opposite aptitude: putting the pieces together, or what I call Symphony. What's in greatest demand today isn't analysis but synthesis—seeing the big picture, crossing boundaries, and being able to combine disparate pieces into an arresting new whole.

4. ***Not just logic but also EMPATHY.*** The capacity for logical thought is one of the things that makes us human. But in a world of ubiquitous information and advanced analytic tools, logic alone won't do. What will distinguish those who thrive will be their ability to understand what makes their fellow woman or man tick, to forge relationships, and to care for others.

5. ***Not just seriousness but also PLAY.*** Ample evidence points to the enormous health and professional benefits of laughter, lightheartedness, games, and humor. There is a time to be serious, of course. But too much sobriety can be bad for your career and worse for your general well-being. In the Conceptual Age, in work and in life, we all need to play.

6. ***Not just accumulation but also MEANING.*** We live in a world of breathtaking material plenty. That has freed hun-

dreds of millions of people from day-to-day struggles and liberated us to pursue more significant desires: purpose, transcendence, and spiritual fulfillment.

Design. Story. Symphony. Empathy. Play. Meaning. These six senses increasingly will guide our lives and shape our world. Many of you no doubt welcome such a change. But to some of you, this vision might seem dreadful—a hostile takeover of normal life by a band of poseurs in black unitards who will leave behind the insufficiently arty and emotive. Fear not. The high-concept, high-touch abilities that now matter most are fundamentally human attributes. After all, back on the savannah, our cave-person ancestors weren't taking SATs or plugging numbers into spreadsheets. But they were telling stories, demonstrating empathy, and designing innovations. These abilities have always comprised part of what it means to be human. But after a few generations in the Information Age, these muscles have atrophied. The challenge is to work them back into shape. (That's the idea behind the Portfolio section at the end of each chapter. This collection of tools, exercises, and further reading materials will send you on your way to developing a whole new mind.) Anyone can master the six Conceptual Age senses. But those who master them first will have a huge advantage. So let's get started.

Four

DESIGN

The late Gordon MacKenzie, a longtime creative force at Hallmark Cards, once told a story that quickly entered the folklore among designers. MacKenzie was a public-spirited fellow who often visited schools to talk about his profession. He'd open each talk by telling students he was an artist. Then he'd look around the classroom, notice the artwork on the walls, and wonder aloud who created the masterpieces.

"How many artists are there in the room?" MacKenzie would ask. "Would you please raise your hands?"

The responses always followed the same pattern. In kindergarten and first-grade classes, every kid thrust a hand in the air. In second-grade classes, about three-fourths of the kids raised their hands, though less eagerly. In third grade, only a few children held up their hands. And by sixth grade, not a single hand went up. The kids just looked around to see if anybody in the class would admit to what they'd now learned was deviant behavior.

Designers and other creative types repeated MacKenzie's tale—often over drinks, usually in a wistful tone—to show how little the wider world valued their work. And when MacKenzie related the story himself to large audiences, people would slowly shake their heads. What a shame, they would mutter. Too bad, they would cluck. But their reaction was, at most, a lament.

In fact, they should have been outraged. They should have raced to their local school and demanded an explanation. They should have consoled their children, confronted the principal, and ousted the school board. Because MacKenzie's story is not some teary saga about underfunded art programs.

It is a cautionary tale for our times.

The wealth of nations and the well-being of individuals now depend on having artists in the room. In a world enriched by abundance but disrupted by the automation and outsourcing of white-collar work, everyone, regardless of profession, must cultivate an artistic sensibility. We may not all be Dali or Degas. But today we must all be designers.

It's easy to dismiss design—to relegate it to mere ornament, the prettifying of places and objects to disguise their banality. But that is a serious misunderstanding of what design is and why it matters—especially now. John Heskett, a scholar of the subject, explains it well: "[D]esign, stripped to its essence, can be defined as the human nature to shape and make our environment in ways without precedent in nature, to serve our needs and give meaning to our lives."[1]

Look up from this page and cast your eyes around the room you're in. Everything in your midst has been designed. The typeface of these letters. The book you hold in your hands. The clothes that cover your body. The piece of furniture on which you're sitting. The building that surrounds you. These things are part of your life because someone else imagined them and brought them into being.

Design is a classic whole-minded aptitude. It is, to borrow Heskett's terms, a combination of *utility* and *significance.* A graphic designer must whip up a brochure that is easy to read. That's utility. But at its most effective, her brochure must also transmit ideas or emotions that the words themselves cannot convey. That's significance. A furniture designer must craft a table that stands up properly and supports its weight (utility). But the table must also possess an aesthetic appeal that transcends functionality (significance). Utility is akin to L-Directed Thinking; significance is akin to R-Directed Thinking. And, as with those two thinking styles, today utility has become widespread, inexpensive, and relatively easy to achieve—which has increased the value of significance.

"I think designers are the alchemists of the future."

—RICHARD KOSHALEK, *president, Art Center College of Design*

Design—that is, utility enhanced by significance—has become an essential aptitude for personal fulfillment and professional success for at least three reasons. First, thanks to rising prosperity and advancing technology, good design is now more accessible than ever, which allows more people to partake in its pleasures and become connoisseurs of what was once specialized knowledge. Second, in an age of material abundance, design has become crucial for most modern businesses—as a means of differentiation and as a way to create new markets. Third, as more people develop a design sensibility, we'll increasingly be able to deploy design for its ultimate purpose: changing the world.

I saw all three of these reasons converge one brisk February morning, half a block from Independence Hall in downtown Philadelphia, at a place that Gordon MacKenzie must be smiling down on from heaven.

IT'S 10 A.M. in Mike Reingold's design studio. As soothing music is piped through the air, one student is posing on a chair that sits atop a table, while her nineteen classmates sketch her form on their large drawing pads. The scene is straight out of a tony arts academy, except for one thing: the young men and women sketching away are all tenth-graders, and most of them come from some of the roughest neighborhoods in Philadelphia.

Welcome to CHAD—the Charter High School for Architecture and Design—a tuition-free Philadelphia public school that is demonstrating the power of design to expand young minds, while also puncturing the myth that design is the province of a select few.

Before they came to CHAD as ninth-graders, most of these students had never taken an art class, and one-third read and did math at a third-grade level. But now, if they follow the route of those in the senior class, 80 percent of them will go on to two- or four-year colleges—and some of them will enroll at places like the Pratt Institute and the Rhode Island School of Design.

When it was founded in 1999 as the country's first public high school with a design-centered curriculum, CHAD's goal wasn't merely to train a new generation of designers and to diversify a largely white profession. (Three out of four CHAD students are African-American; 88 percent are racial minorities.) The aim was also to use design to teach core academic subjects. Students here spend 100 minutes each day in a design studio. They take courses in architecture, industrial design, color theory, and painting. But equally important, the school marries design to math, science, English, social studies, and other subjects. For example, when they study the Roman Empire, rather than only read about the Roman water delivery process, the students build a model aqueduct. "They're learning to bring disparate things together to a solution. That's what designers do," says Claire Gallagher, a former architect who previously served as the school's supervisor of curriculum and instruction. "Design is interdisciplinary. We're producing people who can think holistically."

One student who has flourished in this whole-minded atmosphere is Sean Canty, a junior. He's a smart, skinny kid who is as poised as a veteran designer, yet as gangly as a typical sixteen-year-old. When I talk to him after classes let out, he tells me that in his rough-and-tumble middle school, "I was the kid who always sketched in class. I was the kid who was always good in art class. But you're always the oddball because the artistic person in the classroom is the weird one." Since enrolling as a freshman, he has found his comfort zone and gained a range of experience unusual for someone his age. He interns two afternoons a week at a local architecture firm. He's traveled to New York to design a poster with the help of an architect mentor he met through CHAD. He's built models of "two cool towers" he'd like to see constructed one day. Yet Canty says the most important thing he's learned at CHAD is broader than any particular skill: "I've learned how to work with people and how to be inspired by other people."

"Good design is a renaissance attitude that combines technology, cognitive science, human need, and beauty to produce something that the world didn't know it was missing."

—PAOLA ANTONELLI, *curator of architecture and design, Museum of Modern Art*

Indeed, merely walking the halls here is inspiring. Student artwork is on display in the lobby. The hallways sport furniture donated by the Cooper-Hewitt Museum. And throughout the school are the works of designers such as Karim Rashid, Kate Spade, and Frank Gehry, some of which are presented in lockers CHAD students have converted into display cases. The students all wear blue button-down shirts and tan pants. The boys also wear ties. "They feel and look like young architects and designers," the school's development director, Barbara Chandler Allen, tells me, no small feat in a school where a substantial portion of the student body is eligible for free lunches.

For many of the students, the school is a haven in a harsh world—a place that's safe and orderly and where the adults care and have high expectations. While the typical Philadelphia public high school has a daily attendance rate of 63 percent, at CHAD it's 95 percent. Equally revealing is what isn't here. CHAD is one of the only high schools in Philadelphia without metal detectors. Instead, when stu-

CHAD student Quincy Ellis, who graduated in 2005 and enrolled at the Rhode Island School of Design.

dents, teachers, and visitors pass through the front door on Sansom Street, they're greeted by a colorful mural crafted by the American minimalist Sol Lewitt.

Although CHAD is a pioneer, it is not the only school of its kind. Miami's public school system boasts Design and Architecture Senior High, New York City has the High School of Art and Design. Washington, D.C., has a charter elementary school called the Studio School, where many of the teachers are professional artists. And beyond the elementary and secondary level, design education is positively booming. In the United States, as we learned in Chapter 3, the MFA is becoming the new MBA. In the United Kingdom, the number of design students climbed 35 percent between 1995 and 2002. In Asia, the sum total of design schools in Japan, South Korea, and Singapore thirty-five years ago was . . . zero. Today, the three countries have more than twenty-three design schools among them.[2]

At these schools, as at CHAD, many students ultimately might not become professional designers. That's fine, says deputy principal Christina Alvarez. "We're building an awareness in students of what design is and how it can affect their lives," she tells me. "I see the design curriculum as providing a modern version of a liberal arts education for these kids." No matter what path these students pursue, their experience at this school will enhance their ability to solve problems, understand others, and appreciate the world around them—essential abilities in the Conceptual Age.

The Democracy of Design

Frank Nuovo is one of the world's best-known industrial designers. If you use a Nokia cell phone, chances are good Nuovo helped design it. But as a younger man, Nuovo had a difficult time explaining his career choice to his family. "When I told my father I wanted to be a designer, he said, 'What does that mean?'" Nuovo told me in an interview. We "need to reduce the nervousness" surrounding design, Nuovo says. "Design in its simplest form is the activity of creating solutions. Design is something that everyone does every day."

From the moment some guy in a loincloth scraped a rock against a piece of flint to create an arrowhead, human beings have been designers. Even when our ancestors were roaming the savannah, our species has always harbored an innate desire for novelty and beauty. Yet for much of history, design (and especially its more intimidating cousin, Design) was often reserved for the elite, who had the money to afford such frivolity and the time to enjoy it. The rest of us might occasionally dip our toes into significance, but mostly we stayed at the utility end of the pool.

In the last few decades, however, that has begun to change. Design has become democratized. If you don't believe me, take this test. Below are three type fonts. Match the font on the left with the correct font name on the right.

1. A Whole New Mind	a. Times New Roman
2. A Whole New Mind	b. Arial
3. A Whole New Mind	c. Courier New

My guess, having conducted this experiment many times in the course of researching this book, is that most of you completed the task quickly and correctly.* But had I posed this challenge, say, twenty-five years ago, you probably wouldn't have had a clue. Back then, fonts were the specialized domain of typesetters and graphic designers, something that regular folks like you and me scarcely recognized

*The correct answers are: 1-b, 2-c, 3-a

and barely understood. Today we live and work in a new habitat. Most Westerners who can read, write, and use a computer are also literate in fonts. "If you are a native of the rain forest, you learn to distinguish many sorts of leaves," says Virginia Postrel. "We learn to distinguish many different typefaces."[3]

Fonts, of course, are just one aspect of the democratization of design. One of the most successful retail ventures of the last decade is Design Within Reach, a network of thirty-one studios whose mission is to bring great design to the masses. In DWR's studios and catalogs are the sort of beautiful chairs, lamps, and desks that the wealthy have always purchased but that are now available to wider segments of the population. Target, a family visit to which I described in Chapter 2, has gone even further in democratizing design, often obliterating the distinction between high fashion and mass merchandise, as it has with its Isaac Mizrahi clothing line. In the pages of *The New York Times*, Target advertises its $3.49 Philippe Starck spill-proof baby cup alongside ads for $5,000 Concord LaScala watches and $30,000 Harry Winston diamond rings. Likewise, Michael Graves, whose cerulean toilet brush I purchased during that Target trip, now sells kits that buyers can use to construct stylish gazebos, studios, and porches. Graves, who has designed libraries, museums, and multimillion-dollar homes, is too expensive for most of us to hire to build out the family room. But for $10,000, we might be able to buy one of his Graves Pavilions and enjoy the beauty and grace of one of the world's finest architects literally in our own backyard.

**"Aesthetics matter.
Attractive things work better."**

—DON NORMAN, *author and engineering professor*

The mainstreaming of design has infiltrated beyond the commercial realm. It's no surprise that Sony has four hundred in-house designers. But how about this? There are sixty designers on the staff of the Church of Jesus Christ of Latter-day Saints.[4] And while God is bringing artists into the room, Uncle Sam is redoing the room itself. The General Services Administration, which oversees the construction of U.S. government buildings, has a "Design Excellence" program that aims to turn drab federal facilities into places more pleasant to work in and more beautiful to view. Even U.S. diplomats have responded to the age's new imperatives. In 2004, the U.S. State Department declared that it was abandoning the font it had used for years—Courier New 12—and replacing it with a new standard font that would henceforth be required in all documents: Times New Roman 14. The internal memorandum announcing the change explained that the Times New Roman font "takes up almost exactly the same area on the page as Courier New 12, while offering a crisper, cleaner, more modern look."[5] What was more remarkable than the change itself—and what would have been unthinkable had the change occurred a generation ago—was that everybody in the State Department understood what the memo was talking about.

Design Means Business/ Business Means Design

The democratization of design has altered the competitive logic of businesses. Companies traditionally have competed on price or quality, or some combination of the two. But today decent quality and reasonable price have become merely table stakes in the business game—the entry ticket for being allowed into the marketplace.

Once companies satisfy those requirements, they are left to compete less on functional or financial qualities and more on ineffable qualities such as whimsy, beauty, and meaning. This insight isn't terribly new. Tom Peters, whom I quoted in the last chapter, was making the business case for design before most businesspeople knew the difference between Charles Eames and Charlie's Angels. ("Design," he advises companies, "is the principal difference between love and hate.") But as with the State Department's font memo, what's remarkable about the business urgency of design isn't so much the idea but how widely held it has become.

"Businesspeople don't need to understand designers better. They need to be designers."

—ROGER MARTIN, *dean, Rotman School of Management*

Consider two men from separate countries and different worlds. Paul Thompson is the director of the Cooper-Hewitt Museum in New York City. Norio Ohga is the former chairman of the high-tech powerhouse Sony.

Here's Thompson: "Manufacturers have begun to recognize that we can't compete with the pricing structure and labor costs of the Far East. So how can we compete? It has to be with design."[6]

Here's Ohga: "At Sony, we assume that all products of our competitors have basically the same technology, price, performance, and features. Design is the only thing that differentiates one product from another in the marketplace."[7]

Thompson's and Ohga's arguments are increasingly borne out on corporate income statements and stock tables. For every percent of sales invested in product design, a company's sales and profits rise by an average of 3 to 4 percent, according to research at the London Business School.[8] Similarly, other research has shown that the stocks of companies that place a heavy emphasis on design outperform the stocks of their less design-centric counterparts by a wide margin.[9]

Cars are a good example. As I noted in Chapter 2, the United States now has more autos than drivers—which means that the vast majority of Americans who want a car can have one. That ubiquity has brought down prices and boosted quality, leaving design as a key criterion for consumer decisions. U.S. automakers have slowly learned this lesson. "For a long time, going back to the 1960s, marketing directors were more focused on science and engineering, gathering data and crunching numbers, and they neglected the importance of the other side of the brain, the right side," says Anne Asenio, a design director for GM. And that eventually proved disastrous for Detroit. It took mavericks like Bob Lutz, whom we heard from in Chapter 3, to show that utility requires significance. Lutz famously declared that GM was in the art business—and worked to make designers the equals of engineers. "You need to differentiate or you cannot survive," says Asenio. "I think designers have a sixth sense, an antenna, that allows them to accomplish this better than other professionals."[10]

Other car companies have shifted gears and headed in this same direction. BMW's Chris Bangle says, "We don't make 'automobiles.'" BMW makes "moving works of art that express the driver's love of quality."[11] One Ford vice president says that "in the past, it was all about a big V-8. Now it's about harmony and balance."[12] So frenzied are the car companies to differentiate by design that "in Detroit's macho culture, horsepower has taken a back seat to ambience," as *Newsweek* puts it. "The Detroit Auto Show . . . might as well be renamed the Detroit Interior Decorating Show."[13]

"Design correctly harnessed can enhance life, create jobs, and make people happy—not such a bad thing."

—PAUL SMITH, *fashion designer*

Your kitchen offers further evidence of the new premium on design. We see it, of course, in those high-end kitchens with gleaming Sub-Zero refrigerators and gargantuan Viking ranges. But the phenomenon is most evident in the smaller, less expensive goods that populate the cabinets and countertops of the United States and Europe. Take the popularity of "cutensils"—kitchen utensils that have been given personality implants. Open the drawer in an American or European home and you'll likely find a bottle opener that looks like a smiling cat, a spaghetti spoon that grins at you and the pasta, or a vegetable brush with googly eyes and spindly legs. Or just go shopping for a toaster. You'll have a hard time finding a plain old model, because most of the choices these days are stylized, funky, fanciful, sleek, or some other adjective not commonly associated with small appliances.

Some pundits might write off these developments as mass manipulation by wily marketers or further proof that well-off Westerners are mesmerized by style over substance. But that view misreads economic reality and human aspiration. Ponder that humble toaster. The typical person uses a toaster at most 15 minutes per day. The remaining 1,425 minutes of the day the toaster is on display. In other words, 1 percent of the toaster's time is devoted to utility, while 99 percent is devoted to significance. Why *shouldn't* it be beautiful, especially when you can buy a good-looking one for less than forty bucks? Ralph Waldo Emerson said that if you built a better mousetrap, the world would beat a path to your door. But in an age of abundance, nobody will come knocking unless your better mousetrap also appeals to the right side of the brain.

Design has also become an essential aptitude because of the quickened metabolism of commerce. Today's products make the journey from L-Directed utility to R-Directed significance in the blink of an eye. Think about cell phones. In less than a decade, they've gone from being a luxury for some to being a necessity for most to becoming an accessorized expression of individuality for many. They've morphed from "logical devices" (which emphasize speed and specialized function) to "emotional devices" (which are "expressive, customizable, and fanciful"), as Japanese personal electronics executive Toshiro Iizuka puts it.[14] Consumers now spend nearly as much on decorative (and nonfunctional) faceplates for their cell phones as they do on the phones themselves. Last year, they purchased about $4 billion worth of ring tones.[15]

Indeed, one of design's most potent economic effects is this very capacity to create new markets—whether for ring tones, cutensils, photovoltaic cells, or medical devices. The forces of Abundance, Asia, and Automation turn goods and services into commodities so quickly that the only way to survive is by constantly developing new innovations, inventing new categories, and (in Paola Antonelli's lovely phrase) giving the world something it didn't know it was missing.

Designing Our Future

Design can do more than supply our kitchens with cooking implements that stir both our sauces and our souls. Good design can change the world. (And so, alas, can bad design.)

> **"It's not true that what is useful is beautiful. It is what is beautiful that is useful. Beauty can improve people's way of life and thinking."**
>
> —ANNA CASTELLI FERRIERI, *furniture designer*

Take health care. Most hospitals and doctors' offices are not exactly repositories of charm and good taste. And while physicians and administrators might favor changing that state of affairs, they generally consider it secondary to the more pressing matters of prescribing drugs and performing surgery. But a growing body of evidence is showing that improving the design of medical settings helps patients get better faster. For example, in a study at Pittsburgh's Montefiore Hospital, surgery patients in rooms with ample natural light required less pain medication, and their drug costs were 21 percent lower, than their counterparts in traditional rooms.[16] Another study compared two groups of patients who suffered identical ailments. One group was treated in a dreary conventional ward of the hospital. The other was treated in a modern, sunlit, visually appealing ward. Patients in the better-designed ward needed less pain medicine than those in the less inviting ward and were discharged on average nearly two days early. Many hospitals are now redesigning their facilities to include greater amounts of natural light, waiting rooms that provide both privacy and comfort, and an array of design features such as meditative gardens and labyrinths that physicians now realize can speed the healing process.

Similar potential exists in bringing a new design sensibility to two other settings where beauty has long taken a backseat to bureaucracy—public schools and public housing. A study at Georgetown University found that even if the students, teachers, and educational approach remained the same, improving a school's physical environment could increase test scores by as much as 11 percent.[17] Meanwhile, public housing, notorious for its abominable aesthetics, may be in the very early stages of a renaissance. A nice example is architect Louise Braverman's Chelsea Court in New York City. Constructed on an austere budget, the building has colorful stairwells, airy apartments, and a roof deck with Philippe Starck furniture—all for tenants who are low-income or (formerly) homeless.

Design can also deliver environmental benefits. The "green design" movement is incorporating the principles of sustainability in the design of consumer goods. This approach not only creates products from recycled materials but also designs the products with an

Chelsea Court rooftop terrace in New York City. SCOTT FRANCES

eye to their eventual disposal as well as their use. Architecture is likewise going green—in part because architects and designers are understanding that in the United States, buildings generate as much pollution as autos and factories combined. More than 1,100 buildings in the United States have applied to the U.S. Green Building Council to be certified as environmentally friendly.[18]

If you're still unconvinced that design can have consequences beyond the carport and cutting board, point your memory back to the 2000 U.S. presidential elections and the thirty-six-day snarl over whether Al Gore or George W. Bush won the most votes in Florida. That election and its aftermath may seem like a bad dream today. But buried in that brouhaha was an important, and mostly ignored, lesson. Democrats alleged that the U.S. Supreme Court, by halting the recount of ballots, handed the election to George W. Bush.

Republicans claimed that their opponents tried to steal the election by urging voting officials to count chads—those little rectangular ballot pieces—that were not fully punched out. But the truth is that both sides are wrong.

According to an exhaustive examination of all of Florida's ballots that several newspapers and academics conducted a year after the election—and whose findings were largely lost amid the coverage of the September 11, 2001, terrorist attacks and utterly forgotten after Bush's 2004 reelection—what determined who won the U.S. presidency in 2000 was this:

Bruce Weaver, Getty Images

This is the infamous butterfly ballot that voters in Palm Beach County used to mark their choice for President. In Palm Beach County—a heavily Democratic enclave populated by tens of thousands of elderly Jewish voters—ultraconservative fringe candidate Pat Buchanan received 3,407 votes, three times as many votes as he did in any other county in the state. (According to one statistical analysis, if the voting pattern of the state's other sixty-six counties had held in Palm Beach, Buchanan would have won only 603 votes.)[19] What's more, 5,237 Palm Beach County voters marked ballots for *both* Al Gore and Pat Buchanan, and therefore had their ballots invalidated. Bush carried the entire state by 537 votes.

What explained Buchanan's stunning performance and the thousands of invalidated ballots?

Bad design.

The nonpartisan investigation found that what decided the outcome in Palm Beach County—and therefore determined who would become leader of the free world—wasn't an evil Supreme Court or recalcitrant chads. *It was bad design.* The bewildering butterfly ballot confused thousands of voters and cost Gore the presidency, according to the professor who headed the project. "Voters' confusion with ballot instruction and design and voting machines appears to have changed the course of U.S. history."[20] Had Palm Beach County had a few artists in the room when it was designing its ballot, the course of U.S. history would likely have been different.*

Now, intelligent people can argue whether the butterfly ballot and the confusion it wrought ultimately produced a good or bad result for the country. And this isn't partisan sniping from somebody—full disclosure—who worked for Al Gore ten years ago and who remains a registered Democrat. Bad design could have worked to Democrats' advantage and the Republicans' chagrin—and one day it likely will. But whatever our own partisan persuasion, we should consider the butterfly ballot the Conceptual Age equivalent of the Sputnik launch. It was a surprising, world-changing event that re-

*Less well known is the ballot in Duval County in which the presidential ballot showed five candidates on one page and another five candidates on the next page, along with instructions to "vote every page." In that county, 7,162 Gore ballots were tossed out because voters selected two candidates for President. Had the instructions been clearer, Duval County, too, would have provided Gore the margin of victory.

vealed how weak Americans were in what we'd now discovered was a fundamentally important strength—design.

DESIGN IS a high-concept aptitude that is difficult to outsource or automate—and that increasingly confers a competitive advantage in business. Good design, now more accessible and affordable than ever, also offers us a chance to bring pleasure, meaning, and beauty to our lives. But most important, cultivating a design sensibility can make our small planet a better place for us all. "To be a designer is to be an agent of change," says CHAD's Barbara Chandler Allen. "Think of how much better the world is going to be when CHAD kids pour into the world."

PORTFOLIO

II

Design

Story

Symphony

Empathy

Play

Meaning

Keep a Design Notebook.

Buy a small notebook and begin carrying it with you wherever you go. When you see great design, make a note of it. (Example: my $6.95 Hotspot silicone trivet—a thin, flexible square that doubles as a pot holder, triples as a jar opener, and looks cool.) Do the same for flawed design. (Example: the hazard light button in my car, which is so close to the gearshift that I often turn on the hazards when I put the car in PARK.) Before long, you'll be looking at graphics, interiors, environments, and much more with greater acuity. And you'll understand in a deeper way how design decisions shape our everyday lives. Be sure to include the design of experiences as well—buying a cup of coffee, taking a trip on an airplane, going to an emergency room. If you're not a note-taker, carry around a small digital camera or camera cell phone instead and snap photos of good and bad design.

Channel Your Annoyance.

1. Choose a household item that annoys you in any way.
2. Go by yourself to a café with pen and paper, but without a book and without a newspaper, and, for the duration of your cup of coffee, think about improving the poorly designed item.
3. Send the idea/sketch as it is to the manufacturer of your annoying household item.

You never know what might come of it.

The above from Stefan Sagmeister, graphic design impresario. (More info: www.sagmeister.com)

Read Design Magazines.

Professional designers read (and obsess over) design magazines. So should you (except for the obsess part). Reading design magazines—or just leafing through them—can sharpen your eye and inspire your mind. While hundreds of design magazines—many of which merely fetishize expensive things—fill the newsstands, these eight are on my must-read list:

Ambidextrous—A project of Stanford University's d. school, this quirky magazine explores the craft of design and the nuances of design thinking. *(More info: www.ambidextrousmag.com)*

Dwell—One of the most respected shelter magazines, *Dwell* has an ethic of public service and environmental responsibility that helps it stand out. *(More info: www.dwellmag.com)*

HOW—This terrific magazine mostly focuses on graphic design. It also has lots of smart business advice, reading recommendations, and an annual design competition that's a great source of ideas. *(More info: www.howdesign.com)*

iD—This award-winning magazine is well known for its Annual Design Review, which singles out the year's best designs—and for the iD 40, which introduces readers to up-and-coming designers. *(More info: www.idonline.com)*

Metropolis—With a strong emphasis on construction and materials, this magazine offers tremendous insight into the built environment. I also like its coverage of sustainable design. *(More info: www.metropolismag.com)*

***O* Magazine**—Oprah Winfrey's publication, which bears its creator's design sensibility, is one of my three favorite magazines of any kind. Period. Read it, know it, live it. *(More info: www.oprah.com/omagazine)*

Print—Another great graphic design magazine, this one is known for its voluminous Regional Design Annual. *(More info: www.printmag.com)*

Real Simple—One designer I know calls this magazine her bible. Its theology is straightforward: "to bring clarity to everyday tasks, so readers can focus on what really adds meaning to their lives." *(More info: www.realsimple.com)*

Be Like Karim.

In response to my request for advice on how those of us who aren't professional designers can incorporate a design sensibility into our lives, Karim Rashid sent me his "Karimanifesto," a fifty-point guide to life and design. Here are some excerpts:

1. Don't specialize.
5. Before giving birth to anything physical, ask yourself if you have created an original idea, an original concept, if there is any real value in what you disseminate.
6. Know everything about the history of your profession and then forget it all when you design something new.
7. Never say "I could have done that" because you didn't.
24. Consume experiences, not things.
33. Normal is **not** good.
38. There are three types of beings—those who create culture, those who buy culture, and those who don't give a shit about culture. Move between the first two.
40. Think extensively, not intensively.
43. Experience is the most important part of living, and the exchange of ideas and human contact is all life really is. Space and objects can encourage increased experiences or distract from our experiences.
50. Here and now is all we got.

The above from Karim Rashid, one the most world's most versatile, prolific, and celebrated designers. (More info: www.karimrashid.com)

Become a Design Detective.

It's a favorite hobby of the real estate–obsessed and the just plain nosy: visiting open houses. Follow their example and spend a Sunday walking through other people's homes. Scour the real estate ads in search of residences likely to yield an eclectic mix of design ideas and insights. Tour a half dozen homes and look for design trends and commonalities, as well as unique or quirky expressions of the owners' personalities and tastes. Take a page from architect Sarah Susanka, author of *The Not So Big House*, and "notice what constitutes the spaces that feel good to you. Try to determine if they appeal on an emotional level or in a physical way. And try to articulate why."

Perhaps turn this into a group outing by collecting several friends and heading off to different open houses. Gather at the end of the day to compare notes. And be sure to take advantage of decorator show homes and neighborhood house tours. They can provide a healthy dose of design diversity in just a few hours.

The snooping approach can also work on the job. Next time you're at someone else's workplace, look around. How does the physical environment make you feel? Would you be productive and happy in this kind of setting? How do the layout, the lighting, and the furniture enhance or impede how people interact and communicate? What design elements would you incorporate into your own workplace?

Participate in the "Third Industrial Revolution."

If we're all designers, what better way to get started than by designing something yourself? "In the future," says Italian designer Gaetano Pesce, "customers will expect original objects. What I call the third industrial revolution will give people the opportunity to have a unique piece." You can sample the revolution by designing your own Nike shoe—with the color, pattern, and image that's right for you. *(More info: nikeid.nike.com)* You can also do the same with Vans skate shoes. *(More info: www.vans.com)* Or, for the ultimate expression of individuality, use your handwriting to create your very own font. *(More info: www.fontifier.com)* "The proliferation of mass customization of consumer products," designer David Small told me, "will have a powerful and empowering effect on how ordinary people see design."

Visit a Design Museum.

Fine art has always found a home in museums. But applied art—that is, design—has often been consigned to rickety file cabinets and designers' basements. Fortunately, that's changing. Several large cities now boast museums devoted to industrial, graphic, interior, and architectural design. These museums, rich with examples and explanations, offer a great way to deepen your design sensibility. Here are ten of the best.

Cooper-Hewitt, National Design Museum (New York City)—The Cooper-Hewitt's extraordinary permanent collection is one of the largest design troves in the world, featuring everything from a Michelangelo drawing to Eva Zeisel saltshakers. The exhibits are always wonderful, especially those that include pieces from the National Design Triennial, which the Cooper-Hewitt hosts.

(More info: www.ndm.si.edu)

Design Exchange (Toronto)—This museum and research center takes its name from its building, the site of Toronto's first stock exchange. Today the museum serves a dual purpose: touting the best of Canadian design and teaching visitors about the variety of design in the world. *(More info: www.dx.org)*

Design Museum (London)—The brainchild of Sir Terence Conran, this two-floor museum features rotating exhibits of twentieth- and twenty-first-century design. The gift shop and children's activities are first-rate. Its location near the Tower of London introduced me to a part of London I'd never explored.

(More info: www.designmuseum.org)

Eames House (Los Angeles)—The husband and wife team of Charles and Ray Eames are perhaps the most famous furniture designers of the twentieth century. The home that they built as a case study, and that they lived in much of their lives, is now a showcase of their work. You can view it only by appointment. But once or twice a year, Eames officials will open the house for public tours.

(More info: www.eamesoffice.org/visit_house.html)

Herbert Lubalin Study Center of Design and Typography (New York City)—Visit this quiet place in New York's East Village and you'll never look at graphic design the same way. The center, dedicated to preserving seminal works of graphic design, serves mostly as a research facility for students and faculty of the Cooper Union. While it sometimes has public exhibitions, you'll need to make an appointment to see the good stuff.

(More info: www.cooper.edu/art/lubalin)

Museum of Modern Art, Architecture and Design Department (New York City)—MoMA, of course, is one of the world's finest art museums. But it was also one of the first U.S. museums to devote display space to design and architecture. Its permanent collection—which has everything from sports cars to furniture to posters to appliances—is a required stop for your design education. *(More info: www.moma.org/collection/depts/arch_design/)*

National Building Museum (Washington, D.C.)—This is one of the most beautiful museums in Washington, worth visiting simply to step into the Great Hall and gaze at the ceiling for five minutes. But if you stay longer, you'll usually find excellent exhibitions on architecture and urban design, often with a public-spirited bent. The children's programs also are excellent.

(More info: www.nbm.org)

Victoria and Albert Museum (London)—Britain's cavernous national museum of art and design features some two thousand years of extraordinary design—from tenth-century Egyptian vases to twentieth-century Eames storage units. Great kids' activities here, too. *(More info: www.vam.ac.uk)*

Vitra Design Museum (Weil am Rhein, Germany)—Located in a building designed by Frank Gehry, this museum offers regular exhibitions on the best industrial design in Europe.

(More info: www.design-museum.de)

William F. Eisner Museum of Advertising and Design (Milwaukee, Wisconsin)—This fascinating contemporary museum is part of the Milwaukee Institute of Art & Design. Most of the exhibits highlight print design, but you can find some interesting industrial design here as well. *(More info: www.eisnermuseum.org)*

C-R-A-P-ify Your Graphic Design.

Robin Williams (no, not that one) is one of today's best design writers. Her book, *The Non-Designer's Design Book: Design and Typographic Principles for the Visual Novice,* is a gem, in no small measure because she spells out the four basics of effective graphic design:

1. ***Contrast.*** "If the elements (type, color, size, line thicknesses, shape, space, etc.) are not the *same*, then make them **very different.**"
2. ***Repetition.*** Repeating visual elements "helps develop the organization and strengthens the unity" of your brochure, newsletter, or letterhead.
3. ***Alignment.*** "Nothing should be placed on the page arbitrarily. Every element should have some visual connection with another element on the page."
4. ***Proximity.*** "Items relating to each other should be grouped close together."

Check out Williams's book for examples. If you heed her C, R, A, and P, you'll avoid printed materials that look like, uh, not very good.

(More info: www.ratz.com)

Put It on a Table.

Find an object in your life that holds a special place in your heart—an old shirt from your college days, a perfectly butt-conforming wallet, a favorite serving spoon, a cool new watch. Place it on a table in front of you or hold it in your hand. Then explore the following questions:

1. When you look at or use this object, what does it make you think of? Past experiences? The skill with which you can use it? The person who made it? There will be some satisfying experience or feeling that you may be able to uncover.
2. How does this object affect each of your five senses? There will be a series of details or aspects of design that will trigger your senses.
3. Think of how you have connected the sensory clues you receive from the object to the way you think and feel about it. Can you see the connections you have made?

Try this exercise with other objects, maybe objects that you don't have a particular connection with. What about these objects is different? Why don't they tickle the emotions?

Developing the ability to consciously select designs that connect with our emotions should help us populate our lives with meaningful, satisfying objects and not just more stuff.

The above from Dan Buchner, director of industrial design, Design Continuum. (More info: www.dcontinuum.com)

Be Choosy.

Choose things in your life that will endure, that are a pleasure to use. Classic clothes never go out of style. Furniture should get better with age. Choose things because they delight you, not because they impress others. And never let things be more important than your family, friends, and your own spirit.

The above from Marney Morris, founder and president, Animatrix, and instructor in interactive design, Stanford University.

(More info: www.animatrix.com)

Five

STORY

Time for a pop quiz.

Back in Chapter 2, when I was presenting the three forces nudging us into the Conceptual Age, I offered some evidence to support my arguments. Let's see how much you remember with this two-question midbook midterm.

> ***Question 1.*** In the section on Asia, we learned that large amounts of white-collar work are going to places like India, China, and the Philippines. According to the research I cited, how many dollars in American wages are expected to shift to these low-cost locales over the next ten years?

Question 2. In the section on Automation, we learned that powerful software was reconfiguring, and often eliminating, the jobs of many knowledge workers in the West. Who is the John Henry of the Conceptual Age?

Unless you've got a photographic memory or a peculiar fascination with lost wages, you probably missed Question 1 and nailed Question 2.* Why? In Question 1, I asked you to recall a fact. In Question 2, I asked you to remember a story.

Our difficulty retrieving that isolated factoid, and our relative ease summoning the sad saga of Garry Kasparov, aren't signs of flaccid intelligence or impending Alzheimer's. They merely demonstrate how most minds work. Stories are easier to remember—because in many ways, stories are *how* we remember. "Narrative imagining—story—is the fundamental instrument of thought," writes cognitive scientist Mark Turner in his book *The Literary Mind.* "Rational capacities depend on it. It is our chief means of looking into the future, of predicting, of planning, and of explaining. . . . Most of our experience, our knowledge and our thinking is organized as stories."[1]

Story is just as integral to the human experience as design. Think about that loincloth-draped prehistoric guy I mentioned last chapter—the one scraping flint against a rock and becoming a designer. When evening fell and he and his buddies returned home, they probably sat around the campfire trading tales about escaping saber-toothed tigers or renovating the family cave. His brain, like ours, had an internal "story grammar" that helped him understand the world

*The answers: Question 1—$136 billion. Question 2—Chess grand master Garry Kasparov.

not as a set of logical propositions but as a pattern of experiences. He explained himself and connected to others through stories.

But as important as story has been throughout humanity, and as central as it remains to how we think, in the Information Age it got something of a bad rap. Hollywood, Bollywood, and other entertainment centers revere story. But the rest of society, to the extent anyone even thinks about it, considers it fact's less dependable younger sibling. Stories amuse; facts illuminate. Stories divert; facts reveal. Stories are for cover; facts are for real. The trouble with this view is twofold. First, as that pop quiz gave us a quick glimmer, it runs counter to how our minds actually work. Second, in the Conceptual Age, minimizing the importance of story places you in professional and personal peril.

Finding facts wasn't always so easy. Until recently, much of the world's data and information was piled on the dusty shelves of physical libraries. And the rest of it was housed in proprietary databases that only deep pocketed institutions could afford and well-trained experts could access. But today facts are ubiquitous, nearly free, and available at the speed of light. If you had wanted to find that lost-wages factoid, you probably could have typed a few words into Google, hit RETURN, and looked at what appeared on the screen a few seconds later. What's unsurprising today would have seemed preposterous just fifteen years ago: an English-speaking thirteen-year-old in Zaire who's connected to the Internet can find the current temperature in Brussels or the closing price of IBM stock or the name of Winston Churchill's second finance minister as quickly and easily as the head librarian at

"Humans are not ideally set up to understand logic; they are ideally set up to understand stories."

—ROGER C. SCHANK, *cognitive scientist*

Cambridge University. That's glorious. But it has enormous consequences for how we work and live. When facts become so widely available and instantly accessible, each one becomes less valuable. What begins to matter more is the ability to place these facts in *context* and to deliver them with *emotional impact.*

And that is the essence of the aptitude of Story—context enriched by emotion.

Story exists where high concept and high touch intersect. Story is high concept because it sharpens our understanding of one thing by showing it in the context of something else. For instance, the John Henry parable helps us understand in a tightly compressed way what happened in the early stages of the Industrial Age. The Garry Kasparov tale then relates that story in a new context—thus conveying a complex idea in a more memorable and meaningful way than if, say, I had tortured you with a PowerPoint presentation on the automation of work. Story is high touch because stories almost always pack an emotional punch. John Henry perishes. Garry Kasparov is humbled. To paraphrase E. M. Forster's famous observation, a fact is "The queen died and the king died." A story is "The queen died and the king died of a broken heart."

In his book *Things That Make Us Smart*, Don Norman crisply summarizes Story's high-concept and high-touch essence:

> Stories have the felicitous capacity of capturing exactly those elements that formal decision methods leave out. Logic tries to generalize, to strip the decision making from the specific context, to remove it from subjective emotions. Stories capture the context, capture the emotions. . . . Stories are important cognitive events, for they encapsulate, into one compact package, information, knowledge, context, and emotion.[2]

The ability to encapsulate, contextualize, and emotionalize has become vastly more important in the Conceptual Age. When so much routine knowledge work can be reduced to rules and farmed out to fast computers and smart L-Directed thinkers abroad, the more elusive abilities embodied by Story become more valuable. Likewise, as more people lead lives of abundance, we'll have a greater opportunity to pursue lives of meaning. And stories—the ones we tell *about* ourselves, the ones we tell *to* ourselves—are often the vehicles we use in that pursuit. In the rest of this chapter, I'll examine how the high-concept and high-touch capacity to weave events into an emotionally compelling narrative has become an essential aptitude in business, medicine, and personal life.

But first I need to tell you a story.

ONCE UPON A TIME, in a far-off land, lived a hero who was prosperous, happy, and respected by all. One day, three visitors arrived. They began pointing out the hero's many flaws and told him he was unfit to remain. The hero resisted, but to no avail. He was ousted from his land and sent off to a new world. There, adrift and alone, he floundered. But with the help of a few he met during his exile, he transformed himself and vowed to make his way back. And eventually he did return, where he was welcomed to a place he scarcely recognized, but that he still understood was home.

Does that story sound familiar? It should. It's a variation on what Joseph Campbell called "the hero's journey." In his 1949 book, *The Hero with a Thousand Faces*, Campbell argued that all myths—across time and across cultures—contain the same basic ingredients and follow the same general recipe. There are never any new stories, he said—just the same stories retold. And the one overarching story, the blueprint for tales since humankind's earliest days, is the "hero's journey." The hero's journey has three main parts: Departure, Initiation, and Return. The hero hears a call, refuses it at first, and then crosses the threshold into a new world. During Initiation, he faces stiff challenges and stares into the abyss. But along the way—usually with the help of mentors who give the hero a divine gift—he transforms and becomes at one with his new self. Then he returns, becoming the master of two worlds, committed to improving each. This structure underlies Homer's *Odyssey*, the story of Buddha, the legend of King Arthur, the story of Sacagawea, *Huckleberry Finn*, *Star Wars*, *The Matrix*, and, Campbell would have argued, just about every other epic tale.

But there's something else about the hero's journey that you might not have noticed—and that I wasn't conscious of myself until very recently. The hero's journey is the underlying story of this book. It begins with the knowledge worker, the master of L-Directed aptitudes. She faces a transformative crisis (wrought by Abundance, Asia, and Automation) and must answer the call (of a new way to work and live.) She resists the call at first (protesting outsourcing, denying that things need to change). But eventually she crosses the threshold (into the Conceptual Age). She faces challenges and difficulties (mastering R-Directed aptitudes). But she perseveres, acquires those capabilities, and returns as someone who can inhabit both worlds (she has a whole new mind).

> **"The story—from Rumplestiltskin to *War and Peace*—is one of the basic tools invented by the human mind for the purpose of understanding. There have been great societies that did not use the wheel, but there have been no societies that did not tell stories."**
>
> —URSULA K. LE GUIN

Now, I'm not suggesting that *A Whole New Mind* has some mythic stature. Hardly. Indeed, my point is just the opposite. It's to show that stories in general, and the story structure of the hero's journey in particular, lurk everywhere. Our tendency to see and explain the world in common narratives is so deeply ingrained that we often don't notice it—even when we've written the words ourselves. In the Conceptual Age, however, we must awaken to the power of narrative.

The Story Business

Robert McKee is one of the most influential figures in Hollywood, but you'll never see his face on the screen or his name on the closing credits. For the past fifteen years, in three-day seminars in the United States and Europe, McKee has taught aspiring screenwriters how to craft a compelling story. Some forty thousand people have plunked down $600 for his Story Seminar. And his students have gone on to win twenty-six Academy Awards. Anybody who hopes to write a screenplay begins by reading his book—*Story: Substance, Structure, Style, and The Principles of Screenwriting.* But in recent years, McKee has attracted a following among people whose only connection to the movie business comes when they buy a ticket and a tub of popcorn at the local multiplex: the executives, entrepreneurs, and workers of traditional business.

Why do they seek McKee's counsel?

I'll let the irascible master answer in his own words: "Although businesspeople are often suspicious of stories . . . the fact is that statistics are used to tell lies and damned lies, while accounting reports are often BS in a ball gown. . . . If a businessperson understands that his or her own mind naturally wants to frame experience in a story, the key to moving the audience is not to resist this impulse but to embrace it."[3]

Story, businesses are realizing, means big money. Economists Deirdre McCloskey and Arjo Klamer calculate that persuasion—advertising, counseling, consulting, and so on—accounts for 25 percent of U.S. gross domestic product. If, as some posit, Story is a component of half those persuasive efforts, then Story is worth about $1 trillion a year to the U.S. economy.[4] So organizations are embracing the story ethic espoused by McKee and others—often in unlikely ways.

The clearest example is a nascent movement called "organizational storytelling," which aims to make organizations aware of the stories that exist within their walls—and then to use those stories in pursuit of organizational goals. One of the founders of the movement is Steve Denning, an Australian who began his career as a lawyer in Sydney and later became a midlevel executive at the World Bank. "I was a left brain person," he says. "Big organizations love that kind of person."

Then one day, in a World Bank shake-up, he was booted from a job he loved and banished to the organizational equivalent of Siberia: a department known as "knowledge management," corporate jargon for how a company organizes its vast reserves of information and experience. Denning became the department's chief. And—grudgingly at first—he underwent a transformation. (Sounds like a hero's journey, doesn't it?) As he sought to understand what the World Bank knew—that is, what knowledge required management—Denning discovered that he learned more from trading stories in the cafeteria than he did from reading the bank's official documents and reports. An organization's knowledge, he realized, is contained in its stories. And that meant that if he was really going to be the top knowledge honcho at the bank, he had to go well beyond the L-Directed lawyer-executive approach he'd learned in the first twenty-five years of his career. So he made the World Bank a leader in knowledge management by making it a pioneer in using stories to contain and convey knowledge. "Storytelling doesn't replace analytical thinking," he says. "It supplements it by enabling us to imagine new perspectives and new worlds. . . . Abstract analysis is easier to understand when seen through the lens of a well-chosen story."[5] Now Denning is spreading his message—and telling his story—to organizations worldwide.

Denning isn't the only one taken with stories' business possibilities. 3M gives its top executives storytelling lessons. NASA has begun using storytelling in its knowledge management initiatives. And Xerox—recognizing that its repair personnel learned to fix machines by trading stories rather than by reading manuals—has collected its stories into a database called Eureka that *Fortune* estimates is worth $100 million to the company. In addition, several ventures have emerged to help existing companies harvest their internal stories. One such firm is StoryQuest, based in suburban Chicago. It dispatches interviewers to a company, records the stories of that company's employees, and then produces a CD that uses these personal narratives to yield broader insights about the company's culture and mission. In the United Kingdom, Richard Olivier, the son of Laurence Olivier and Joan Plowright and a former Shakespearean theater director, now advises large companies about how to integrate Story into their operations. Olivier calls his technique "mythodrama." His clients read and act Shakespeare's plays to elicit lessons in leadership and corporate governance. "Logical and analytical abilities alone can no longer guarantee success," Olivier says.[6] Successful businesspeople must be able to combine the science of accounting and finance with the art of Story.

> **"Myth is the secret opening through which the inexhaustible energies of the cosmos pour into human manifestation."**
>
> —JOSEPH CAMPBELL

It's easy to make fun of a purchasing manager pretending to be Titus Andronicus. But the fact that slow-moving, change-resistant large organizations have begun wrestling with Story—a word that itself would have made someone an executive suite laughingstock a decade ago—is telling. And it speaks to that innate capacity that I mentioned earlier. As Alan Kay, a Hewlett-Packard executive and cofounder of Xerox PARC, puts it: "Scratch the surface in a typical boardroom and we're all just cavemen with briefcases, hungry for a wise person to tell us stories."

STORY IS having another important impact on business. Like design, it is becoming a key way for individuals and entrepreneurs to distinguish their goods and services in a crowded marketplace. The best way to explain this phenomenon is to tell you a couple of stories from my own consumer life.

The first example of story-as-differentiator arrived in the mail. My family's neighborhood in northwest Washington, D.C., is in the midst of a slow generational turnover. The people who bought their houses decades ago and raised their kids in tidy brick colonials have started to retire. Meantime, young couples with children want to move into the neighborhood because it offers the conveniences of a suburb without actually having to live in one. Since prospective buyers far outnumber potential sellers, prices have been climbing. And so, to entice a few more of the older folks to get up and go, realtors frequently send postcards to every address in the neighborhood touting the latest sky-high price they've gotten for one of these modest homes. But in the mail one day came a realtor postcard that was different. I nearly threw it out at first. On one side it had the usual photo—a house a few blocks away that the realtor had just sold. But on the other side, instead of the sales price in 72-

point type followed by a row of exclamation points, it had the following:

> *Florence Skretowicz and her husband bought this delightful home in 1955. They paid $20,000 in cash for it and loved the many special details like solid oak floors, large windows including many with leaded glass, oak millwork around the doors, . . . an Old English fireplace mantle, and a garden pond. At age 91, Florence moved to Brighton Gardens, a retirement community in Friendship Heights, and the Fernandez sisters, neighbors and old family friends, asked me to sell this jewel. I was honored. Florence let us clear out the house, paint it inside and out, refinish the floors, and wash the windows.*
>
> *Now please take a minute to welcome Scott Dresser and Christie Constantine, the new residents who love the house just as much and plan to be in it forever and ever.*

The postcard didn't mention the sale price of the home. That seemed like an oversight at first, but it was actually a deft bit of Conceptual Age marketing. The price the house sold for is easy to find—in the newspaper, on the Internet, in neighborhood chitchat. Besides, the houses here are similar enough that their selling prices don't vary all that much. So despite realtors' persistent efforts, it's doubtful that a postcard celebrating a high price would be enough on its own to persuade a potential seller to sign up with a particular realtor. But selling a house you've lived in for half a century is not simply a financial decision; it's also an emotional one. And what better way to make that high-touch connection—and for this realtor to distinguish her services from her number-happy competitors—than with a story?

Or take another example of narrative's role in a time of abundance. I was at the store one afternoon picking up food for dinner, and I decided to grab a few bottles of wine. The selection was good but modest—maybe fifty bottles in all. And I quickly zeroed in on three inexpensive reds. All three were about the same price—nine or ten dollars each. All three seemed roughly the same quality. How to decide? I looked at the bottles. Two of them had labels filled with those fancy wine adjectives. But the third bottle—2 Brothers Big Tattoo Red—told me a story:

> *The idea for this wine comes from two brothers, Erik and Alex Bartholomaus. They wanted to sell a great wine, sourced by Alex, labeled with Erik's art, in a non-serious way for a good cause. Their goal was to pay homage to their late mother who suffered an untimely death due to cancer. . . . Alex and Erik will donate 50 cents from the sale of each bottle of Big Tattoo Red to Hospice of Northern Virginia and/or various cancer research funds in the name of Liliana S. Bartholomaus. Thanks to your support we have donated approximately $75,000 from the sales of our first release, and hopefully much more in the future. Alex and Erik thank you for purchasing a bottle of Big Tattoo Red in honor of their mother.*

Guess which wine I bought?

The Story of Healing

Modern medicine is a marvel. Powerful machines, like the MRI that took pictures of my brain, are letting us glimpse our body's inner workings. New drugs and medical devices are saving many lives and improving many more. Yet, those spectacular advances have often come at the expense of a more mundane, though no less important, aspect of care. The medical system can "completely eliminate the person's story," says Dr. Jack Coulehan of Stony Brook University Hospital in New York. "Unfortunately, medicine sees anecdote as the lowest form of science."[7] You've probably had this experience yourself. You're waiting in the exam room at your doctor's office. When the doctor comes in, two things are almost certain to happen next. You'll begin telling a story. And your doctor will interrupt you. Twenty years ago, when researchers videotaped doctor-patient encounters in an exam room, they found that doctors interrupted their patients after an average of twenty-one seconds. When another set of researchers repeated the study more recently, doctors had improved. They now waited an average of twenty-three seconds before butting in.

But that rushed just-the-facts approach to patient care may be changing, thanks in large part to the work of Dr. Rita Charon, a Columbia University Medical School professor who is attempting to place story at the heart of diagnosis and healing. When Charon was a young internist doing rounds at a hospital, she made a startling discovery: much of what she did as a doctor revolved around stories. Patients explained their ailments in narratives. Doctors repeated stories of their own. Illness itself unfolded as a narrative. Narrative was everywhere. Everywhere—except in the medical school curriculum or the consciousness of students and teachers. So Charon picked up a PhD in English to go with her MD—and then set about reforming medical

> **"Stories—that's how people make sense of what's happening to them when they get sick. They tell stories about themselves. Our ability as doctors to treat and heal is bound up in our ability to accurately perceive a patient's story. If you can't do that, you're working with one hand tied behind your back."**
>
> —DR. HOWARD BRODY, *family practice physician*

education. She launched the narrative medicine movement in a 2001 article in the *Journal of the American Medical Association* that called for a whole-minded approach to medical care:

> A scientifically competent medicine alone cannot help a patient grapple with the loss of health or find meaning in suffering. Along with scientific ability, physicians need the ability to listen to the narratives of the patient, grasp and honor their meanings, and be moved to act on the patient's behalf.[8]

Today, at Columbia, all second-year medical students take a seminar in narrative medicine in addition to their hard-core science classes. There they learn to listen more empathically to the stories their patients tell and to "read" those stories with greater acuity. Instead of asking a list of computerlike diagnostic questions, these young doctors broaden their inquiry. "Tell me where it hurts" becomes "Tell me about your life." The goal is empathy, which studies have shown declines in students with every year they spend in medical school. And the result is both high touch and high concept. Studying narrative helps a young doctor relate better to patients and to assess a patient's current condition in the context of that person's full life story. Being a good doctor, Charon says, requires narrative competence—"the competence that human beings use to absorb, interpret, and respond to stories."[9]

Narrative medicine is part of a wider trend to incorporate an R-Directed approach into what has long been a bastion of L-Directed muscle-flexing. Fifteen years ago, about one out of three American medical schools offered humanities courses. Today, three out of four do.[10] Bellevue, the legendary New York City public hospital, publishes its own journal—the *Bellevue Literary Review.* (Literary journals have also popped up at medical schools at Columbia, Penn State University, and the University of New Mexico.) The editor in chief of the Bellevue journal, Dr. Danielle Ofri, who teaches med students, requires her young charges to write up at least one of their patient histories as a narrative—to tell the patient's story from the patient's point of view. "That's not different from what the novelist wants to do," Ofri says. "I think we can take people who are basically empathetic and well-meaning and give them better skills to connect with their patients."[11]

Of course, narrative competence cannot replace technical expertise. A doctor who listens empathically to her patient's story but forgets to take his blood pressure or prescribes the wrong drug is not long for the profession. But Charon's approach can help young physicians imbue their work with greater empathy. (I'll discuss empathy in greater detail in Chapter 7.) For example, Charon's students all keep two charts on each patient. On one chart, they include the quantitative information and medical lingo of a typical hospital chart. But on the other—what she calls the "parallel chart"—students write narratives about their patients and chronicle their own emotions. According to the first study to test this method's effectiveness, students who kept a parallel chart had better relationships with patients—and better interviewing and technical skills—than their counterparts who did not.[12] Stories alone won't cure the sick. But combined with modern technology, they have an undeniable healing power. This may be the future of medicine: physicians who can both think rigorously and feel empathically,

"If stories come to you, care for them. And learn to give them away where they are needed. Sometimes a person needs a story more than food to stay alive."

—BARRY LOPEZ,
author of Arctic Dreams

physicians who can both analyze a test and appreciate a story—physicians with a whole new mind.

We are our stories. We compress years of experience, thought, and emotion into a few compact narratives that we convey to others and tell to ourselves. That has always been true. But personal narrative has become more prevalent, and perhaps more urgent, in a time of abundance, when many of us are freer to seek a deeper understanding of ourselves and our purpose.

More than a means to sell a house or even to deepen a doctor's compassion, Story represents a pathway to understanding that doesn't run through the left side of the brain. We can see this yearning for self-knowledge through stories in many places—in the astonishingly popular "scrapbooking" movement, where people assemble the artifacts of their lives into a narrative that tells the world, and maybe themselves, who they are and what they're about, and in the surging popularity of genealogy as millions search the Web to piece together their family histories.

What these efforts reveal is a hunger for what stories can provide—context enriched by emotion, a deeper understanding of how we fit in and why that matters. The Conceptual Age can remind us what has always been true but rarely been acted upon—that we must listen to each other's stories and that we are each the authors of our own lives.

PORTFOLIO

Design

Story

Symphony

Empathy

Play

Meaning

Write a Mini-Saga.

Writing anything is hard work. Writing a short story is really hard work. And writing a novel, a play, or a screenplay can take years. So go easy on yourself by writing a mini-saga. Mini-sagas are *extremely* short stories—just fifty words long . . . no more, no less. Yet, like all stories, they have a beginning, a middle, and an end. London's *Telegraph* newspaper once sponsored an annual mini-saga contest—and the results showed how much creativity a person can pack into exactly fifty words. Try writing a mini-saga yourself. It's addicting. Here are two excellent examples to hook you:

A Life

BY JANE ROSENBERG, BRIGHTON, UNITED KINGDOM

Joey, third of five, left home at sixteen, travelled the country and wound up in Nottingham with a wife and kids. They do shifts, the kids play out and ends never meet. Sometimes he'd give anything to walk away but he knows she's only got a year and she doesn't.

A Dream So Real

BY PATRICK FORSYTH, MALDON, UNITED KINGDOM

Staying overnight with friends, his sleep was disturbed by a vivid dream: a thief broke in, stole everything in the flat—then carefully replaced every single item with an exact replica.

"It felt so real," he told his friends in the morning.

Horrified, uncomprehending, they replied, "But who are you?"

Enlist in StoryCorps.

In the middle of New York's Grand Central Terminal sits a strange-looking square hut. It's called a StoryBooth, and if you're in New York, you should check it out. For ten dollars you can book an hour in the booth and record a broadcast-quality interview with someone (your ninety-year-old great-grandmother, zany Uncle Ted, the mysterious guy down the street) whose story you're eager to hear and preserve. It's all part of StoryCorps, an extraordinary national project "to instruct and inspire Americans to record each other's stories in sound." The effort, the brainchild of MacArthur fellow David Isay, is modeled after the Works Progress Administration oral history project of the 1930s. All the stories submitted end up in the StoryCorps archives at the U.S. Library of Congress's American Folklife Center, where they will be available for posterity. But you needn't go to

Grand Central, or even New York, to participate. The StoryCorps Web site offers StoryKits to help you do it yourself. "StoryCorps celebrates our shared humanity and collective identity," the organizers say. "It captures and defines the stories that bond us. We've found that the process of interviewing a friend, neighbor, or family member can have a profound impact on both the interviewer and interviewee. We've seen people change, friendships grow, families walk away feeling closer, understanding each other better. Listening, after all, is an act of love." *(More info: www.storycorps.net)*

Whip Out the Tape Recorder.

If StoryCorps is too complicated for your tastes, try a more modest version of your own. Find a friend or relative, sit him down, turn on a tape recorder, and begin asking him questions about his life. *How did you and your spouse meet? What was your first job? When was the first time you were away from home overnight? Who was the worst teacher you ever had? What was the happiest day of your life? The saddest? The most terrifying? What was the best decision you ever made?* You'll be amazed at the stories that pour out—and you'll be thrilled to have them recorded for yourself and others.

Visit a Storytelling Festival.

A great way to sample the incredible diversity of stories and storytellers in the world is to visit one of the growing number of storytelling festivals. At these two- or three-day gatherings, hundreds of people—some professionals, some not—take the stage to tell tales. Some of the storytellers at these events are a bit shellacked—in a twangy cornpone kind of way. But you're almost certain to stumble upon some amazing stories and some fascinating people recounting them. Here are seven of the best festivals.

National Storytelling Festival—The granddaddy of American storytelling festivals, attended each year by more than ten thousand people.
Where: Jonesborough, Tennessee
When: October
More info: www.storytellingcenter.com

Yukon International Storytelling Festival—Now in its second decade, this festival features storytellers from the "circumpolar world"—the Yukon, Greenland, Iceland—telling stories under the endless sun of early spring. Some of the participants tell their stories in dying native languages in an effort to keep those languages alive.
Where: Whitehorse, Yukon, Canada
When: June
More info: www.storytelling.yk.net

Bay Area Storytelling Festival—This weekend of outdoor storytelling is one of the best festivals in the western United States.
Where: El Sobrante, California
When: May
More info: www.bayareastorytelling.org

Digital Storytelling Festival—A wonderful gathering with an array of speakers and entertainers using computers and other digital tools to craft compelling tales. (See "Experiment with Digital Storytelling" on page 125.) The festival was launched by digital storytelling pioneer Dana Atchley, who died well before his time.

Where: Sedona, Arizona

When: June

More info: www.dstory.com

Cape Clear Island International Storytelling Festival—Held on Ireland's southernmost island, this festival attracts an eclectic mix of storytellers from all over the world. Most of the stories are in English, but some are in Irish.

Where: Cape Clear Island, Republic of Ireland

When: September

More info: www.indigo.ie/~stories

Sharing the Fire, New England Storytelling Conference—One of the oldest regional festivals in the United States, this event draws the best storytellers in the eastern United States.

Where: Cambridge, Massachusetts

When: September

More info: www.lanes.org/stf/sharing_the_fire.html

Get *One Story.*

Reading short stories is a fine way to sharpen your Story aptitude, but how can you find the good ones without poring through dozens of highbrow literary journals? One answer: let Maribeth Batcha and Hannah Tinti do the sifting for you with their innovative *One Story.* This publication delivers exactly what its title promises. Every three weeks or so, Batcha and Tinti send subscribers . . . one story. It's printed as a pocket-sized booklet that's easy to stick in your pocket or toss in your bag. The stories are usually great. And there's an elegant simplicity to reading a single story all by itself—rather than jammed between a bunch of other stories or wedged between a ten-thousand-word article about Kazakhstan and a review of the anniversary edition of *Jude the Obscure* in the *New Yorker.* I've subscribed to *One Story* for a few years now—and given subscriptions (a mere $21 per year) as gifts. *(More info: www.one-story.com)*

Riff on Opening Lines.

Call me Ishmael. That's not my name—but Herman Melville's famous opening line does offer some guidance for sharpening your narrative capabilities. Begin by underlining a sentence in a book or magazine. Then craft a story that evolves from this "opening line." Or do your own form of storytelling improv by asking someone else to feed you an opening line—and then use it as a springboard for your story. You can also turn this into a group activity. Ask everyone to write an opening line on an index card. Toss the cards into a hat. Then, taking turns, have each person draw a card and, on the spot, tell a story that begins with the line on the card. In a business setting, apply this exercise to a particular product, service, or experience in your company. How can an opening line chosen more or less at random lead to a compelling tale about your offering? This ad-hoc, story-based approach might help you harpoon the big ideas swimming around on the right side of your brain.

Play Photo Finish.

Instead of using words, turn to pictures for story inspiration. Select a photo (from a newspaper, a magazine, even a dusty shoebox) and fashion a tale about what is happening in the picture. Challenge yourself not only to describe the obvious, but also to tell the "back story," the part that isn't there or isn't initially apparent. Art and photography on display in museums (or on museum web sites) offer another rich source of material.

Experiment with Digital Storytelling.

Story is an ancient art—but like all art, it can be enhanced with modern tools. Digital cameras, inexpensive audio and video editing programs, Photoshop, and CD burners are allowing anyone with a story in their hearts to tell it with pictures and sound. A good place to learn these new techniques is at the Storytelling Bootcamp at the annual Digital Storytelling Festival (see page 122). (I've gone through the boot camp myself—and it was worth the time and money.) The Center for Digital Storytelling also has classes and lots of background material *(more info: www.storycenter.org)*. For other ways that technology is turbocharging stories, check out the online storytelling community, the Fray *(more info: www.fray.com)*, as well as the City Stories Project *(more info: www.citystories.com)* and I Used to Believe *(more info: www.iusedtobelieve.com)*, a fascinating collection of childhood beliefs.

Ask Yourself: "Who Are These People?"

Do you ever find yourself in large public places (airports, shopping malls, movie theaters, or sports stadiums) looking around and wondering who all these people are? Next time you're in this situation, don't just ask the question. Answer it. Make up a story about two of the people in your proximity. Who are they? What are their names? Are they coworkers? Lovers? Siblings? Enemies? Why are they here? Where are they going next? If you're out with friends, together select a few people, craft your own stories, and then compare the results. What do you ignore that your friend emphasizes? Which details do you focus on that they might not even see? People often interpret the same clues very differently based on their own life experiences. This exercise can help you challenge assumptions, bypass stereotypes, and broaden the stories you create in your interactions with family, friends, and colleagues. If nothing else, it can make waiting for a bus a bit more entertaining.

Read These Books.

The best method for heightening your aptitude for Story is just to read great stories—particularly the archetypal stories found in Aesop's fables; Greek, Nordic, Native American, South Asian, and Japanese myths; the Bible; and Shakespeare's plays. But if you're looking for a broader view of Story itself, the following five books are must-reads.

Story: Substance, Structure, Style, and the Principles of Screenwriting *by Robert McKee*—Even if you don't plan to write the next great screenplay, McKee's book is valuable reading. It explains the basic structure of the cinematic story—from how characters drive narrative to the twenty-six different types of story genres. This book will also change the way you watch movies.

Stealing Fire from the Gods: A Dynamic New Story Model for Writers and Filmmakers *by James Bonnet*—Drawing on the work of Carl Jung, Joseph Campbell, and others, Bonnet demonstrates how to use story archetypes and the "natural storymaking process" to create modern narratives of any kind.

Beyond Bullet Points: Using Microsoft PowerPoint to Create Presentations That Inform, Motivate, and Inspire *by Cliff Atkinson*—PowerPoint. Just the word makes my eyelids droop. But since this slide program has infiltrated every organization in every part of the world, we might as well make the best of it. Throw away those room-emptying left-brain slides and use Atkinson's book to turn your PowerPoint presentation into an epic.

Understanding Comics: The Invisible Art *by Scott McCloud*—People laugh at me when I say this is one of the best books I've ever read, but they just don't get it. Scott McCloud's masterpiece (yeah, it is) explains how comics work—how the stories unfold, how the pictures and words work together, and how the readers supply much of the meaning. And get this: McCloud wrote it in the form of a book-length comic. Amazing.

The Hero with a Thousand Faces *by Joseph Campbell*—Campbell's book introduces the idea of the "hero's journey," something that every aspiring writer—not to mention, any self-actualizing human—ought to understand. For another avenue into Campbell's mind, look for his famous late-1980s interviews with Bill Moyers, which are available on CD, DVD, and video. A collection of Campbell lectures and writings is also available from the foundation established in his name.

(*More info: www.jcf.org/works.php*)

Six

SYMPHONY

This is me.

Actually, it's not me precisely. It's a drawing of me, in which I'm both the subject and the artist. A self-portrait. Pretty awful, isn't it? (And those nostrils? Don't even ask.)

I was never very good at drawing, so one week I decided to learn. But instead of enrolling in a conventional art class, I opted for an approach closer to the heart of this book: drawing on the right side of the brain, the method pioneered by Betty Edwards and described in her similarly titled book. The self-portrait above is like those "before" pictures in weight-loss ads. I drew it on the first day of class—before the instruction began. Five days later, as you'll see later in this chapter, my artwork came out different. And in the process, I learned a lot about our next high-concept aptitude.

Symphony, as I call this aptitude, is the ability to put together the pieces. It is the capacity to synthesize rather than to analyze; to see relationships between seemingly unrelated fields; to detect broad patterns rather than to deliver specific answers; and to invent something new by combining elements nobody else thought to pair. Symphony is also an attribute of the brain's right hemisphere in the literal, as well as the metaphorical, sense. As I explained in Chapter 2, the neuroscience research conducted with functional MRIs has shown that the right hemisphere operates in a simultaneous, contextual, and symphonic manner. It concerns itself not with a particular spruce but with the whole forest—not with the bassoon player or the first violinist but with the entire orchestra.

Symphonic thinking is a signature ability of composers and conductors, whose jobs involve corralling a diverse group of notes, instruments, and performers and producing a unified and pleasing sound. Entrepreneurs and inventors have long relied on this ability. But today Symphony is becoming an essential aptitude for a much wider swath of the population. The reasons go back to the three forces propelling us out of the Information Age. Automation has taken over many of the routine analytic tasks that knowledge workers once performed. Many of those tasks are also heading to Asia, where they can be done equally well for much less. That is freeing (and in some cases forcing) professionals to do what computers and low-wage foreign technicians have a more difficult time replicating: recognizing patterns, crossing boundaries to uncover hidden connections, and making bold leaps of imagination. Meantime, a world teeming with information, individual choices, and just plain stuff is putting a premium on this aptitude in our personal lives as well. Modern life's glut of options and stimuli can be so overwhelming that those with the ability to see the big picture—to sort out what really matters—have a decided advantage in their pursuit of personal well-being.

One of the best ways to understand and develop the aptitude of Symphony is to learn how to draw—a skill that, as that self-portrait demonstrates, wasn't exactly my forte.

ON THE MORNING of the first day of drawing class, before we open our sketchbooks or sharpen our pencils, we learn the essence of our craft, distilled to a single sentence that will be repeated for the next five days. "Drawing," says Brian Bomeisler, "is largely about relationships."

Bomeisler is my instructor. He'll be teaching me and six other students—a far-flung group that includes a lawyer from the Canary Islands and a pharmacist from New Zealand—the techniques developed by Betty Edwards in *Drawing on the Right Side of the Brain.* Bomeisler comes to the job with considerable street cred. He's an accomplished painter in New York. His works (and works-in-progress) adorn the walls of the sixth-floor SoHo loft that will be our classroom. He's been teaching this course for twenty years. He's also Betty Edwards's son.

Like his mother, with whom he developed this five-day workshop, Bomeisler believes drawing is about seeing. "The naming of things is where you get into trouble," he says. And to prove the point, as well as to benchmark our abilities, he gives us an hour to draw a self-portrait. We prop up our little mirrors, open our oversized sketchbooks, and begin to draw. I finish before the others—and Bomeisler immediately identifies me as the four-hundred-pound Cheez Doodle fiend making his inaugural visit to Weight Watchers: I've got a long way to go—but since things can't get much worse, they'll likely get a little better.

My problem, Bomeisler tells me as he squints at my artwork, is that I'm not drawing what I'm seeing. I'm drawing "remembered symbols from childhood." To grasp what he means, turn back to page 129 and if you can bear it, look at that self-portrait again. My lips don't *really* look like that. Nobody's lips look like that. I've drawn a *symbol* for lips—a symbol, as a matter of fact, that comes from childhood. Those penciled lips look a lot like the Magikist sign that used to beckon from I-94 when, as a kid, my family drove to visit my grandparents in Chicago. In a sense, I've merely written "lips" in modern hieroglyphics instead of truly seeing my lips and recognizing how they relate to the totality of my face.

Later that first day, Bomeisler shows us a Picasso line drawing and asks us to copy it. But before we begin, he tells us to turn Picasso's sketch upside down—so "you know nothing about what you're drawing." The goal is to trick the left hemisphere and clear the way for the right. When the left brain doesn't know what the right brain

is doing, the mind is free to see relationships and to integrate those relationships into a whole. In many ways, this is the core of learning how to draw—as well as the key to mastering the aptitude of Symphony. For example, one of the reasons my self-portrait looks so strange is that the relationships are skewed. In class, we seven students learn—and, more important, we *see*—that on a human face, the distance from the center line of the eyes to the bottom of the chin is equal to the distance from the center line of the eyes to the top of the head. I drew my eyes much higher on the head than they are in reality—and by botching that one relationship, I've distorted the entire picture.

Bomeisler is a sympathetic teacher with the gentle manner of Mr. Rogers had Mr. Rogers done time on Paris's left bank. During each drawing exercise, he glides around the room offering encouragement. "I'm here to keep your left hemisphere quiet," he murmurs. One day he teaches us about negative space—that is, the area between and around an image. He shows us the logo of FedEx, like the one below.

Look at the white space between the "E" and the "x" in "Ex." See the arrow? That's negative space. When we draw portraits of our classmates later in the week, we begin by lightly shading our large piece of paper—and then *erasing* the part that's *not* the outline of our subject's head in order to reveal it. "Negative space is a powerful drawing tool," Bomeisler says. "It's one of the secrets to learning how to draw."

Over the next four days, we learn to see several of these relationships—between space and negative space, between light and shadow, between angles and proportions—in ways that many of us never noticed. We draw stools propped on tables, the wrinkles on our hands, and the shadows that caress the corners of Bomeisler's studio. Throughout Bomeisler repeats his mantra that "drawing is largely about relationships" that, when combined, create the whole. And so, in some sense, is this course. All of our exercises in relationships lead to the final afternoon, when we must integrate our newly acquired understanding into a big picture—a second attempt at a self-portrait.

Seeing Relationships

Like drawing, Symphony is largely about relationships. People who hope to thrive in the Conceptual Age must understand the connections between diverse, and seemingly separate, disciplines. They must know how to link apparently unconnected elements to create something new. And they must become adept at analogy—at seeing one thing in terms of another. There are ample opportunities, in other words, for three types of people: the boundary crosser, the inventor, and the metaphor maker.

THE BOUNDARY CROSSER

What's the most prevalent, and perhaps most important, prefix of our times? *Multi.* Our jobs require multitasking. Our communities are multicultural. Our entertainment is multimedia. While detailed knowledge of a single area once guaranteed success, today the top rewards go to those who can operate with equal aplomb in starkly different realms. I call these people "boundary crossers." They develop expertise in multiple spheres, they speak different languages, and they find joy in the rich variety of human experience. They live *multi* lives—because that's more interesting and, nowadays, more effective.

Boundary crossers are people like Andy Tuck, a philosophy professor and pianist who applies the skills he honed in those fields to run his own management consulting firm. They include people such as Gloria White-Hammond, a pastor and pediatrician in Boston; Todd Machover, who composes operas and builds high-tech music equipment; and Jhane Barnes, whose expertise in mathematics informs her intricate clothing designs.[1] Mihalyi Csikszentmihalyi, the University of Chicago psychologist who wrote the classic book *Flow: The Psychology of Optimal Experience* as well as *Creativity: Flow and the Psychology of Discovery and Invention*, has studied the lives of creative people and found that "creativity generally involves crossing the boundaries of domains."[2] The most creative among us see relationships the rest of us never notice. Such ability is at a premium in a world where specialized knowledge work can quickly become routinized work—and therefore be automated or outsourced away. Designer Clement Mok says, "The next 10 years will require people to think and work across boundaries into new zones that are totally different from their areas of expertise. They will not only have to cross those boundaries, but they will also have to identify opportunities and make connections between them."[3]

> **"What I do is pattern recognition. I try to recognize the pattern before anyone else does."**
>
> —CAYCE POLLARD, *protagonist of William Gibson's novel* Pattern Recognition

For example, the offshoring of computer jobs to India will create new demand for people who can manage the relationship between the coders in the East and the clients in the West. These whole-minded professionals must be literate in two cultures, comfortable in both the hard science of computing and the soft science of sales and marketing, and able to move between different, and sometimes antagonistic, groups with the ease of a diplomat. Such multifaceted people can often solve problems that flummox the experts. "Many engineering deadlocks have been broken by people who are not engineers at all," says Nicholas Negroponte of MIT. "This is because perspective is more important than IQ. The ability to make big leaps of thought is a common denominator among the originators of breakthrough ideas. Usually this ability resides in people with very wide backgrounds, multidisciplinary minds, and a broad spectrum of experiences."[4]

Boundary crossers reject either/or choices and seek multiple options and blended solutions. They lead hyphenated lives filled with hyphenated jobs and enlivened by hyphenated identities. (Example: Omar Wasow, a Nairobi-born, African-American-Jewish entrepreneur–policy wonk–television analyst.) They help explain the growing ranks of college students with double majors—and the proliferation of academic departments that dub themselves "interdisciplinary."

Csikszentmihalyi has also uncovered a related dimension of the boundary crosser's talent: those who possess it often elude traditional gender role stereotyping. In his research, he found that "when tests of masculinity/femininity are given to young people, over and over one finds that creative and talented girls are more dominant and tough than other girls, and creative boys are more sensitive and less aggressive than their male peers." This bestows unique advantages, according to Csikszentmihalyi. "A psychologically androgynous person in effect doubles his or her repertoire of responses and can interact with the world in terms of a much richer and varied spectrum of opportunities."[5]

In other words, as Samuel Taylor Coleridge said two hundred years ago and as boundary crossers remind us today, great minds are androgynous.

THE INVENTOR

In the 1970s, Hershey Food Corp. ran a series of goofy television commercials that inadvertently contained a crucial lesson in R-Directed Thinking. In the ads, a person walks along dreamily while munching a chocolate bar. Someone else, equally oblivious, strolls about while eating peanut butter. The two collide.

"Hey, you got peanut butter on my chocolate," the first person complains.

"And you got chocolate on my peanut butter," the other replies.

Each then samples the results. To their surprise, they discover they've created a masterpiece. "Reese's Peanut Butter Cups," the announcer intones. "Two great tastes that taste great together."

R-Directed thinkers understand the logic of this confectionary fender-bender. They have an intuitive sense of what I call the "Reese's Peanut Butter Cup Theory of Innovation": sometimes the most powerful ideas come from simply combining two existing ideas nobody else ever thought to unite. Take John Fabel, an avid cross-country skier. He loved the sport, but his backpack straps always bruised his shoulders. One day on a trip to New York, he passed by the Brooklyn Bridge—and saw the solution to his problem. In an act of what cognitive scientists Gilles Fouconnier and Mark Turner call "conceptual blending," Fabel combined the structure of a suspension bridge with the components of a traditional backpack—and invented a new, easier-to-tote, and now popular pack called the Ecotrek.

> "The key to success is to risk thinking unconventional thoughts. Convention is the enemy of progress. As long as you've got slightly more perception than the average wrapped loaf, you could invent something."
>
> —TREVOR BAYLIS, *inventor*

The ability to forge these kinds of inspired, inventive relationships is a function of the right side of our brains. Cognitive neuroscientists at Drexel and Northwestern universities have found that the flashes of insight that precede "Aha!" moments are accompanied by a large burst of neural activity in the brain's right hemisphere. However, when we work out problems in a more methodical L-Directed way, this "eureka center" remains quiet.[6] Our ability to activate this right hemisphere capacity has become more urgent as we transition out of the Information Age. In business today, the journey from innovation to commodity is so swift that successful individuals and organizations must be relentless. They must focus maniacally on invention—while outsourcing or automating much of the execution. This requires those with the ability and fortitude to experiment with novel combinations and to make the many mistakes that inevitably come with an inspiration-centered approach. Fortunately, despite what some might believe, all of us harbor this capacity to invent. Listen to Trevor Baylis, the British stuntman-turned-inventor who invented a windup radio that can be used without batteries or electricity: "Invention isn't some impenetrable branch of magic: anyone can have a go." Most inventions and breakthroughs come from reassembling existing ideas in new ways. Those willing to have a go at developing this symphonic ability will flourish in the Conceptual Age.

THE METAPHOR MAKER

Suppose you're at the office one day and your boss says, "Lend me your ears." As we learned in Chapter 1, because the literal meaning of those four words computes only in a gruesome way, the left hemisphere will get a bit panicky and look beseechingly across the corpus callosum for assistance. The right hemisphere will then calm its partner, put the phrase in context, and explain that "lend me your ears" is a metaphor. The boss doesn't really want you to pull a Van Gogh. He just wants you to listen to what he's about to say.

Metaphor—that is, understanding one thing in terms of something else—is another important element of Symphony. But like so many aspects of R-Directed Thinking, it struggles against an undeserved reputation. "The Western tradition . . . has excluded metaphor from the domain of reason," writes the prominent linguist George Lakoff. Metaphor is often considered ornamentation—the stuff of poets and other frilly sorts, flowery words designed to perfume the ordinary or unpleasant. In fact, metaphor is central to reason—because, as Lakoff writes, "Human thought processes are largely metaphorical."[7]

In a complex world, mastery of metaphor—a whole-minded ability that some cognitive scientists have called "imaginative rationality"—has become ever more valuable. Each morning, when we rise from our slumber and flick on the lights, we know we'll spend much of the day paddling through a torrent of data and information. Certain kinds of software can sort these bits and offer glimpses into patterns. But only the human mind can think metaphorically and see relationships that computers could never detect.

Likewise, in a time of abundance, when the largest rewards go to those who can devise novel and compelling creations, metaphor-making is vital. For instance, Georges de Mestral noticed how burrs stuck to his dog's fur and, reasoning metaphorically, came up with the idea for Velcro.[8] A computer couldn't have done that. "Everything you create is a representation of something else; in this sense, everything you create is enriched by metaphor," writes choreographer Twyla Tharp. She encourages people to boost their metaphor quotient, or MQ, because "in the creative process, MQ is as valuable as IQ."[9]

> **"Metaphor is the lifeblood of all art."**
>
> —TWYLA THARP

Metaphorical thinking is also important because it helps us understand others. That's one reason that marketers are supplementing their quantitative research with qualitative investigations into the metaphorical minds of their customers.[10] For instance, a method developed by Harvard Business School professor Gerald Zaltman supplements polls and focus groups by asking subjects to bring in pictures that describe their feelings toward particular goods and services—and then to fashion those pictures into a collage. Through this technique, Zaltman elicits the metaphors customers use to think of products—coffee as an "engine," a security gizmo as a "companionable watchdog," and so on.

But the benefits go well beyond the commercial realm. Today, thanks to astonishing improvements in telecommunications, wider access to travel, and increasing life spans, we come into contact with a larger and more diverse set of people than any humans in history. Metaphorical imagination is essential in forging empathic connections and communicating experiences that others do not share. Finally—and perhaps most important—is metaphor's role in slaking the thirst for meaning. The material comforts brought forth by abundance ultimately matter much less than the metaphors you live by—whether, say, you think of your life as a "journey" or as a "treadmill." "A large part of self-understanding," says Lakoff, "is the search for appropriate personal metaphors that make sense of our lives."[11] The more we understand metaphor, the more we understand ourselves.

Seeing the Big Picture

In any symphony, the composer and the conductor have a variety of responsibilities. They must make sure that the brass horns work in synch with the woodwinds, that the percussion instruments don't drown out the violas. But perfecting those relationships—important though it is—is not the ultimate goal of their efforts. What conductors and composers desire—what separates the long remembered from the quickly forgotten—is the ability to marshal these relationships into a whole whose magnificence exceeds the sum of its parts. So it is with the high-concept aptitude of Symphony. The boundary crosser, the inventor, and the metaphor maker all understand the importance of relationships. But the Conceptual Age also demands the ability to grasp the *relationships between relationships.* This meta-ability goes by many names—systems thinking, gestalt thinking, holistic thinking. I prefer to think of it simply as seeing the big picture.

Seeing the big picture is fast becoming a killer app in business. While knowledge workers of the past typically performed piecemeal assignments and spent their days tending their own patch of a larger garden, such work is now moving overseas or being reduced to instructions in powerful software. As a result, what has become more valuable is what fast computers and low-paid overseas specialists cannot do nearly as well: integrating and imagining how the pieces fit together. This has become increasingly evident among entrepreneurs and other successful businesspeople.

For instance, one remarkable recent study found that self-made millionaires are four times more likely than the rest of the population to be dyslexic.[12] Why? Dyslexics struggle with L-Directed Thinking and the linear, sequential, alphabetic reasoning at its core. But as with a blind person who develops a more acute sense of hearing, a dyslexic's difficulties in one area lead him to acquire outsized ability in others. As Sally Shaywitz, a Yale neuroscientist and specialist in dyslexia, writes, "Dyslexics think differently. They are intuitive and excel at problem-solving, seeing the big picture, and simplifying. . . . They are poor rote reciters, but inspired visionaries."[13] Game-changers such as Charles Schwab, who invented the discount brokerage, and Richard Branson, who has shaken up the retail music and airline industries, both cite their dyslexia as a secret to their success. It forced them to see the big picture. Because of their difficulty analyzing the particulars, they became adept at recognizing the patterns. Michael Gerber, who has studied entrepreneurs of all sorts, has reached similar conclusions: "All great entrepreneurs are Systems Thinkers. All who wish to become great entrepreneurs need to learn how to become a Systems Thinker . . . to develop their innate passion for seeing things whole."[14]

"The guy who invented the wheel was an idiot. The guy who invented the other three, he was a genius."

—SID CAESAR

Both academic studies and firsthand observations are showing that pattern recognition—understanding the relationships between relationships—is equally important for those who aren't intent on building their own empire. Daniel Goleman writes about a study of executives at fifteen large companies: "Just one cognitive ability distinguished star performers from average: pattern recognition, the 'big picture' thinking that allows leaders to pick out the meaningful trends from a welter of information around them and to think strategically far into the future."[15] These star performers, he found, "relied less on deductive, if-then reasoning" and more on the intuitive, contextual reasoning characteristic of Symphony. The shifting terrain is already prompting some archetypal L-Directed workers to recast who they are and what they do. One example: Stefani Quane of Seattle, who calls herself a "holistic attorney," dedicated to taking care of your will, trust, and family matters by viewing them in context rather than isolation, and examining how your legal concerns relate to the entirety of your life.

More and more employers are looking for people who possess this aptitude. Sidney Harman is one of them. The eightysomething multimillionaire CEO of a stereo components company says he doesn't find it all that valuable to hire MBAs. Instead,

> I say, "Get me some poets as managers." Poets are our original systems thinkers. They contemplate the world in which we live and feel obliged to interpret and give expression to it in a way that makes the reader understand how that world turns. Poets, those unheralded systems thinkers, are our true digital thinkers. It is from their midst that I believe we will draw tomorrow's new business leaders.[16]

Business and work, of course, are far from the only places where seeing the big picture is helpful. This aspect of Symphony has also become crucial for health and well-being. Take the growing appeal of integrative medicine, which combines conventional medicine with alternative and complementary therapies, and its cousin, holistic medicine, which aims to treat the whole person rather than the particular disease. These movements—grounded in science but not dependent solely on science's often L-Directed approach—have achieved mainstream recognition, including their own branch of the National Institutes of Health. They move beyond the reductionist, mechanistic approach of conventional medicine toward one that, in the words of one physicians' professional association, integrates "all aspects of well-being, including physical, environmental, mental, emotional, spiritual and social health; thereby contributing to the healing of ourselves and our planet."[17]

The capacity to see the big picture is perhaps most important as an antidote to the variety of psychic woes brought forth by the remarkable prosperity and plentitude of our times. Many of us are crunched for time, deluged by information, and paralyzed by the weight of too many choices. The best prescription for these modern maladies may be to approach one's own life in a contextual, big-picture fashion—to distinguish between what really matters and what merely annoys. As I'll discuss in the final chapter, this ability to perceive one's own life in a way that encompasses the full spectrum of human possibility is essential to the search for meaning.

ON THE FINAL DAY of drawing class, we approach the week's crescendo. After lunch, we each tape our small mirrors to the wall. We position our chairs about eight inches away and begin to draw our self-portraits once again. Bomeisler warns us of the perils lurking in the looking glass. "We've used the mirror to prepare ourselves to face the world. Clear your mind of any thoughts you've had about that and concentrate on the shapes, the lights, and the relationships," he says. "You want to see what your face looks like on this particular day in this particular place."

At lunch, I swap my glasses for contact lenses so I won't have to draw the shadows cast by my spectacles. Given my performance on the first self-portrait, I'll take any edge I can get. I begin with my eyes—really looking at them, seeing what shape they are, where the color ends and the whites of my eyeballs begin, realizing that the width between my two eyes is exactly the same as the width of each individual eye. My nose, though, gives me fits—in part because I keep *thinking* of a nose instead of just seeing what's plain on my face. I skip that part—and for the longest time, my self-portrait has a big empty spot in the center, a Venus de Milo of proboscises. When I get to the mouth, I draw and redraw it nine times until I get it right because the early renditions keep looking like that Magikist sign. But the shape of the head comes easily because I just erase the negative space around it.

To my amazement, what emerges on the sketchpad begins to look a little like me on that particular day in that particular place. Bomeisler checks in on my progress, touches my shoulder, and whispers, "Fantastic." I almost believe he means it. And as I pencil in the finishing touches, I experience a tiny hint of the kind of feeling a terrified mother must have after she's lifted a Buick off her child and wonders where her strength came from.

When I'm done, after seeing the relationships and integrating those relationships into the big picture, this is me.

PORTFOLIO

II

Design

Story

Symphony

Empathy

Play

Meaning

Listen to the Great Symphonies.

Listening to symphonies, not surprisingly, is an excellent way to develop your powers of Symphony. Here are five classics the experts recommend. (Of course, particular recordings—with different conductors and orchestras—will vary in style, interpretation, and sound.)

Beethoven's 9th Symphony—One of the most famous symphonies of all time, Beethoven's "Ode to Joy" is always a treat. I've found that on each listening something new surfaces—in part because the context in which I've listened alters and shapes the meaning.

Mozart's Symphony No. 35, "Haffner Symphony"—Notice how Mozart brings in the woodwinds at the end to create a whole that dramatically surpasses the sum of the parts.

Mahler's 4th Symphony in G Major—I doubt that inspiration was Mahler's aim, but his 4th Symphony always sounds inspiring to me.

Tchaikovsky's 1812 Overture—You've heard this one many times before. But next time, get a recording that uses actual church bells and cannons—and listen carefully to how the components fit together.

Haydn's Symphony No. 94 in G Major, "Surprise"—To master the aptitude of Symphony, you must be open to surprise. When you listen to this, marvel at how Haydn uses surprise to broaden and deepen the music.

Hit the Newsstand.

One of my favorite exercises in conceptual blending is the "newsstand roundup." If you're stymied on how to solve a problem, or just want to freshen your own thinking, visit the largest newsstand you can find. Spend twenty minutes browsing—and select ten publications that you've never read and would likely never buy. That's the key: buy magazines you never noticed before. Then take some time to look through them. You don't have to read every page of every magazine. But get a sense of what the magazine is about and what its readers have on their minds. Then look for connections to your own work or life. For instance, when I did this exercise, I figured out a better way to craft my business cards thanks to something I saw in *Cake Decorating*—and came up with a new idea for a newsletter because of an article in *Hair for You.* Warning: your spouse might give you uncomfortable looks when you come home toting *Trailer Life*, *Teen Cosmo*, and *Divorce Magazine.*

Draw.

A great way to expand your capacity for Symphony is to learn how to draw. As I discovered myself, drawing is about seeing relationships—and then integrating those relationships into a whole. I'm partial to the Betty Edwards approach, because it proved so valuable to me. About a dozen times a year, Brian Bomeisler (and other Edwards disciples) teach courses like the one I took. If you can spare the time, the five-day workshop is well worth the investment. If you can't, Edwards and Bomeisler have a *Drawing on the Right Side of the Brain* video. And Edwards's classic book, *Drawing on the Right Side of the Brain*, is available at most booksellers. *(More info: www.drawright.com)* For those of you with more curiosity than patience, consider playing around with a five-line self-portrait—that is, drawing your self-portrait using only five lines. It's a great big-picture exercise and plenty of fun. Here's one of mine:

Keep a Metaphor Log.

Improve your MQ (metaphor quotient) by writing down compelling and surprising metaphors you encounter. Try it for a week and you'll understand the power of this exercise. Keep a small notebook with you and scribble when you read a newspaper columnist write that pollsters have "colonized" the minds of our leaders—or when your friend says, "I don't feel rooted." You'll be amazed. When I last kept a log, I came upon such an array of metaphors that the world seemed richer and more vivid. It will also inspire you to create your own metaphors in writing, thought, or other parts of your life.

Follow the Links.

Play your own version of six degrees of separation courtesy of the Internet. Choose a word or a topic you find interesting, type it into a search engine, and then follow one of the links. From the initial site you visit, select one of *its* links, and venture on. Repeat this process seven or eight times, always clicking a new link from the site you're currently viewing. At the end of your journey, reflect on what you learned about your original topic and the diversions you encountered along the way. What did you encounter because of your casual detours that you might otherwise not have found? What patterns or themes (if any) emerged? What unusual connections between seemingly unrelated thinking did you accidentally discover? Following the links is a commitment to learning by serendipity. A variation: Go with pure chance by using a random web site generator like U Roulette (*www.uroulette.com*) or Random Web Search (*www.randomwebsearch.com*). Beginning with a site you never would have visited can take you to places you never expected—and enhance your appreciation for the symphonic relationships between ideas.

Look for Solutions in Search of Problems

Problems need solutions. That's elementary. But sometimes smart solutions need a few more problems. In their lively and engaging book, *Why Not?: How to Use Everyday Ingenuity to Solve Problems Big and Small,* Yale professors Barry Nalebuff and Ian Ayres suggest we examine existing solutions and ask two questions:

1. ***Where else would it work?*** Sometimes we can export fixes from one realm to another. For instance, the authors ask, if the movie industry can create a PG version of its films to show on airplanes, why not offer the same recut and sanitized version on DVD for parents concerned about what their kids are watching? If U.S. taxpayers can make deductible IRA contributions past the tax year and until April 15, why not permit the same for charitable deductions and "allow people to make more informed choices about their generosity?"

2. ***Would flipping it work?*** Changing the default option is a simple step that can achieve excellent results. Consider organ donation. In the U.S., Nalebuff and Ayres write, potential donors must affirmatively indicate their desire to donate their organs. Although polls show most Americans are willing to do so, inertia and circumstance often stand in the way. But if organ donation were opt-out instead of opt-in—that is, when people applied for their driver's licenses, they were automatically signed up unless they explicitly said

they didn't want to become an organ donor, as is the practice in several other countries—the U.S. could chip away at lengthy transplant waiting lists and save thousands of lives.

Asking "Why?" can lead to understanding. Asking "Why not?" can lead to breakthroughs.

(More information: www.whynot.net)

Create an Inspiration Board.

When you're working on a project, empty your bulletin board and turn it into an inspiration board. Each time you see something that you find compelling—a photo, a piece of fabric, the page of a magazine—tack it to the board. Before long, you'll start seeing connections between the images that will enliven and expand your work. Fashion designers have long used these boards, forming wild collages that serve as mind expanders and conceptual guides. You can do the same.

Read These Books.

Here are six books to help you hone your powers of Symphony:

Beethoven's Anvil: Music in Mind and Culture *by William Benzon*—An excellent exploration of how the mind processes music, in particular how music draws on all parts of the brain in a whole-minded, symphonic fashion.

Powers of Ten *by Charles and Ray Eames*—Created by the well-known husband-wife team, this flip book contains seventy-six pages, each with one image, each of which is seen ten times closer than its predecessor. Start at the beginning of the book with an image of the earth viewed from ten million light-years away. Then flip through the pages with your thumb, and zero in on a man at a picnic on Chicago's lakefront—and descend into the man's skin, one of the skin's cells, the cell's DNA, all the way to a single proton.

Dialogue: The Art of Thinking Together *by William Isaacs*—Collaborating with colleagues to cross boundaries, identify patterns, and connect ideas may require new ways of talking with each other. This book explores principles and practices that can help individuals move beyond simply reporting their own thoughts to truly thinking together and building collective wisdom.

Metaphors We Live By *by George Lakoff and Mark Johnson*—This short, accessible work is the best book available about metaphor as a thought process.

No Waste *(A project by Laboratorio De Creacion Maldeojo)*—A TV aerial made out of discarded metal cafeteria trays. Toy cars fashioned from spent plastic shampoo, ink, and glue containers. Those are just two of the images in this remarkable collection of photographs of ingeniously repurposed items from the streets of Cuba. A stunning display of combinatorial thinking.

How to See: A Guide to Reading Our Man-made Environment *by George Nelson*—First published in the mid-seventies, and reissued in 2003, this book is an amazing tutorial in looking critically at the world around us, making connections between what we see, and conceiving of human creations in a broader context.

Do Some Real Brainstorming.

You've been in this meeting. The boss asks everyone to "brainstorm"—and after fifteen frustrating minutes the effort produces few inspired ideas and many dispirited employees. Why does this happen? Because you weren't following the rules. Effective brainstorming sessions aren't random and haphazard. They follow a particular structure that's proven to elicit good ideas.

To brainstorm properly, abide by these rules (which are drawn from Tom Kelley's excellent book, *The Ten Faces of Innovation*):

1. *Go for Quantity*. Good ideas emerge from lots of ideas. Set a numerical goal—say, a total of one hundred ideas.
2. *Encourage Wild Ideas*. Extremism is a virtue. The right idea often flows from what initially seems outlandish.
3. *Be Visual*. Pictures unlock creativity.
4. *Defer Judgment.* There's no such thing as a bad idea, so banish the naysayers. Think creatively first and critically later.
5. *One Conversation at a Time.* Listen, be polite, and build on others' suggestions.

As people shout out their ideas, or expand others' thoughts, capture everything in writing. (It helps to have one person serve as scribe and another as facilitator.) At the end of a half-hour, you'll have a long list of ideas. Take a break. Then begin evaluating what's on the list. Most of the ideas won't be very good. Some will be downright ridiculous. But it's almost certain that you'll come up with a handful of ideas you'd never have arrived at otherwise.

If you want to brainstorm from your own private Idaho of a computer, check out the Web site Halfbakery, to which people around the world have contributed all manner of ideas for products, services, and businesses. Some of the ideas are raw. But others are surprisingly well done. *(More info: www.halfbakery.com)*

Celebrate Your Amateurness.

I am best at what I can't do.

It has become my ability to feel strong and confident in these situations. I feel free to move, to listen to my heart, to learn, to act even if that means I will make mistakes.

If you want a creative life, do what you can't and experience the beauty of the mistakes you make.

The above from Marcel Wanders, designer and self-described "professional amateur." (More info: www.marcelwanders.com)

Look for Negative Spaces.

Negative space is the part of the big picture we often overlook. So train your eyes to see it. When you take a walk or browse a store or page through a magazine, peer past what's prominent and examine what's between, beyond, and around it. Being aware of negative space will change how you look at your surroundings—and it will make the positive space snap into focus. It's also a way to be surprised. For instance, on a package of Hershey's Kisses, of all things, I found an unexpected and whimsical negative space. Do you see it?

Seven

EMPATHY

Yesterday was rough. I worked nonstop from the time I awoke, straining to meet a couple of deadlines, trying to squirm out of an unexpected new assignment, and contending with a seven-year-old with a runny nose, a five-year-old with a loose tooth, and an eighteen-month-old who was teaching himself cause-and-effect by pushing ceramics off a counter. In the afternoon I ran five miles. After a rushed dinner, I returned to my office and worked a few more hours, until I was too tired to concentrate. At about 10:00—bone tired—I went to bed. Except I couldn't sleep. I read a little, then tried again. No go. So around 1 A.M., I went downstairs, poured myself a glass of wine, and read the previous day's newspaper. Then another glass of wine. Then another newspaper. At 2:15 I went back upstairs and tried again. Finally, I did fall asleep, sometime after 3:06, the last numbers I remember seeing on the clock radio beside my bed.

About three hours later, the eighteen-month-old stood up in his crib and began bellowing his traditional morning milk chant. By 7 A.M., the house had erupted into full morning mania. And by 8 A.M., I was back in my office, where I now sit, facing another day of deadlines. I'm tired, really tired. In fact, I just yawned. And as I think about the day before me, I'm yawning again. Despite the three cups of coffee I've just guzzled, I could fall asleep in about thirty seconds. But sleep will have to wait. Too much to do. So I soldier on—and I yawn.

Stop for a moment. In the past minute, have you yawned? When you read my account of sleepiness, and then pictured me yawning, did you feel an inkling of a yawn creep toward your jaw? If so, you probably have a natural inclination for the next essential aptitude—Empathy. (If not, in order to trigger this innate capacity, you may need a story more emotionally compelling than my boo-hoo tale of overworking and undersleeping.)

Empathy is the ability to imagine yourself in someone else's position and to intuit what that person is feeling. It is the ability to stand in others' shoes, to see with their eyes, and to feel with their hearts. It is something we do pretty much spontaneously, an act of instinct rather than the product of deliberation. But Empathy isn't sympathy—that is, feeling bad *for* someone else. It is feeling *with* someone else, sensing what it would be like to be that person. Empathy is a stunning act of imaginative derring-do, the ultimate virtual reality—climbing into another's mind to experience the world from that person's perspective.

And because it requires attuning oneself to another, Empathy often involves an element of mimicry, which is why some of you yawned a moment ago. Contagious yawning, says Drexel University cognitive neuroscientist Steven Platek, is likely a "primitive empathic mechanism."[1] His research has found that contagious yawners score high on various tests that measure levels of Empathy. Such people—some of you, no doubt—are so in tune with what others are going through that they can't help but mimic that behavior.

Empathy is mighty important. It helped our species climb out of the evolutionary muck. And now that we're upright and bipedal—the big animals on campus—it still helps us get through the day. Empathy allows us to see the other side of an argument, comfort someone in distress, and bite our lip instead of muttering something snide. Empathy builds self-awareness, bonds parent to child, allows us to work together, and provides the scaffolding for our morality.

But Empathy—like many of the other high-concept, high-touch aptitudes—wasn't always given its proper due in the Information Age. It was often considered a softhearted nicety in a world that demanded hardheaded detachment. To undermine an argument or dismiss an idea, you just had to call it "touchy-feely." Or look at the drubbing former U.S. president Bill Clinton took when he uttered these four words: "I feel your pain." Some critics thought Clinton was dissembling when he said that. But the roughest criticism came from those who considered the comment laughably unpresidential and even a tad unmanly. Americans pay presidents to think, not to feel—to strategize, not to empathize. Or so it has long been. The era of sharp-minded knowledge workers and briskly efficient high-tech companies prized emotional distance and cool reason—the ability to step back, assess the situation, and make a decision unimpeded by emotion. But as with so many other attributes of L-Directed Thinking,

"Leadership is about empathy. It is about having the ability to relate and to connect with people for the purpose of inspiring and empowering their lives."

—OPRAH WINFREY

we are beginning to see the limits of such a single-minded approach. Daniel Goleman's book *Emotional Intelligence*, published about the same time that Clinton uttered his empathic words, signaled the beginning of this shift. Goleman argued that emotional abilities are even more important than conventional intellectual abilities—and the world took to his message.

But ten years later, the Conceptual Age is increasing the stakes. When Goleman wrote his book, the Internet was in its infancy and those highly skilled Indian programmers of Chapter 2 were in elementary school. Today, cheap and widespread online access, combined with all those overseas knowledge workers, are making the attributes measurable by IQ much easier to replace—which, as we have seen in earlier chapters, has meant that aptitudes more difficult to replicate are becoming more valuable. And the one aptitude that's proven impossible for computers to reproduce, and very difficult for faraway workers connected by electrons to match, is Empathy.

Facing the Future

In 1872, thirteen years after he published *On the Origin of Species*, Charles Darwin published another book that scandalized Victorian society. The book was called *The Expression of the Emotions in Man and Animals*—and it made some controversial claims. Most notably, Darwin said that all mammals have emotions and that one way they convey these emotions is through their facial expressions. A dog with a lugubrious look on its face probably is sad, just as a person who's frowning probably is unhappy.

Darwin's book caused a stir when it came out. But for the next century it languished in obscurity. The assumption in the world of psychology and science was that our faces did express emotion—but that those expressions were products of culture rather than nature. But in 1965, Paul Ekman—then a young psychologist and now a legendary one—came along. Ekman, an American, traveled to Japan, Argentina, Brazil, and Chile. He showed people there photos of faces fixed in various expressions, and he found that Asians and South Americans interpreted the expressions the same way Americans did. He was intrigued. Perhaps these common interpretations were due to television or Western influence, he thought. So Ekman journeyed to the highlands of New Guinea and showed the same set of facial expression photos to tribespeople who'd never seen television, or even a Westerner, before. They read the faces the same way all of Ekman's previous subjects did. And that led him to a groundbreaking conclusion: Darwin was right after all. Facial expressions were universal. Raising eyebrows indicated surprise in midtown Manhattan, just as it did in suburban Buenos Aires, just as it did in the highlands of New Guinea.

Ekman has devoted much of his career to studying facial expressions. He created the set of photographs that I looked at back in Chapter 1 when I was getting my brain scanned. His work is enormously important for our purposes. Empathy is largely about emotion—feeling what another is feeling. But emotions generally don't reveal themselves in L-Directed ways. "People's emotions are rarely put into words; far more often they are expressed through other cues," writes Goleman. "Just as the mode of the rational mind is words, the mode of the emotions is nonverbal."[2] And the main canvas for displaying those emotions is the face. With forty-three tiny muscles that tug and stretch and lift our mouth, eyes, cheeks, eyebrows, and forehead, our faces can convey the full range of human feeling. Since Empathy depends on emotion and since emotion is conveyed nonverbally, to enter another's heart, you must begin the journey by looking into his face.

As we learned in Chapter 1, reading facial expressions is a specialty of our brain's right hemisphere. When I looked at extreme expressions, unlike when I looked at scary scenes, the fMRI showed that the right side of my brain responded more robustly than my left. "We both express our own emotions and read the emotions of others primarily through the right hemisphere," says George Washington University neurologist Richard Restak. That's why, according to research at the University of Sussex, the vast majority of women—regardless of whether they are right-handed or left-handed—cradle babies on their left side. Since babies can't talk, the only way we can understand their needs is by reading their expressions and intuiting their emotions. So we depend on our right hemisphere, which we enlist by turning to the left. (Recall from Chapter 1 that our brains are contralateral.)[3] People with damage to their right hemisphere have great difficulty recognizing the emotions on others' faces. (The same is often true for those with autism, which in some cases entails a malfunction of the right hemisphere.) By contrast, people with damage to the left side of the brain—the side that, in most people, processes language—are actually *better* at reading expressions than the rest of us. For instance, both Ekman and Nancy Etcoff, a psychologist at Massachusetts General Hospital in Boston, have shown that most of us are astonishingly bad at detecting when someone is lying. When we try to determine from another's facial expressions or tone of voice if that person is fibbing, we don't do much better than if we had offered random guesses. But aphasics—people with damage to their brain's left hemisphere that compromises their ability to speak and understand language—are exceptionally good lie detectors. By reading facial cues, Etcoff found, they can spot liars more than 70 percent of the time.[4] The reason: since they can't receive one channel of communication, they're better at interpreting the other, more expressive channel.

The Conceptual Age puts a premium on this more elusive, but more expressive, channel. Endowing computers with emotional intelligence has been a dream for decades, but even the best scientists in the field of "affective computing" haven't made much progress. Computers still do a shabby job of even distinguishing one face from another—let alone detecting the subtle expressions etched onto them. Computers have "tremendous mathematical abilities," says Rosalind Picard of MIT, "but when it comes to interacting with people, they are autistic."[5] Voice recognition software can now decipher our words—whether we tell our laptop to "Save" or "Delete" or whether we request "Aisle" or "Window" to an automated airline attendant. But the most sophisticated software on the planet running on the world's most powerful computers can't divine our emotions. Some newer applications are getting better at spotting the *existence* of emotion. For instance, some kinds of voice recognition software used in call centers can detect big changes in pitch, timing, and volume, all of which signal heightened emotion. But what happens when the software recognizes these signals? It transfers the call to an actual human being.

That example is a microcosm for work in the Conceptual Age. Work that can be reduced to rules—whether the rules are embedded in a few lines of software code or handed to a low-paid overseas worker—requires relatively little Empathy. Such work will largely disappear from countries like the United States, Canada, and the United Kingdom. But the work that remains will demand a much deeper understanding of the subtleties of human interaction than ever before. No surprise, then, that students at Stanford Business School are flocking to a course officially called "Interpersonal

"People who lean on logic and philosophy and rational exposition end by starving the best part of the mind."

—WILLIAM BUTLER YEATS

Dynamics" but known around campus as "Touchy-feely." Or consider a field not typically known for emotional literacy—the practice of law. Much basic legal research can now be done by English-speaking lawyers in other parts of the world. Likewise, software and Web sites, as I explained in Chapter 3, have eliminated the monopoly lawyers once had on certain specialized information. So which lawyers will remain? Those who can empathize with their clients and understand their true needs. Those who can sit in a negotiation and figure out the subtext of the discussion that's coursing beneath the explicit words. And those who can look at a jury, read their expressions, and instantly know whether they're making a persuasive case. These empathic abilities have always been important to lawyers—but now they've become the key point of differentiation in this and other professions.

But Empathy is much more than a vocational skill necessary for surviving twenty-first–century labor markets. It's an ethic for living. It's a means of understanding other human beings—as Darwin and Ekman found, a universal language that connects us beyond country or culture. Empathy makes us human. Empathy brings joy. And, as we'll see in Chapter 9, Empathy is an essential part of living a life of meaning.

MANY OF US can boost our powers of Empathy. And nearly all of us can improve our ability to read faces. Over the years, Ekman has compiled an atlas of facial expressions—likely all the facial expressions that human beings throughout the world use to convey emotions. And he's found that seven basic human emotions have clear facial signals: anger, sadness, fear, surprise, disgust, contempt, and happiness. Sometimes these expressions are full and intense. Many other times they are less conspicuous. There's what Ekman calls the "slight expression," which is usually the first prickle of an emotion or the failed attempt to hide that emotion. There's the "partial expression." And there's the "micro expression," which flashes across the face in less than one-fifth of a second and often occurs "when a person is consciously trying to conceal all signs of how he or she is feeling."[6] Ekman has taught face-reading skills to agents from the FBI, CIA, and ATF, as well as to police officers, judges, lawyers, and even illustrators and animators. And now I'm going to teach you one aspect of Ekman's techniques. (You can learn more of them in the Portfolio at the end of this chapter.)

I've always been irritated by what I think are fake smiles—but I've never been sure whether someone is grinning because he's charmed by my wit or smiling precisely because he isn't. Now I know. A smile of true enjoyment is what Ekman calls the "Duchenne smile," after the French neurologist Duchenne de Boulogne, who conducted pioneering work in this field in the late 1800s. A genuine smile involves two facial muscles: (1) the zygomatic major muscle, which stretches from the cheekbone and lifts the corners of the mouth; and (2) the outer part of the obicularis oculi muscle, which orbits the eye, and is involved in "pulling down the eyebrows and the skin below the eyebrows, pulling up the skin below the eye, and raising the cheeks."[7]

Artificial smiles involve only the zygomatic major. The reason: we can control that muscle, but we can't control the relevant part of the obicularis oculi muscle. It contracts spontaneously—and only when we're actually experiencing enjoyment. As Duchenne himself put it, "The emotion of frank joy is expressed on the face by the combined contraction of the zygomaticus major muscle and the obicularis oculi. The first obeys the will but the second is only put into play by the sweet emotions of the soul."[8]

In other words, to detect a fake smile, look at the eyes. If the outer muscle of the orbicularis isn't contracting, the person beaming at you is a false friend.

Here's an example—two smiling photos of yours truly.

Can you tell in which one I'm squeezing out an insincere smile and in which I'm smiling in response to something funny my wife said? It's not easy, but if you look carefully at my eyes, you can figure out the answer. The second photo is the true enjoyment photo. The eyebrows are a little lower. The skin under the eyes is pulled a little higher. The eyes themselves are bit narrower. In fact, if you cover up everything but the eyes, the answer is clearer. You just can't fake a Duchenne smile. And while you can improve your empathic powers, you can't fake Empathy either.

A Whole New Health Care

Empathy is not a stand-alone aptitude. It connects to the three high-concept, high-touch aptitudes I've already discussed. Empathy is an essential part of Design, because good designers put themselves in the mind of whoever is going to experience the product or service they're designing. (It should be no surprise that one of the items in the Empathy Portfolio comes from a design firm.) Empathy is related to Symphony—because empathic people understand the importance of context. They see the whole person much as symphonic thinkers see the whole picture. Finally, the aptitude of Story also involves empathy. As we saw in the section on narrative medicine, stories can be pathways to Empathy—especially for physicians.

But Empathy is also reshaping medicine more directly. Several leaders in the medical field are urging that the profession shift its overarching approach from "detached concern to empathy," as bioethicist Jodi Halpern puts it. The detached scientific model isn't inappropriate, they say. It's insufficient. As I've mentioned, much of medical practice has been standardized—reduced to a set of repeatable formulas for diagnosing and treating various ailments. While some doctors have criticized this development as "cookbook medicine," it has many strengths. Rules-based medicine builds on the accumulated evidence of hundreds, and sometimes thousands, of cases. It helps ensure that medical professionals don't reinvent the therapeutic wheel with each patient. But the truth is, computers could do some of this work. What they can't

> **"Trust your intuition, it's just like going fishin'."**
>
> —PAUL SIMON

do—remember, when it comes to human relations, computers are "autistic"—is to be empathic.

Empathy can be a powerful force in medicine. For example, a few years ago, two postal workers went to different health care centers complaining of similar symptoms. One man told his doctor he felt achy and ill and he believed he'd been exposed to anthrax, which had recently been found at the postal facility where he worked. The doctor telephoned the relevant public health departments, which told him that anthrax was not a risk and that he needn't prescribe antibiotics. So he followed the rules and sent his patient home with orders to take some Tylenol. A few days later, the patient died—of anthrax. Meanwhile, the other postal worker went to an emergency room at a different hospital, just a few miles away. His doctor—who didn't know about the patient above—examined the worker and suspected that he'd contracted pneumonia. But then the man told her that he worked at the postal facility hit with an anthrax scare. So she ordered another test, and even though she didn't think that he had anthrax, something still nagged at her. She gave the man a prescription for Cipro, the antibiotic prescribed for anthrax, just in case. And instead of sending him home, as she had initially planned, she kept him at the hospital and referred him to an infectious-disease specialist. As it turned out, the man did have anthrax. And as it also turned out, the doctor's empathic listening, intuition, and willingness to deviate from the rules meant the difference between life and death. "I just listened to my patient," she told the *Wall Street Journal.* "He said, 'I know my body and something's just not right.'" Empathy—his doctor's ability to intuit what someone else was feeling—saved his life.

"Physicians express empathy not only by making accurate comments about a patient's feelings, but by their timing, vocal tones, pauses, and overall attunement to the affective style of a patient," says Halpern. "Empathy supplements objective knowledge, and the use of technology, and other tools for making accurate diagnoses."[9] As this new view of doctoring takes hold, the aptitude of Empathy is moving to the forefront of the medical profession. It is giving way to a new generation of health care professionals like that emergency room physician—people who can combine rule-based detachment with emotion-based empathy into a whole new medicine.

The board that accredits medical schools now makes communicating effectively and empathically with patients a factor in a student doctor's overall evaluation. That may seem like a commonsense move, and it is—but in the heavily L-Directed medical profession, it's a sea change. Meantime, stage actress Megan Cole travels to medical schools across the United States teaching a course called "The Craft of Empathy." In the class, she instructs doctors-in-training how to use nonverbal cues such as facial expression, intonation, body language, as well as other acting techniques, to better grasp what ails patients and to better convey concern for them. Students at Vanderbilt University School of Medicine take courses in communicating—and apologizing for—their mistakes.[10] And Jefferson Medical College in Philadelphia, which I mentioned in Chapter 3, has even developed a measure of this aptitude—the Jefferson Scale of Physician Empathy (JSPE).

Although it is relatively new, the JSPE has produced some intriguing results. For example, high scores on the Empathy test generally correlated with high marks on clinical care. That is, all other things being equal, a patient was more likely to get better with an empathic doctor than with a detached one. What's more, scores on the Empathy test bore no relation to scores on the MCAT or on medical licensing tests—which means that the traditional measures of physician aptitude aren't necessarily relevant to determining who's the best doctor.[11] The differences in who scored high on the JSPE (and who didn't) were also interesting. Women generally scored higher than men. And certain kinds of health care professionals scored better than others. For instance, nurses generally had high scores—much higher than physicians with hospital-based specialties.[12]

The growing recognition of empathy's role in healing is one reason why nursing will be one of the key professions of the Conceptual Age workforce. Nurses do much more than just empathize, of course. But the sort of emotionally intelligent care they often provide is precisely the sort of thing that's impossible to outsource or automate. Radiologists in Bangalore can read X-rays. But it's hard to deliver Empathy—touch, presence, and comfort—via fiber-optic cable. And with the aging of the population in the advanced world, nurses are in huge demand. In the United States, nursing will account for more new jobs over the next decade than any other profession. U.S. health facilities will need one million additional nurses.[13] Nurses have many complaints about being overworked and having to juggle too many patients. But their empathic nature keeps them in high esteem—and increasingly brings them higher salaries. Nursing consistently rates as the most honest and ethical profession in the United States, according to an annual Gallup survey—and its pay is rising faster than nearly every other job category.[14]

The rise of Empathy has even begun to color parental advice. In a recent survey of Australian information technology managers, 90 percent said they would *not* recommend that their own children pursue careers in the L-Directed field of software engineering. What would they recommend their children do instead? "I'd rather my kids opt for nursing as a profession," said James Michaels, who works for a telecommunications company in Sydney. "It has both global and local demand."[15]

Men, Women, and Empathy

Who's more empathic? Men or women? The politically correct answer is to say neither—that empathy depends on the individual. And to a large extent, that's true. But a growing body of research has begun making that politically correct view untenable. Dozens of studies, for instance, have shown that women are generally better at reading facial expressions and at detecting lies.[16] Even as early as age three, girls are better at inferring what others are thinking and at divining emotions from the expression on someone's face.[17] Summarizing this research, psychologist David G. Myers writes:

> When surveyed, women are far more likely to describe themselves as empathic, as being able to rejoice with those who rejoice and weep with those who weep. To a lesser extent, the gender gap in empathy extends to observed behavior. Women are somewhat more likely to cry or report feeling distressed at another's distress. The empathy difference helps explain why both men and women report their friendships with women to be more intimate, enjoyable and nurturing than their friendships with men. When seeking empathy and understanding, both men and women usually turn to women.[18]

Simon Baron-Cohen, a Cambridge University psychologist, has a theory that explains this apparent gender gap. He states it plainly on page one of his 2003 book, *The Essential Difference*: "The female brain is predominantly hard-wired for empathy. The male brain is predominantly hard-wired for understanding and building systems."[19]

Baron-Cohen is quick to note that not all women have "female" brains, and not all men have "male" brains. But he marshals an array of support for his central point: that more males than females have brains that systematize and that more females than males have brains that empathize.[20] The differences in the two thinking styles, as Baron-Cohen describes them, are intriguing. "Systematizing involves exactness, excellent attention to local detail," and an attraction to fixed rules independent of context, he says. "To systematize, you need detachment."[21] (Baron describes autism as an "extreme" male brain.)

> **"The great gift of human beings is that we have the power of empathy."**
>
> —MERYL STREEP

But empathizing is different. "To empathize you need some degree of attachment in order to recognize that you are interacting with a person, not an object, but a person with feelings, and whose feelings affect your own." Empathy, he says, "involves inexactness (one can only ever approximate when one ascertains another's mental state), attention to the larger picture (what one thinks he thinks or feels about other people, for example), context (a person's face, voice, action, and history are all essential information in determining that person's mental state), with no expectation of lawfulness (what made her happy yesterday may not make her happy tomorrow)."[22]

Read those descriptions again. The male brain sounds a little like L-Directed Thinking. And the female brain sounds a lot like the high-concept, high-touch approach of R-Directed Thinking. (The two thinking styles also sound like the differing approaches of the two doctors treating anthrax patients I mentioned earlier—one of whom happened to be a man, and the other a woman.)

Does this mean that we all need to get in touch with the feminine side of our brains—especially those of us with hairy arms and deep voices? Yes. But it doesn't mean rejecting the systematizing side of our brains. Empathy is neither a deviation from intelligence nor the single route to it. Sometimes we need detachment; many other times we need attunement. And the people who will thrive will be those who can toggle between the two. As we've seen again and again, the Conceptual Age requires androgynous minds.

PORTFOLIO

Design

Story

Symphony

Empathy

Play

Meaning

Test Yourself.

Psychologists have developed an array of tests to measure individual empathy and related qualities. Many of these tests are available free on the Web—and they're an excellent introduction to the subject as well as a fun way to learn more about yourself. But caveat test-taker. The Web is full of self-assessments, many of which have all the scientific validity of phrenology. So begin your Empathy testing regimen with these:

Empathy Quotient—Measure your EQ with Simon Baron-Cohen's sixty-question instrument, which will determine whether you have a "female brain." If you want to check your "male brain" bona fides, also take the test that measures your systematizing quotient, or SQ. *(More info on EQ: tinyurl.com/dbsd8; more info on SQ: tinyurl.com/7taj8)*

Spot the Fake Smile—Take the BBC's ten-minute, twenty-question test, based on Paul Ekman's research, to see how good you are at detecting the difference between a fake smile and a real one. *(More info: tinyurl.com/2u7sh)*

Mind in the Eyes Test—Another test from Simon Baron-Cohen, this one measures your ability to identify a facial expression from only a person's eyes. *(More info: tinyurl.com/ckrj3)*

Mayer-Salovey-Caruso Emotional Intelligence Test—This is probably the most widely respected emotional intelligence test available today. But unlike the others I mentioned, to take this one, you'll have to pay. It's not the place to start your inquiry, but it is a great option for those who want to dig deeper. *(More info: www.emotionalintelligencemhs.com/MSCEIT.htm)*

Study Ekman.

As I noted earlier in this chapter, the world's leading expert on facial expressions is Paul Ekman. Do yourself a favor and study his work. Read his latest book, *Emotions Revealed* (Times Books, 2003). It's an excellent overview of the science of expression. And it's a first-rate guide to learning the techniques to decipher the emotions revealed on someone else's face. Ekman's daughter, Eve, is the model for many of the emotions pictured in the book, and she has an uncanny ability to get the expressions just right. If you like *Emotions Revealed*, also check out Ekman's earlier book, *Telling Lies* (W.W. Norton, reissued 2001)—which, among other things, explains how to detect when someone is fibbing. Then, for your graduate degree in Ekmanship, pick up his two interactive CD-ROM tutorials. One, the Micro Expression Training Tool, teaches you to spot those fleeting microexpressions. The other, the Subtle Expression Training Tool, teaches you to spot the seemingly undetectable expressions that occur when someone is just beginning to feel an emotion. The tutorials include pretests to measure your current ability—and at the end, final tests to see how much you've improved. Both are useful—not to mention fascinating. One warning, though, to my fellow Mac users: as of press time, these CD-ROMs worked only with PCs.

(More info: www.paulekman.com)

Eavesdrop

Several years ago, writer and former literary escort Naomi Epel published a small paperback book and companion card set called *The Observation Deck*. Epel's package is a wonderful trove of writing tips assembled from authors she shepherded on book tours. One of those tips is also a fine way to develop greater powers of Empathy: Eavesdrop.

Listening to the conversations of those nearby has a bad reputation. But we all do it, so we might as well make it worthwhile. Next time you're in a position to eavesdrop, listen carefully to what your targets are saying. Then imagine yourself as one of those people in that situation. What are you (that is, him or her) thinking and feeling at that moment? What emotions, if any, are coursing through your body? How did you end up in this particular place at this particular time?

"Many writers are notorious eavesdroppers," Epel writes, citing, among others, F. Scott Fitzgerald, who kept a notebook in which he recorded "overheard conversations." But the practice is valuable—if done in moderation and within the boundaries of the law, of course—to a range of professions. It's an excellent way to put yourself in another's shoes and see the world through that person's eyes—if only for a few moments. One variation: Listen to a conversation without looking at the people who are talking. Then guess who the people are—their ages, their ethnicities, their clothing style. Turn around to see how accurate you are. You might be surprised.

Play "Whose Life?"

IDEO is one of the world's most respected design firms—the creator of everything from those fat-handled toothbrushes for kids to Apple Computer's first mouse to the Palm V. How do they do it? The secret would make an MBA squirm: *Empathy.* In the IDEO universe, great design doesn't begin with a cool drawing or a nifty gadget. It begins with a deep and empathic understanding of people. Here's an exercise in Empathy that I learned when I visited IDEO's Palo Alto, California, headquarters:

Ask someone in your organization to lend you her purse, briefcase, or backpack. Also ask that person to remove the things inside that bear her name. Then gather a group of five or six other people and review the contents, without knowing who the person is, to try to determine what sort of life—personal, professional, emotional—the person lives. For instance, is the bag crammed with things or is it spare and neat? Is everything inside related to work? Or are there items that indicate a family life or other interests? How much money is in the wallet? Does this person carry any photographs? Pick through the artifacts like a purse-snatching archaeologist—and you can really begin to imagine what it's like to be that person. Added bonus: "Whose Life?" is a lot of fun.

Also, IDEO has collected some of its other techniques and stamped them onto fifty-one funky oversized cards that are available online and in a few American stores for $49. These IDEO Method Cards detail an array of strategies—borrowed from anthropology, psychology, biomechanics, and other disciplines—for putting Empathy at the center of the design process. Like conventional playing cards, the Method Cards are organized into four "suits" that represent four methods of empathizing with people: Learn, Look, Ask, and Try. Each individual card explains a particular technique—say, "Camera Journal" or "Bodystorming"—with a photo on one side and on the other an account of how IDEO has used the technique with a client. These cards are almost as fun as rifling through someone's purse.

(More info: www.ideo.com)

Empathize on the Job.

Even though we all say we believe in empathy, we often fail to demonstrate it with the very people who surround us for most of our daylight hours: our coworkers. Here are two techniques for increasing empathy within your organization and team.

1. *A Day in the Life*

   Do you know what work is really like for your colleagues? This activity will help you find out. It's easy to do and great for staff meetings or retreats.

   Have each participant write her name on a piece of flipchart paper and then list four categories: my highs, my lows, my frustrations, my rewards. Post all these sheets on the walls.

Then ask everyone to walk around the room and write what they think the answers are for their colleagues. What's the biggest frustration of the senior vice president? What's the greatest reward for the fellow in the mailroom? Once people write what they think, each person reclaims his own sheet. Then everyone takes a turn responding to his colleagues' guesses and explaining what a workday is *really* like. A variation: Organize people by departments and have each group try to describe a day in the life of the other departments.

2. *How Did I Get Here?*
   Sometimes you work near people for years but have little idea about the path that brought them alongside of you. Understanding these personal histories is the goal of an activity that Kevin Buck, a senior consultant with Leading Initiatives Worldwide Inc., uses with groups of physicians. He invites doctors to pair up and tell the story of why they chose the arduous path of medicine. Each doctor relates her own story, listens to her partner's story, and then retells the partner's story to the rest of the group—a process that Buck says is "always very powerful and renewing." After the storytelling, he elicits the common themes from the community of physicians, the result of which is a new narrative that runs counter to "the dominant story of disdain and negativity that most felt in the health care community." Buck has used this technique with other groups of professionals with similar success.

Take An Acting Class.

Americans of a certain age will remember the television commercial that began, "I'm not a doctor, but I play one on TV." These days that piece of Americana is being turned upside down. Doctors are pretending to be actors. Increasing numbers of physicians are working to understand and deepen their Empathy by taking acting classes. It sounds either dubious or duplicitous, I know. But think about what actors do. They try to inhabit the mind and the heart of another person—and that makes acting a great way to understand emotion and emotional expression. Most local colleges and community centers offer evening classes. And while the instructors aren't exactly Lee Strasberg, you're not exactly Al Pacino. So if you're game, give it a try. You might learn something.

Get *Mind Reading.*

If taking an acting class is too much—or if you find this Empathy stuff really perplexing—consider the CD-ROM *Mind Reading.* Designed by a team of scientists at Cambridge University, the CD-ROM shows real people demonstrating with sound, expression, and gesture more than four hundred different emotions. It's designed partly for people (those on the "autism spectrum," for instance) who have difficulty reading emotions and want to learn how. But it has also become popular among actors, illustrators, and others who need a keener insight into facial expression, intonation, and emotion more generally. It's not cheap—about $125—but it is encyclopedic.

(More info: www.jkp.com/mindreading)

Don't Outsource Your Empathy.

Are you still buying greeting cards that broadcast someone else's sentiments about life's most important moments? Show others how much they really mean to you (and demonstrate your empathy) by creating your own cards for various occasions: birthdays, graduations, illnesses or deaths, anniversaries. Kids know how to do this. And so do you. Just fire up your computer's word processing program and get started. Even better, do it by hand with some blank cards and colored pencils.

Anybody can grab a mass-produced card along with the week's groceries. It takes a special person to spend the time really thinking about what message to send and how best to convey it. Put the power of the personal to work.

Volunteer.

Another great way to sharpen your empathic powers is to volunteer somewhere in your community that serves people whose experiences are far different from your own. If you volunteer at a homeless shelter, for instance, it would be hard not to imagine yourself in the situation of someone there.

Another approach is to combine volunteer work with a vacation. Immersing yourself into someone else's world and working beside that person is a great way to connect with others and gain insight into their lives. Several organizations provide information about these types of experiences: Global Volunteers (*www.globalvolunteers.org*), Cross Cultural Solutions (*www.crossculturalsolutions.org*), and Transitions Abroad. Volunteering vacations have long been popular with college students, many of whom participate in programs offered by their campus chapter of Break Away, an alternative spring break organization (*www.alternativebreaks.org*).

Seeing another human in distress—and thinking, "There but for the grace of God go I"—will hone your powers of empathy. But that's not the reason to do this, of course. It's an ancillary benefit of something more valuable: helping another human being.

Eight

PLAY

Why is this man laughing?

The explanation is more complicated than you might expect. This is Madan Kataria, a physician in Mumbai, India. Dr. Kataria likes to laugh. A lot. In fact, he believes that laughter can function like a benevolent virus—that it can infect individuals, communities, even nations. So a few years ago he scaled back his medical practice and refashioned himself as the Typhoid Mary of laughter. His mission: to trigger an international laughter epidemic that he says can improve our health, increase our profits, and maybe even bring world peace. His means of transmission: laughter clubs—small groups of people who come together early each morning at parks, village greens, and shopping centers to spend a half hour laughing.

Kataria's plan to change the world by making it laugh can seem, well, laughable. But if you visit a laughter club, as I did one damp morning in Mumbai, you can see there's a method to his mirth. Today about 2,500 laughter clubs convene regularly around the world. Many of them are in India, including nearly one hundred clubs in Mumbai and even more in the high-tech haven of Bangalore. But others have sprung up in the West—in the United Kingdom, Germany, Sweden, Norway, Denmark, Canada, and several hundred clubs in the United States. The fastest-growing venue for these clubs is the workplace.

I'll come back to this self-anointed guru of giggles later in this chapter. But his popularity around the world, and especially the gradual acceptance of laughter clubs in offices and boardrooms, reveals another important dimension of the Conceptual Age—a move away from sober seriousness as a measure of ability and the elevation of the next essential high-concept, high-touch aptitude: Play. "The whole purpose of the laughter club is to be more playful," Kataria told me. "When you are playful, you are activating the right side of your brain. The logical brain is a limited brain. The right side is unlimited. You can be anything you want."

Contrast Kataria's movement, and the workplace laughter clubs it has spawned, with the Ford Motor Company of the 1930s and 1940s. At Ford's River Rouge plant, laughter was a disciplinary offense—

and humming, whistling, and smiling were evidence of insubordination. As British management scholar David Collinson recounts:

> In 1940 John Gallo was sacked because he was "caught in the act of smiling," after having committed an earlier breach of "laughing with the other fellows," and "slowing down the line maybe half a minute." This tight managerial discipline reflected the overall philosophy of Henry Ford, who stated that "When we are at work we ought to be at work. When we are at play we ought to be at play. There is no use trying to mix the two."[1]

Work and play, Ford feared, was a toxic combination. If they weren't quarantined, each would poison the other. But in the Conceptual Age, as abundance releases organizations from the post-Depression grimness that gripped the River Rouge plant, commingling work and play has become both more common and more necessary. At times, it is even an explicit corporate strategy. Take the airline business. Southwest Airlines is one of today's most successful carriers, earning a regular profit while many of its competitors wobble on the edge of insolvency. The company's mission statement offers clues to its stellar performance. It says, "People rarely succeed at anything unless they are having fun doing it"—a 180-degree turn from Ford's mandated joylessness. And it's not just one zany American corporation that is supplementing the work ethic with a Play ethic.[2] According to

> **"The opposite of play isn't work. It's depression. To play is to act out and be willful, exultant and committed as if one is assured of one's prospects."**
>
> —BRIAN SUTTON-SMITH, *professor of education (emeritus), University of Pennsylvania*

the *Wall Street Journal*, more than fifty European companies—including less-than-zany firms such as Nokia, Daimler-Chrysler, and Alcatel—have brought in consultants in "Serious Play," a technique that uses Lego building blocks to train corporate executives.[3] British Airways has even hired its own "corporate jester" to imbue the airline with a greater sense of fun.[4]

Like its five sibling senses, Play is emerging from the shadows of frivolousness and assuming a place in the spotlight. *Homo ludens* (Man the Player) is proving to be as effective as Homo sapiens (Man the Knower) in getting the job done. Play is becoming an important part of work, business, and personal well-being, its importance manifesting itself in three ways: games, humor, and joyfulness. Games, particularly computer and video games, have become a large and influential industry that is teaching whole-minded lessons to its customers and recruiting a new breed of whole-minded worker. Humor is showing itself to be an accurate marker for managerial effectiveness, emotional intelligence, and the thinking style characteristic of the brain's right hemisphere. And joyfulness, as exemplified by unconditional laughter, is demonstrating its power to make us more productive and fulfilled. In the Conceptual Age, as we'll see, fun and games are not just fun and games—and laughter is no laughing matter.

Games

Here's a screen shot from a popular video game called *America's Army*:

AFP, Getty Images

When you play this game, you navigate a treacherous environment, trying to knock off bad guys while avoiding getting whacked yourself. You earn points for nailing opposing soldiers and for helping your side elude harm, a format and structure similar to most games in this genre. So here's a question: Which company makes the game? Nintendo? Sega? Electronic Arts? Nope. The organization that created, manufactured, and distributed *America's Army* is . . . America's Army, the United States military.

A few years ago Colonel Casey Wardynski, a West Point professor who specializes in military manpower, was working on ways to boost recruiting for the armed forces, which had fallen to dismal levels. Because the draft had ended in the 1970s and the size of the military had shrunk after the end of the Cold War, potential recruits knew much less than previous generations about what it was like to serve in the armed forces. While chewing on this problem, Wardynski noticed that the cadets he was teaching at West Point were obsessed with video games. And in a flash of right-brain inspiration, he glimpsed a possible solution.

What if, Wardynski wondered, the military tried reaching young people where they live—on Sony PlayStations, Microsoft Xboxes, and personal computers? Since gauzy television ads and person-to-person persuasion couldn't give recruits a feel for the reality of military service, perhaps the Army could, as Wardynski put it, substitute "virtual experiences for vicarious insights" by creating a video game. He presented his plan to the Pentagon brass, which, concerned about a shortfall in personnel, was willing to try anything. They gave Wardynski a healthy budget, and he began formulating a game that he thought would convey the substance of Army life while also being engaging and challenging to play. Over the next year, he and a team from the Naval Postgraduate School, with the help of several programmers and artists, built *America's Army* and released it for free on the GoArmy.com Web site on July 4, 2002. That first weekend, demand was so great that it crashed the Army's servers. Today the game, which is also distributed on disk at recruiting offices and in gaming magazines, has more than two million registered users. On a typical weekend nearly a half-million people sit in front of computer screens, maneuvering through simulated military missions.[5]

America's Army says it's different from many other martial games because of its emphasis on "teamwork, values, and responsibility as a means of achieving the goals." Players go through basic training, advance to multiplayer games where they work in small units, and, if they're successful, move on to become Green Berets. Most of the missions are team endeavors—rescuing a prisoner of war, protecting a pipeline, thwarting a weapons sale to terrorists. Players earn points not only for killing enemies but also for protecting other soldiers and for completing a mission with everyone in the unit still alive. If you try something stupid—for instance, gunning down civilians or ignoring orders—you can end up in a virtual Leavenworth prison or find yourself banished from the game altogether. And like any producer with a hit on its hands, the Army has produced a sequel—a new edition of the game called *America's Army: Special Forces.*

This ought to throw a bucket of cold water on the overheated belief that Play is an aptitude only for the hackey-sack set. The reality is more surprising: just as General Motors is in the art business, the U.S. military is in the game business. (Indeed, had the military sold the game at a price comparable to other video games, the Army would have earned about $600 million in the first year.[6])

> **"Games are the most elevated form of investigation."**
>
> —ALBERT EINSTEIN

The military's embrace of video games is just one example of the influence of these games. From their humble beginnings thirty years ago, when *Pong*, one of the very first, made its appearance in arcades, video games (that is, games played on computers, on the Web, and on dedicated platforms such as PlayStation and Xbox) have become a booming business and a prominent part of everyday life. For example:

- Half of all Americans over age six play computer and video games. Each year, Americans purchase more than 220 million games, nearly two games for every U.S. household. And despite the common belief that gaming is a pastime that requires a Y chromosome, today more than 40 percent of game players are women.[7]
- In the United States, the video game business is larger than the motion picture industry. Americans spend more on video games than they do on movie tickets. On average, Americans

devote seventy-five hours a year to playing video games, double the time they spent in 1977 and more time than they spend watching DVDs and videos.[8]

- One game company, Electronic Arts, is now part of the Standard & Poor's 500 Index. In 2004, EA earned nearly $3 billion, more than the combined revenue of the year's ten top-grossing movies. Nintendo's *Mario* series of video games has earned more than $7 billion over its lifetime—double the money earned by all the *Star Wars* movies.[9]

Still, unless they live in a home with thumb-twitching teenagers, many adults haven't fully comprehended the significance of these games. For a generation of people, games have become a tool for solving problems as well as a vehicle for self-expression and self-exploration. Video games are as woven into this generation's lives as television was into that of their predecessors. For example, according to several surveys, the percentage of American college students who say they've played video games is 100.[10] On campuses today you'd sooner find a short-tailed tree frog taking calculus than an undergrad who's never fired up *Myst*, *Grand Theft Auto*, or *Sim City*. As two Carnegie Mellon University professors write, "We routinely poll our students on their experience with the media, and typically we cannot find a single movie that all fifty students in the course have seen (only about a third have usually seen *Casablanca*, for instance). However, we typically find at least one video game that every student has played, like *Super Mario Brothers.*"[11]

Some people—many of them members of my own fortysomething geezer set—tend to despair over such information, fearing that each minute spent wielding a joystick represents a step backward for individual intelligence and social progress. But that attitude misunderstands the power of these games. In fact, James Paul Gee, a professor at the University of Wisconsin and author of *What Video Games Have to Teach Us About Learning and Literacy*, argues that games can be the ultimate learning machine. "[Video games] operate with—that is, they build into their designs and encourage—good principles of learning, principles that are better than those in many of our skill-and-drill, back-to-basics, test-them-until-they-drop schools."[12] That's why so many people buy video games, and then spend fifty to one hundred hours mastering them, roughly the length of a college semester.[13] As Gee writes, "The fact is when kids play video games they can experience a much more powerful form of learning than when they're in the classroom. Learning isn't about memorizing isolated facts. It's about connecting and manipulating them."[14]

Indeed, a growing stack of research is showing that playing video games can sharpen many of the skills that are vital in the Conceptual Age. For instance, an important 2003 study in the journal *Nature* found an array of benefits to playing video games. On tests of visual perception, game players scored 30 percent higher than nonplayers. Playing video games enhanced individuals' ability to detect changes in the environment and their capacity to process information simultaneously.[15] Even doctors can benefit from a little time at the GameCube. One study found that physicians "who spent at least three hours a week playing video games made about 37 percent fewer mistakes in laparoscopic surgery and performed the task 27 percent faster than their counterparts who did not play."[16] Another study even found that playing video games at work can boost productivity and enhance job satisfaction.[17]

> **"Play will be to the 21st century what work was to the last 300 years of industrial society—our dominant way of knowing, doing and creating value."**
>
> —PAT KANE, *author of* The Play Ethic

There's also evidence that playing video games enhances the

right-brain ability to solve problems that require pattern recognition.[18] Many aspects of video gaming resemble the aptitude of Symphony—spotting trends, drawing connections, and discerning the big picture. "What we need people to learn is how to think deeply about complex systems (e.g., modern workplaces, the environment, international relations, social interactions, cultures, etc.) where everything interacts in complicated ways with everything else and bad decisions can make for disasters," says Gee. Computer and video games can teach that. In addition, the fastest growing category of games isn't shooter games like *America's Army* but role-playing games, which require players to assume the identity of a character and to navigate a virtual world through the eyes of that figure. Experiences with those simulation games can deepen the aptitude of Empathy and offer rehearsals for the social interactions of our lives.

What's more, games have begun to reach the medical field. For example, children with diabetes can now use GlucoBoy, which hooks up to a Nintendo Game Boy, to monitor their glucose levels. And at California's Virtual Reality Medical Center, therapists are treating phobias and other anxiety disorders with video games that simulate driving, flying, heights, tight spaces, and other fear-inducing situations.

To be sure, games aren't perfect. Some evidence points to a correlation between game-playing and aggressive behavior, though it's unclear whether a causal link exists. And certain games are utter time-wasters. But video games are much more valuable than handwringing parents or family-values moralists would want you to believe. And the aptitudes players are mastering are especially well suited to an age that relies on the right side of the brain.

Along with being an avocation of millions, gaming is becoming a vocation for hundreds of thousands—and an especially whole-minded vocation at that. The ideal hire, says one game-industry recruiter, is someone who can "bridge that left brain-right brain divide."[19] Companies resist segregating the disciplines of art, programming, math, and cognitive psychology and instead look for those who can piece together patches of many disciplines and weave them together into a larger tapestry. And both the maturation of games and the offshoring of routine programming work to Asia are changing the emphasis of the gaming profession. As one gaming columnist writes: "Changes in the way games are built indicate less of a future demand for coders, but more of a demand for artists, producers, story tellers and designers. . . . 'We've moved away from relying simply on code,' said [one game developer]. 'It's become more of an artistic medium.' "[20]

That's one reason that many arts schools now offer degrees in game art and design. DigiPen Institute of Technology, near Seattle, which awards a four-year degree in video gaming, is, as *USA Today* puts it, "fast becoming the Harvard among joystick-clenching students fresh out of high school." The school's nickname: Donkey Kong U.[21] The University of Southern California's renowned School of Cinema-Television now offers a master of fine arts degree in game studies. "When USC started a film school 75 years ago, there were skeptics," says Chris Swain, who teaches game design at USC. "We believe games are the literature of the twenty-first century. When you look at games today, it may be difficult to see that. But the pieces are in place for this to happen."[22]

The purest expression of the centrality of gaming in the emerging economy might exist at Carnegie Mellon University's Entertainment Technology Center, a collaboration between its College of Fine Arts and School of Computer Science. Carnegie Mellon offers an entirely new degree: a master's in entertainment technology, which it bills as "a graduate program for the left and right brain." Students study everything from programming to business to improvisational theater—and earn neither an arts degree nor a science degree but an interdisciplinary degree that the school says is "the academic pinnacle of studies in this field, thus having greater significance than the M.A. or M.S., and the equivalent academic weight of the M.F.A. and/or M.B.A. degree." If the MFA is the new MBA, one day soon the MET might be the new MFA. It's a degree that requires and enables a whole new mind.

Humor

With the subject of games fresh in our heads, let's play a game. I call it "Pick the Punch Line." Here's how it works. I'll give you the first part of a joke—the setup. Then you select the correct punch line from four choices. Ready?

It's a Saturday in June and Mr. Jones sees his next-door neighbor, Mr. Smith, outside and walks toward him. "Hey, Smith," Jones asks. "Are you using your lawn-mower this afternoon?" Smith replies warily, "Uh, yes I am." Then Jones says:

(a) "Oh well, can I borrow it when you're done?"
(b) "Great. Then you won't be using your golf clubs. Can I borrow them?"
(c) "Oops!" as he steps on a rake that nearly hits him in the face.
(d) "The birds are always eating my grass seed."

The correct punch line, of course, is (b). Answer (a) is logical but not surprising or funny. Answer (c) is surprising, and its slapstick quality might elicit laughs, but it doesn't follow coherently from the setup. Answer (d) is a complete non sequitur.

I didn't hear this joke at a nightclub or on an HBO comedy special. I plucked it from a 1999 neuroscience study published in the journal *Brain* (which might explain why the joke isn't exactly a side-splitter). To test the role the two hemispheres of the brain play in processing humor, two neuroscientists, Prabitha Shammi and Donald Stuss, conducted an experiment in which they administered this pick-the-punch-line test to a series of subjects. The control group, people with intact brains, chose (b), the punch line you probably selected. But the experimental group, which consisted of people with damage to their right hemisphere (in particular, that hemisphere's frontal lobe), rarely chose that answer. Instead, they usually selected one of the other answers, with a slight preference for answer (c), in which Mr. Jones gets clonked in the nose by a rake.

From their research, the neuroscientists concluded that the right hemisphere plays an essential role in understanding and appreciating humor. When that hemisphere is impaired, the brain's ability to process even semisophisticated comedy suffers. The reason has to do with both the nature of humor and the particular specialties of the right hemisphere. Humor often involves incongruity. A story is moving along when suddenly something surprising and incongruous occurs. The left hemisphere doesn't like surprise or incongruity. ("Golf clubs?" it yelps. "What does that have to do with mowing the lawn? This doesn't make any sense.") So, as with metaphors and nonverbal expression, it calls over for help from its companion hemisphere—which in this case resolves the incongruity by making sense of the comment in a new way. ("You see," explains the right side, "Jones is tricking Smith. Har, har, har.") But if the joke-loving, incongruity-resolving right hemisphere becomes hobbled, the brain has much greater difficulty understanding humor. Instead of surprise being followed by coherence—the chain reaction of an effective joke—the attempted yuk just lingers, an incongruous, confusing set of events.

The importance of this joke-getting specialization goes beyond the ease with which someone can choose the proper punch line.* Shammi and Stuss maintain that humor represents one of the highest forms of human intelligence. "This entire story has profound implications," they write. "The right frontal lobe has been (and in some cases still is) considered the most silent of brain areas. In contrast, it may represent one of the most important human brain regions . . . [and] is critical to the highest and most evolved human cognitive functions."[23]

Humor embodies many of the right hemisphere's most powerful attributes—the ability to place situations in context, to glimpse the big picture, and to combine differing perspectives into new alignments. And that makes this aspect of Play increasingly valuable in the world of work. "More than four decades of study by various researchers confirms some common-sense wisdom: Humor, used skillfully, greases the management wheels," writes Fabio Sala in the *Harvard Business Review.* "It reduces hostility, deflects criticism, relieves tension, improves morale, and helps communicate difficult messages."[24] According to the research, the most effective executives deployed humor twice as often as middle-of-the-pack managers. "A natural facility with humor," Sala says, "is intertwined with, and ap-

"There is no question that a playfully light attitude is characteristic of creative individuals."

—MIHALYI CSIKSZENTMIHALYI

*This study might also shed light on another scientific conundrum: why most men find the Three Stooges funny and most women somehow don't. Recall from the last chapter that the "extreme male brain" often shows right hemisphere impairment. In the pick-the-punch-line study, patients with impaired right hemispheres showed a preference for slapstick humor. So men's preference for the Stooges (and women's disdain for them) might be more about the maleness of our brains than the meagerness of our taste.

pears to be a marker for, a much broader managerial trait: high emotional intelligence."[25]

Humor can be a volatile substance in organizations, of course. "Attempts to manufacture humor can actually suppress it, while the suppression of jocularity may also lead to its resurgence," writes David Collinson, who related the tale of the dour Ford plant and who studies humor in organizations.[26] And it comes in different strengths with varying side effects. Negative humor, for instance, can be especially destructive. It can rip through an organization, carving divisions that are difficult to bridge. "Far from always being a source of social cohesion, humor can reflect and reinforce, articulate and highlight workplace divisions, tensions, conflicts, power asymmetries, and inequalities," Collinson writes.[27]

But used more sensibly, humor can be a clarifying organizational elixir. "Jokes that people tell at the workplace can reveal as much or perhaps more about the organization, its management, its culture, and its conflicts than answers to carefully administered surveys," Collinson says.[28] Thomas A. Stewart, editor in chief of the *Harvard Business Review*, has suggested mining corporate skits for clues about an organization's soul—after he discovered that many of Enron's shady dealings were lampooned at the company's talent show well before auditors had any inkling of wrongdoing at the now notorious energy company.[29] And humor can be a cohesive force in organizations—as anyone who's ever traded jokes at the water cooler or laughed over lunch with colleagues understands. Instead of disciplining the joke-crackers, as Ford did in the last century, organizations should be seeking them out and treating a sense of humor as an asset. It's time to rescue humor from its status as mere entertainment and recognize it for what it is—a sophisticated and peculiarly human form of intelligence that can't be replicated by computers and that is becoming increasingly valuable in a high-concept, high-touch world.

Joyfulness

Everything always starts a little late in India, except the laughter club, which begins exactly on time. At 6:30 A.M., Kiri Agarawal blows her whistle, and forty-three people—including Dr. Kataria, his wife, Madhuri, and I—assemble in a shaggy semicircle. Agarawal pauses—and then all forty-four of us begin walking about, clapping our hands in unison while shouting "Ho-ho, Ha-ha-ha . . . Ho-ho, Ha-ha-ha" over and over again.

We're in the Prabodhan Sports Complex, a few miles from Kataria's home in a residential section of northwest Bombay, where what passes for a "sports complex" is a crumbly concrete wall surrounding a muddy soccer field and a cracked running track. For the next forty minutes, I do things—in public, with strangers—I've never done before. With the other members of the laughing club, I move through a series of exercises that resemble yoga and calisthenics—with a little Method acting thrown in for good measure. One of our first exercises is the "Namaste laugh." We place our palms together, bring them prayerfully before our faces in the traditional Hindu greeting, gaze at another participant, and then laugh. I find it difficult. Self-induced laughter is much tougher than those fake smiles I squeezed out in Chapter 7. So I begin simply bellowing the syllables, "Ha, ha, ha, ha, ha, ha." Then something strange happens. My forced guffaws begin to feel more natural, and the laughter of others seems to call my own out of hiding.

A bit later comes an exercise called "just laughter." I follow the lead of Kataria, who's come decked out in jeans, a diamond earring stud, and a red T-shirt that reads THINK GLOBALLY, LAUGH LOCALLY. He raises his palms upward, walks in circles, and repeats aloud, "I don't know why I'm laughing." I do the same. Kataria's laugh—he

often shuts his eyes tight—seems to transport him to another realm. Then, after each laugh, we do another one-minute round of clapping to the 1-2, 1-2-3 refrain of "Ho-ho, Ha-ha-ha."

The experience is simultaneously weird and invigorating. It's weird to see forty-three people—most of them older women dressed in saris—doing the "lion laughter," in which they stick out their tongues, hold up their hands as if they're claws, and screech like people possessed. But it's invigorating to be outside and to laugh for no reason, because—despite my skepticism—it does feel good.

Later, when we return to his office, Kataria tells me how laughter came to define his life. He was born, the youngest of eight children, in a small village in the state of Punjab. His parents weren't educated, he says, but his mother wanted him to become a doctor. Kataria went to medical school and in the 1980s began practicing internal medicine from a mobile unit that he drove around Bombay. In the early 1990s, he began editing a health magazine, *My Doctor*, along with treating patients. After noticing that patients got better faster when they laughed, he wrote an article in 1995 entitled "Laughter: The Best Medicine."[30]

"If laughing is so good," Kataria says he thought to himself, "why not start a laughter club?" (Roughly one-fourth of the good doctor's sentences seem to include some variation of the "Why not?" formulation.) "The idea came to my mind as a flash at four in the morning on the 13th of March 1995. And within three hours I went to a public park and started asking people if they wanted to laugh with me in a laughing club." He had only four takers. But he explained the benefits of laughing. The five of them told a bunch of jokes, and afterward everybody felt good. They continued each following day, but by day ten they encountered an obstacle: they'd run out of jokes. Kataria was stuck. But then he says he realized that they might not need a joke to laugh. He talked to his wife, a yoga teacher, about creating a series of laughter exercises and concluded, "Why not combine yoga breathing with laughter to make laughter yoga?" And thus a movement was born. "If I were not a doctor, people would have laughed at me," he says. That line always cracks him up. He closes his eyes, throws back his head, and laughs.

For Kataria, humor is not a prerequisite for laughter. The goal of his clubs is "thought-free" laughter. "If you're laughing, you cannot think. That is the objective we achieve in meditation." The meditative mind is the route to joyfulness. Joyfulness differs from happiness, Kataria says. Happiness is conditional; joyfulness is unconditional. "When you depend on something else to make you laugh, the laughter doesn't belong to you. That's a conditional laugh. But in laughter

"He who laughs last doesn't get it."

—HELEN GIANGREGORIO

clubs, the source of laughter is not outside the body; it is within us." Kataria points out that children don't really grasp humor early in life, yet they laugh from the time they are infants. In fact, folklore has it that children laugh hundreds of times a day and adults barely a dozen. Yogic laughter in a group, he says, can help people go from the conditional happiness of adults to the unconditional joyfulness of children. "I want to help people reclaim their childlike playfulness," he tells me.

Now, usually the mere hint that I need to pick up my inner child from the day care of my subconscious makes me roll my eyes and hide my wallet. But the science mostly backs up Kataria's claims about laughter's virtues. Laughter won't cure tuberculosis, but this odd human activity—emitting pulsating paroxysms of air and sound through our piehole—is undeniably good for us. For example, studies by Dr. Lee Berk of the Center for Neuroimmunology at the Loma Linda School of Medicine show that laughter can decrease stress hormones and boost the immune system.[31] Robert Provine, a neuroscientist whose book *Laughter: A Scientific Investigation* offers a thorough account of the anthropology and biology of laughter, notes, "The scientific record offers modest but growing support for the analgesic properties of humor and laughter."[32] What's more, laughter has aerobic benefits. It activates the cardiovascular system, increases the heart rate, and pumps more blood to internal organs. Provine reports that laugh researcher William Fry "found that it took 10 minutes of rowing on his home exercise machine to reach the heart rate produced by one minute of hearty laughter."[33] Perhaps most important, laughter is a social activity—and the evidence is vast that people who have regular, satisfying connections to other people are healthier and happier. Laughter, says Provine, "has more to do with relationships than jokes." We rarely laugh alone. Yet, we often can't help but laugh when others begin to chuckle. Laughter is a form of nonverbal communication that conveys empathy and that is even more contagious than the yawning we did in Chapter 7. Laughter clubs—which, like laughter itself, are always free—combine elements of four good things (yoga, meditation, aerobics, and social contact) into a fifth good thing.

And that's why Kataria believes that the next frontier of laughter clubs is the place where stress runs most rampant: the workplace. "Laughter can play a major role in reducing stress in the workplace," he says. Kataria says that businesses believe that "serious people are more responsible. That's not true. That's yesterday's news. Laughing people are more creative people. They are more productive people. People who laugh together can work together." Companies such as Glaxo and Volvo have gotten the message and organized laughing clubs. And Steve Wilson, a Kataria disciple and self-described "joyologist" in Ohio, is taking the message to corporate America. Says Kataria, "There should be a laughing room at every company. If you can have a smoking room in a company, why not have a laughing room?"

I doubt that IBM will set up a laughing room anytime soon (though there were probably those who doubted whether Fortune 500 execs would ever pay money to play with Legos). But it seems clear that in an age of abundance, laughter provides something the left brain cannot. More broadly, today a play ethic can strengthen and ennoble the work ethic. Games are teaching a variety of whole-minded lessons to a new generation of workers and have given rise to an industry that demands several of the key skills of the Conceptual Age. Humor represents many aspects of the sophisticated thinking required in automated and outsourced times. And just plain laughter can lead to joyfulness, which in turn can lead to greater creativity, productivity, and collaboration.

"The limited brain is a technology," Kataria tells me after we've finished breakfast and the clock is edging toward noon. "You do this, you get this. You do that, you get that. It's mathematics. Laughter I see as a divine mathematics. It doesn't make two plus two equal four. Two plus two can equal sixty-four." Then he laughs.

PORTFOLIO

II

Design

Story

Symphony

Empathy

Play

Meaning

Find a Laughter Club.

One easy way to add some levity to your life is to visit a laughter club. These groups are growing at such a rapid clip that there's probably one near you. (For a list of clubs, go to the Laughter Yoga Web site.) Dr. Madan Kataria, the guru of giggles, has also produced a book, video, and DVD, *Laugh for No Reason*, that explain the basics of laughter yoga as well as the theory and science supporting it. The reading and viewing materials will set you back about $30. But the clubs themselves are free. As Kataria puts it, "No forms, no fee, no fuss." Also, in the springtime, be sure to watch for World Laughter

Day, which is held each year on the first Sunday of May. Repeat after me: Ho-ho, Ha-ha-ha. *(More info: www.laughteryoga.org)*

Play the Cartoon Captions Game.

In Chapter 2, we learned about the Rainbow Project, an alternative SAT devised by Yale's Robert Sternberg that measures more whole-minded abilities. One of the exercises on that anti-SAT asks test takers to supply the captions to *New Yorker* cartoons that have had their captions removed. Try a version of this exercise yourself, preferably with a few other people. Select five or six cartoons from the *New Yorker.* Cut them out of the magazine, but cover up the caption. Then show the captionless cartoon to your pals—and ask them to devise a caption of their own. Lather. Rinse. Repeat. You'll be surprised by how challenging and fun this can be. (It's also good training for the caption contest that appears on the back page of every *New Yorker* issue.) For background on this exercise, and on the broader subject of witty cartoons, consult *New Yorker* cartoon editor Robert Mankoff's book *The Naked Cartoonist.* (And if you're really into this, check out the Mankoff-edited *The Complete Cartoons of The New Yorker*, which includes a companion CD with all 68,647 cartoons ever published in the magazine.) Mankoff says captions require "rhythm, brevity, and surprise." And the humor contained in them depends on a particularly right-brain sensibility. "Most cartoons or funny ideas have this weird combining aspect," he writes. "It is a conceptual blending and overlapping of categories that the conscious mind resists, but that is absolutely necessary to create new ideas. A provocative way to think about it is that it is as if a couple of ideas got together and had sex."

Step on the Humor Scale.

James Thorson, a professor at the University of Nebraska–Omaha, has devised a multidimensional sense of humor scale, which has been used by both researchers and clinicians to measure individuals' level of mirth. The test asks things like whether you use humor to cope and whether your friends consider you a wit. Thorson's research has found that "those who score high on a multidimensional sense of humor scale have lower levels of depression and higher levels of purpose than those who score low in humor." Take the test yourself and see where you stand. *(More info: tinyurl.com/6t7ff)*

Play at Inventing.

Invention and play often have much in common. The best inventors are playful. The best players are inventive. One place to understand the connections is the Smithsonian Institution's traveling "Invention at Play" exhibit, which "focuses on the similarities between the way children and adults play and the creative processes used by innovators in science and technology" and examines the "various playful habits of mind that underlie invention." The exhibit will travel through the United States for a few years. If you can't see it in person, check out the excellent "Invention at Play" Web site.

(More info: www.inventionatplay.org)

Get Your Game On.

You must understand video games. Seriously. You must. So if you don't know a joystick from a jelly roll, spend some time getting up to speed on games played on computers, online, and on special devices such as Game Boys and PlayStations. Ask your kid. Ask your neighbor's kid. Or go into an electronics store such as Best Buy, where the games are usually on display, and ask for a demo. You won't regret it. And you may even become hooked. At the very least, you'll begin to understand the powerful new grammar, narrative pattern, and thinking style these games are teaching. For added nuance about this world, page through any of the many gaming magazines now available. (Look for them near the games in that electronics store.) And investigate the following Web sites, which offer smart primers and some snippets of cool games.

Game Spot—A comprehensive gaming site—one of the best around.
(More info: www.gamespot.com)

Game Talk—An online community for gamers.
(More info: www.gametalk.com)

Game Zone—Another comprehensive gaming site with news and reviews for games on every platform.
(More info: www.gamezone.com)

Newsgaming—Operating at the boundary of gaming and political commentary, this site offers games based on current events.
(More info: www.newsgaming.com)

Open Directory Project, Video Games—A massive list of just about every good gaming site and online game on the Web.

(More info: dmoz.org/Games/Video_Games/full-index.html)

There—This site bills itself as an "online getaway." You become a character—and then hang out with other players on a nifty islandlike setting. This might not ultimately be your cup of chai, but the free trial is worth exploring to get a sense of what role-playing games are like. *(More info: www.there.com)*

Wireless Gaming Review—This site is a great source of information about wireless gaming—games you can play on your cell phone and on other wireless devices. Lots of free downloads, too.

(More info: www.wgamer.com)

Women Gamers—The Internet's largest portal for women gamers, this site features the usual reviews and product announcements as well as great information about industry trends.

(More info: www.womengamers.com)

Yahoo! Games—A good introduction to online games, this site allows you to play everything from backgammon to canasta to Toki Toki Boom with people around the world.

(More info: games.yahoo.com/)

Go Back to School

The best way to get in touch with your inner child is to take it outside for some play. So go back to school . . . or at least, back to the playground. Visit a schoolyard, take a seat on a bench, and watch how the real kids play. See if some of their sense of wonder and curiosity penetrates your adult immune system.

To mix business with pleasure, schedule your next staff retreat in an elementary school. Talking about strategic priorities takes on new meaning when you're in a classroom whose bulletin boards admonish everyone to Play Fair, Don't Hit, and Be Nice. And if this retro approach is really working for you, head to a children's museum for a day of discovery. You'll benefit not only from tackling the hands-on museum exhibits, but also by soaking in the learning and laughter of the little people around you. These places likewise offer a nice alternative for meetings and retreats. Check out the Association of Children's Museum's Web site for links to children's museums around the world (*More info: www.childrensmuseums.org*).

Dissect a Joke.

A nun, a rabbi, and a priest walk into a bar. The bartender looks up at them and says, "What is this? A joke?"

Actually, it is. And, if you ask me, it's a pretty funny joke, too. But why? Giving that question some thought can strengthen your Play muscles. Next time you hear a joke, laugh (if it's funny). Then try to figure out what made it humorous. Was it the ambiguity of a phrase? Was it the sound of a particular word? Was it another instance of the right hemisphere's ability to resolve incongruity?

I don't want you to take a purely clinical approach to humor. (Your popularity among your peers matters to me.) But if you occasionally step back and reverse-engineer a joke or funny line, you'll gain a deeper comprehension of which kinds of humor work—and, more important, which don't.

Play Right-Brain Games.

Two new wireless games are specifically designed to test and enhance R-Directed abilities. Tecmo's *Right Brain Game* features 12 activities that measure whether you're right-brain dominant or left-brain dominant. As of press time, the game was available only in Japan, but it should come to North America and Europe soon. *(More info: www.tecmogames.com)* Right Brain Paradise, which purports to be perhaps "the most brain-stimulating mobile game ever created," moves you through nine increasingly difficult levels that test the capacity of your brain's right hemisphere. *(More info: www.bluelavawireless.com)*

Nine

MEANING

In the early winter of 1942, Austrian authorities in Vienna rounded up and arrested hundreds of Jews, among them a young psychiatrist named Viktor Frankl. At the time Frankl was a rising figure in his field who was developing a new theory of psychological well-being. He and his wife, Tilly, had anticipated the roundup, so they took pains to preserve what was then their most important possession. Before the police marched into their home, Tilly sewed into the lining of Viktor's coat the manuscript of the book he was writing about his theories. Viktor wore the coat when the couple was later dispatched to Auschwitz. He clung to it his first day in the concentration camp. But on day two, the SS guards stripped him down, confiscated all his clothing, and Frankl never saw the manuscript again.

Over the next three years, at Auschwitz and later at Dachau, as his wife, brother, mother, and father perished in the gas ovens, Frankl worked to recreate his text by scratching notes on stolen scraps of paper. And in 1946, one year after Allied forces liberated the concentration camps, those crumpled bits of paper formed the basis of what would become one of the most powerful and enduring works of the last century—Frankl's book, *Man's Search for Meaning.*[1]

In *Man's Search for Meaning*, Frankl describes how he persevered in the face of crushing labor, sadistic guards, and scant food. But his book is more than a narrative of survival. It is both a window into the human soul and a guide to a meaningful life. Drawing on his own experiences in the camps, as well as the experiences and mental states of his fellow prisoners, Frankl elaborated the theory he had begun before his arrest. He argues that "man's main concern is not to gain pleasure or to avoid pain but rather to see a meaning in his life."[2] Our fundamental drive, the motivational engine that powers human existence, is the pursuit of meaning. Frankl's approach—called "logotherapy," for "*logos*," the Greek word for meaning—quickly became an influential movement in psychotherapy.

Frankl and others managed to find meaning and purpose even in the unimaginably ghastly setting of a concentration camp. (In one of my favorite passages, Frankl writes, "I understood how a man who has nothing left in the world still may know bliss, be it only for a brief moment, in the contemplation of his beloved.") He demonstrates that meaning is possible in spite of suffering—indeed, that meaning can sometimes grow from suffering. But he also emphasizes that suffering is not a prerequisite to finding meaning. The search for meaning is a drive that exists in all of us—and a combination of external circumstances and internal will can bring it to the surface.

This last point is the key to the book—and to its relevance today. In the early years of the twenty-first century, several forces have gathered to create the circumstances for the pursuit of meaning on a scale never before imagined. First, while problems of poverty and other social maladies persist, most people in the advanced world have been relieved from true suffering. As I laid out in Chapter 2, we live in an era of abundance, with standards of living unmatched in the history of the world. Freed from the struggle for survival, we have the luxury of devoting more of our lives to the search for meaning. Surely, if Frankl and his fellow prisoners could pursue meaning from the work camps of Auschwitz, we can do the same from the comfort of our abundant lives.

> **"We are born for meaning, not pleasure, unless it is pleasure that is steeped in meaning."**
>
> —JACOB NEEDLEMAN

Other forces are also at work. As I mentioned in Chapter 3, the mammoth baby boom generation is reaching a demographic milestone. The typical boomer now has more of his life behind him than ahead of him, prompting the searching of souls and the reevaluation of priorities. The specter of terrorism hovers, offering reminders of life's fleetingness and raising questions of its purpose. Meantime, technology continues its unrelenting march, deluging us with data and choking us with choices. All these forces have gathered into a perfect storm of circumstances that is making the search for meaning more possible and the will to find meaning the sixth essential aptitude of the Conceptual Age.

Robert William Fogel, the Nobel laureate economist I mentioned briefly in Chapter 2, calls this moment the "Fourth Great Awakening." He writes, "Spiritual (or immaterial) inequity is now as great a problem as material inequity, perhaps even greater."[3] His words echo Frankl's a half-century earlier: "[P]eople have enough to live, but nothing to live for; they have the means but no meaning."[4] Ronald Inglehart, a respected political scientist at the University of

Michigan who has been tracking and comparing public opinion in dozens of countries for the last quarter-century, has detected a similar yearning. Each time he administers his World Values Survey, he finds that respondents express greater concern for spiritual and immaterial matters. For instance, according to one recent survey, 58 percent of Americans say they think often about the meaning and purpose of life. Substantial, though lower, percentages of Germans, British, and Japanese report the same.[5] Inglehart believes that the advanced world is in the midst of a slow change in its operating principles, "a gradual shift from 'Materialist' values (emphasizing economic and physical security above all) toward 'Postmaterialist' priorities (emphasizing self-expression and the quality of life)."[6] Gregg Easterbrook, an American journalist who has written insightfully on this topic, puts it more boldly: "A transition from material want to meaning want is in progress on an historically unprecedented scale—involving hundreds of millions of people—and may eventually be recognized as the principal cultural development of our age."[7]

Whatever we call it—the "Fourth Great Awakening," "Postmaterialist" values, "meaning want"—the consequences are the same. Meaning has become a central aspect of our work and our lives. Pursuing meaning obviously is no simple task. You can't buy a cookbook with the recipe for it—or open a packet of powder and add water and stir. But there are two practical, whole-minded ways for individuals, families, and businesses to begin the search for meaning: start taking spirituality seriously and start taking happiness seriously.

Taking Spirituality Seriously

A little man in a burgundy robe and red sneakers is the last to take the stage. As he emerges from the wings, the audience stands in hushed reverence. He smiles a beatific smile, greets the others, and sits cross-legged on the empty armchair that's waiting for him. The man I'm squinting at from the back rows of a packed 1,300-seat auditorium on the campus of the Massachusetts Institute of Technology—the man who's caused all these people, including Richard Gere, hands pressed together Namaste-style, and Goldie Hawn, hands wiggling by her side, to rise and revere—is Tenzin Gayatso, aka the 14th manifestation of the Buddha of Compassion, aka the Dalai Lama—winner of the Nobel Prize, leader in exile of Tibet, and spiritual rock star who the next evening will fill Boston's Fleet Center with some thirteen thousand adoring fans.

What is the Dalai Lama doing at MIT? He's here for the "Investigating the Mind" conference—a two-day gabfest about what science can learn from Buddhism and what Buddhism can learn from science. Each morning and afternoon the chairs onstage will fill with scientists wearing professorial earth tones and monks wearing rich shades of red and saffron—a visual display of reason breaking bread with spirit, of the left and right sides of our collective brains meeting in the middle. Fifteen years ago, the Dalai Lama began inviting scientists to his home in Dharamsala, India. He was interested in what they were learning about the brain, and they were curious about what was going on in the brains of people who have developed an almost superhuman capacity for meditation and spiritual transcendence. Over the next decade and a half, scientists such as the University of Wisconsin's Richard Davidson began sliding monks into MRI machines like the one I entered in Chapter 1,

> "I believe the very purpose of our life is to seek happiness. That is clear. Whether one believes in religion or not, whether one believes in this religion or that religion, we are all seeking something better in life. So I think the very motion of our life is towards happiness."
>
> —THE DALAI LAMA

to capture images of their meditating brains and to make new insights into emotion, attention, mental imagery, and other cognitive capacities. Monks such as Mathieu Ricard, who originally trained as a molecular biologist, began reading scientific papers to understand the workings of the mind and perhaps the nature of the soul. The meeting that I attended was their first public gathering—a coming-out party of sorts. "Science and Buddhism are very similar," the Dalai Lama told some of us at a press conference before the main event, "because they are exploring the nature of reality, and both have the goal to lessen the suffering of mankind."

What happened at the conference—lots of talk, plans for future research—is less significant perhaps than that it happened. Even MIT is taking spirituality seriously. As the well-known molecular biologist Eric Lander told the crowd, science is merely one way to understand the world. Across many different realms, there's a growing recognition that spirituality—not religion necessarily, but the more broadly defined concern for the meaning and purpose of life—is a fundamental part of the human condition. Indeed, our capacity for faith—again, not religion per se, but the belief in something larger than ourselves—may be wired into our brains. Perhaps not surprisingly, this wiring seems to run through the brain's right hemisphere. For example, Michael Persinger, a neuroscientist at Ontario's Laurentian University, has conducted (somewhat controversial) experiments with a device that's come to be called a "God helmet." Persinger fastens the helmet onto subjects' heads and bathes their brains' right hemispheres in a weak field of electromagnetic radiation. Most of those who have strapped on the apparatus report feeling either the presence of God or a oneness with the universe, suggesting again that spiritual and mystical thoughts and experiences may be part of our neurophysiology.[8] Meantime, at the University of Pennsylvania, Andrew Newberg has scanned the brains of nuns when they have meditated to the point of religious ecstasy and connection with God. His images show that during such moments, the part of the brain that guides a sense of self is less active—thus contributing to the feeling of being unified with something larger. Their work and the work of others have given rise to a new field, neurotheology, which explores the relationship between the brain and spiritual experience. As Caltech neuroscientist Steven Quartz puts it, "Studies of our biological constitution make it increasingly clear that we are social creatures of meaning, who crave a sense of coherence and purpose."[9]

At the very least, we ought to take spirituality seriously because of its demonstrated ability to improve our lives—something that might be even more valuable when so many of us have satisfied (and oversatisfied) our material needs. For instance, some of the maladies of modern life—stress, heart disease, and so on—can be allayed by attending to the spirit. People who pray regularly have been shown to have lower blood pressure, on average, than those who don't, according to research at Duke University. Johns Hopkins researchers have found that attending religious services cut people's risk of death from heart disease, suicide, and some cancers. Other research has found that women to whom life's meaning and purpose was central had higher levels of the types of cells that attack viruses and some kinds of cancer cells. Still other studies have found that the belief that life has some higher purpose can buffer people from heart disease. According to a study at Dartmouth College, one predictor of survival among open-heart patients was how much patients relied on faith and prayer. People who go to church (or synagogue or a mosque) regularly also seem to live longer than those who don't—even controlling for a host of biological and behavioral variables.[10]

This is tricky and controversial territory—in part because so many charlatans have invoked the power of God to heal the infirm. If you depend on spirituality alone to battle cancer or to mend broken bones, you deserve the disastrous results that will follow. But a whole-minded approach—L-Directed reason combined with R-Directed spirit—can be effective. As I noted in Chapter 3, more than half of American medical schools now have courses in spirituality and health. According to *Newsweek*, "72 percent of Americans say they would welcome a conversation with their physician about faith."[11] That's one reason some doctors have even begun taking "spiritual histories" of patients—asking them whether they seek solace in religion, whether they're part of a community of faith, and whether they see a deeper meaning in their lives. It can be a delicate topic, of course. But as Duke University's Dr. Harold Koenig told *Religion News Service*, "We're at the place we were 20 years ago when doctors were asked to take a sexual history." Koenig estimates that between 5 and 10 percent of U.S. physicians take some form of spiritual history.[12] Like narrative medicine, this merging of spirit and health is part of a more sweeping trend in medicine to treat each patient as a whole person rather than as a receptacle for a particular illness.

One other field that has begun to take spirituality more seriously is business. If the Conceptual Age is flowering with postmaterialist values and deepening our "meaning want," it makes sense that the phenomenon would take root in the place where many of us spend most of our waking hours.

Five years ago, Ian Mitroff, a professor at the University of Southern California's Marshall School of Business, and Elizabeth Denton, a consultant, published a report called *A Spiritual Audit of Corporate America.* After interviewing nearly one hundred executives about spirituality in the workplace, they reached some surprising conclusions. Most of the executives defined spirituality in much the same way—not as religion, but as "the basic desire to find purpose and meaning in one's life." Yet, the executives were so understandably concerned that the language of spirit in the workplace would offend their religiously diverse employees that they scrubbed their vocabulary of all such talk. Meanwhile, Mitroff and Denton discovered, the employees were hungering to bring their spiritual values (and thus their whole person rather than one compartment of themselves) to work, but didn't feel comfortable doing so. Read this report and you can almost picture a river of meaning and purpose being dammed outside of corporate headquarters. But here's the kicker: if that spiritual tide had been released, the companies might have been better off. Mitroff and Denton also found that companies that acknowledged spiritual values and aligned them with company goals outperformed those that did not. In other words, letting spirituality into the workplace didn't distract organizations from their goals. It often helped them reach those goals.

As more companies grasp this idea, we are likely to see a rise in spirit *in* business—a growing demand from individuals for workplaces that offer meaning as well as money. According to one recent U.S. survey, more than three out of five adults believe a greater sense of spirituality would improve their own workplace. Likewise, 70 percent of respondents to British think tank Roffey Park's annual management survey said they wanted their working lives to be more meaningful. And in the last few years groups such as the Association for Spirit at Work and events such as the annual international Spirit in Business Conference have emerged.

We'll also see a continued rise in spirit *as* business—commercial ventures that help a meaning-seeking population slake its craving for transcendence. Recall the candle industry of Chapter 2. Or think about the proliferation of yoga studios, evangelical bookstores, and "green" products from the Toyota Prius to the cosmetics of the Body Shop. Rich Karlgaard, the savvy publisher of *Forbes*, says this is the next cycle of business. First came the quality revolution of the 1990s. Then came what Karlgaard calls "the cheap revolution," which dramatically reduced the cost of goods and allowed people around the world to have cell phones and Internet access. "So what's next?" he asks. "Meaning. Purpose. Deep life experience. Use whatever word or phrase you like, but know that consumer desire for these qualities is on the rise. Remember your Abraham Maslow and your Viktor Frankl. Bet your business on it."[13]

Taking Happiness Seriously

"Happiness," Viktor Frankl wrote, "cannot be pursued; it must ensue." But from what does it ensue? That question has vexed humankind since a humankind was around to be vexed. But now the field of psychology has begun to provide some answers—thanks largely to the work of Dr. Martin E. P. Seligman, a professor at the University of Pennsylvania and founder of the "positive psychology" movement.

For most of its history, academic psychology focused on everything *except* happiness. It studied disease, disorder, and dysfunction, and largely ignored what made people satisfied and fulfilled. But when Seligman took the helm of the American Psychological Association in 1998, he slowly began guiding the ship of psych in a new direction. Seligman's research, as well as that of many other scientists who have turned their attention to satisfaction and well-being, has begun to unlock the secrets of what makes people happy—and to encourage the wider world to take happiness seriously.

> **"You're not going to find the meaning of life hidden under a rock written by someone else. You'll only find it by giving meaning to life from inside yourself."**
>
> —DR. ROBERT FIRESTONE, *author and psychotherapist*

According to Seligman, happiness derives from a mix of factors. Part of it depends on biology. We're all born with a relatively fixed natural range of well-being imprinted on our genes. Some of us tilt toward the gloomy end of the spectrum, others toward the cheery end. But all of us can learn how to reach the upper portions of our individual range—where happiness can ensue. Among the things that contribute to happiness, according to Seligman, are engaging in satisfying work, avoiding negative events and emotions, being married, and having a rich social network. Also important are gratitude, forgiveness, and optimism. (What doesn't seem to matter much at all, according to the research, are making more money, getting lots of education, or living in a pleasant climate.)

Marshalling these elements can help create what Seligman calls the "Pleasant Life"—a life full of positive emotions about the past, present, and future. But the Pleasant Life is only one rung on the hedonic ladder. At a higher level is what Seligman calls the "Good Life"—in which you use your "signature strengths" (what you're great at) to achieve gratification in the main areas of your life. This can turn work from what Studs Terkel called "a Monday to Friday sort of dying" into a calling. "A calling is the most satisfying form of work because, as gratification, it is done for its own sake rather than for the material benefits it brings," says Seligman. "Enjoying the resulting state of flow on the job will soon, I predict, overtake material reward as the principal reason for working." The Good Life is good for business, too. "More happiness causes more productivity and higher income," Seligman writes. There's even an emerging school of management thought built around the tenets of positive psychology.

But the Good Life is not the ultimate. "There's a third form of happiness that is ineluctably pursued by humans, and that's the pursuit of meaning . . . knowing what your highest strengths are and deploying them in the service of something larger than you are,"

Seligman says.[14] Going beyond the self in this fashion is not much different from what those meditating nuns and monks were doing. And as rising prosperity and abundance allow more people to engage in this pursuit, and as more of us summon the will to do so, Meaning will move to the center of our lives and our consciousness.

THE BESTSELLING business book of the last decade has been a thin little volume with a strange title. *Who Moved My Cheese?* is a business fable that has sold millions of copies around the world. The book tells the tale of Hem and Haw, two mouselike critters who live in a maze and love cheese. One day, after years of finding their cheese in the same place, Hem and Haw awaken to find their precious cheddar gone. Somebody, yes, has moved their cheese. Hem and Haw react differently to this discovery. Hem, the whiny mouseling, wants to wait until somebody puts the cheese back. Haw, the anxious but realistic mouseling, wants to venture into the maze to discover new cheese. In the end, Haw convinces Hem that they should take action to solve their problem rather than wait for the solution magically to appear. And the micelings live happily ever after (or at least until their cheese moves again). The moral of the story is that change is inevitable, and when it happens, the wisest response is not to wail or whine but to suck it up and deal with it.

I don't disagree with the message of *Who Moved My Cheese?* but I do take issue with the metaphor. In the Conceptual Age, Asia and automation may constantly be moving our cheese, so to speak. But in an age of abundance, we're no longer in a maze. Today the more appropriate metaphor for our times is the labyrinth.

Mazes and labyrinths are often lumped together in the popular imagination, but they differ in important ways. A maze is a series of compartmentalized and confusing paths, most of which lead to dead ends. When you enter, your objective is to escape—as quickly as you can. A labyrinth is a spiral walking course. When you enter, your goal is to follow the path to the center, stop, turn around, and walk back out—all at whatever pace you choose. Mazes are analytic puzzles to be solved; labyrinths are a form of moving meditation. Mazes can be disorienting; labyrinths can be centering. You can get lost in a maze; you can lose yourself in a labyrinth. Mazes engage the left brain; labyrinths free the right brain.

There are now more than 4,000 public and private labyrinths in the United States. They are surging in popularity for many of the reasons I've discussed in this chapter and in the rest of this book. "In an age when many Americans are looking beyond the church pulpit for spiritual experience and solace, a growing number have rediscovered the labyrinth as a path to prayer, introspection, and emotional healing," reports *The New York Times.*[15] You can find them everywhere: in downtown squares in Switzerland; village greens in England; public parks from Indiana to Washington state to Denmark; universities in northern California; jails in southern California; and at houses of worship such as Riverside Church in Manhattan, the National Cathedral in Washington, D.C., Methodist churches in Albany, a Unitarian church in San Jose, and a synagogue in Houston.[16] Labyrinths are also showing up at hospitals and other medical facilities—like the one in the photo on page 229 at the Bayview Medical Center at Johns Hopkins University in Baltimore.

This labyrinth, which I walked one morning not too long ago, is composed of four-inch by four-inch brick squares. Eight concentric circles, formed from similarly sized white squares, orbit a center space that's roughly two feet in diameter. Along the outer edge a few squares have single words stamped onto them: *Create. Faith. Wisdom. Believe.* Visitors often choose one of these words, and then repeat it, like a mantra in meditation, as they circle to the center. I began my labyrinth

walk by heading left and walking through the first ring. As I looked around, I saw a few Medical Center buildings on one side and a parking lot on the other. Nothing transcendent about this. It felt as if I was simply walking in a circle. So I started again. To avoid distractions, I looked down. I focused my sight on the two curving lines that formed the outline of my path, and I began walking—as slowly as I possibly could. The lines curled around me. And after a while it felt a bit like driving on a long empty road. I didn't have to pay much attention, so my mind slipped to a different place—and that had an unexpected calming effect. The experience, perhaps not surprisingly, was similar to the drawing course of Chapter 6 and the laughing club of Chapter 8. It jammed my powers of L-Directed Thinking. "A labyrinth is an escape for the right brain," says David Tolzman, who designed and built the Johns Hopkins labyrinth. "As the left brain engages in the logical progression of walking the path, the right brain is free to think creatively."

The person who most put labyrinths on the cultural map is Dr.

Lauren Artress, an Episcopal priest at Grace Cathedral Church in San Francisco. A few years ago she traveled to Chartres Cathedral in France, site of a forty-two-foot-diameter labyrinth etched into the floor of the nave. When she visited, the labyrinth was covered with chairs and hadn't been used for 250 years. Artress removed the chairs, walked the labyrinth, and then imported the concept to the United States. She installed two now popular labyrinths at Grace Cathedral. And she set up a ministry called Verditas that provides training and labyrinth kits to churches and other organizations.

"We live in such a left brain world . . . and here's this whole other world that we must integrate in order to meet the challenges of the next century," Artress has said. When people walk into a labyrinth, they "shift consciousness from the linear to the non-linear" and bring to the surface "the deep, intuitive, pattern part of ourselves." That experience is different from the experience of being in a maze, she says. "[I]t takes you into an entirely different part of your being than that problem-solving, I-hope-I-make-it feeling." Even the shape of the typical labyrinth is significant. "The circle is an archetype for wholeness or unity. So when people walk into the labyrinth, they begin to see their whole life."[17]

> **"We are not human beings on a spiritual path, but spiritual beings on a human path."**
>
> —DR. LAUREN ARTRESS, *Episcopal priest and labyrinth pioneer*

About forty hospitals and medical centers now have labyrinths—for many of the same reasons that empathy and narrative have begun infiltrating the medical world. There's a growing recognition that the analytical approach to healing, while absolutely necessary, is not always sufficient—and that approaches once dismissed as woo-woo suggestions from New Age whack jobs can help patients get better. That whole-minded thinking led to the labyrinth at Johns Hopkins, one of the finest medical facilities in the world. Its organizers wanted a place where patients, their families, and the medical staff could go to "find physical and mental relaxation." It may be working. At the labyrinth site are two weathered yellow notebooks in which people who have walked the labyrinth can write their thoughts. The notebooks testify to the solace and sense of meaning the labyrinth brings. Doctors and nurses write of coming here after challenging or harrowing experiences. Families of people undergoing surgery describe coming here to pray, to think, and to distract themselves. And in the notebook are moving stories written by patients themselves—entries like this one, which was written just a few days before I arrived:

> *I join in the spirit of all those who have walked the labyrinth and have written on these pages.*
>
> *For me, my surgery, one week ago today, is the beginning of a new phase of life. My word as I walked the labyrinth was "BELIEVE."*
>
> *I believe in a new future.*

Labyrinths won't save the world, of course. Neither will any of the six senses I've discussed in this book. Making the transition from the Information Age to the Conceptual Age, moving from a landscape of L-Directed Thinking to one of R-Directed Thinking, adding the capacity for art and heart to our penchant for logic and analysis, won't be easy. Few worthwhile things ever are. But maybe that's the point. As Viktor Frankl could have told us, the ideal life is not a fear-fueled pursuit of cheese. It's more like walking a labyrinth, where the purpose is the journey itself.

PORTFOLIO

Design

Story

Symphony

Empathy

Play

Meaning

Say Thanks.

Gratitude works. Feelings of gratitude enhance well-being and deepen one's sense of meaning. That's why Martin Seligman, whose work I described earlier in this chapter, advocates "the gratitude visit." It works like this: You think of a person in your life who has been kind or generous to you but whom you've never properly thanked. You write a detailed "gratitude letter" to that person, explaining in concrete terms why you're grateful. Then you visit that person and read the letter aloud. According to Seligman, the ritual is quite powerful. "Everyone cries when you do a gratitude visit. It's very moving for both people."

Seligman's research, as well as the work of the growing ranks of scholars who study positive psychology, suggests that gratitude is a key component of personal happiness. People who are grateful about specific things in their past, who dwell on the sweet triumphs instead of the bitter disappointments, tend to be more satisfied about the present. The gratitude visit, Seligman says, can be an effective way to "increase the intensity, duration and frequency of positive memory."

One reason to give the gratitude visit a try is that it can generate a momentum of its own. Those who are thanked often then start to consider who in their lives they never thanked. So they make their own pilgrimage, as eventually do the recipients of their thanks, resulting in a daisy chain of gratitude and contentment.

Two variations on this theme are the birthday gratitude list and the gratitude one-a-day. The birthday gratitude list is simple. Once a year, on your birthday, make a list of the things for which you're grateful—with the number of items equaling the number of years you're turning that day. (When I did this on my fortieth birthday, my gratitude list included everything from red wine to the fact that my children are healthy to living in a free country.) Your list will grow by one each year—the theory being that the older you get, the more you have to be thankful for. Keep your lists and review them each birthday. It will bring a sense of satisfaction that can soothe the anxiety of time's passage. The gratitude one-a-day is a way to weave thankfulness into your daily routine. Each day, at a certain moment, think of one thing for which you're grateful. Some people do this when they're about to go to sleep. Others do it to accompany some existing routine—when they drink a cup of coffee in the morning, when they make their bed, when they take their first step outside. These gratitude exercises might sound a little touchy-feely to some of you. Give them a try anyway. I guarantee you'll thank me.

Take the 20-10 Test.

I heard this exercise from Jim Collins, author of the blockbuster book *Good to Great.* He encourages people to look at their lives—in particular, their work—and ask themselves whether they would still do what they're doing now if they had $20 million in the bank or knew they had no more than ten years to live. For instance, if you inherited $20 million, no strings attached, would you spend your days the way you spend them now? If you knew you had at most ten years to live, would you stick with your current job? If the answer is no, that ought to tell you something. This test alone obviously can't determine your life course. But the approach is smart—and the answers can be clarifying.

Measure Your Spirit.

In my research, I've encountered two self-assessments that help measure qualities and attitudes associated with Meaning. Neither of these instruments measures exactly what I mean by the elusive ability of Meaning. But both are interesting, useful, and worth exploring.

The first comes from Dr. Ralph Piedmont of Loyola College in Maryland, who's developed what he calls the Spiritual Transcendence Scale. It's much like the other assessments I've mentioned in earlier Portfolios. You answer a series of questions—and when you're through, you tally up your score based on your responses. Piedmont says that "people high on ST believe that there is a larger plan and meaning to life, something beyond our mortal existence. . . . Those low on ST are more concerned with the material aspects of life and see no larger meaning to life other than what life offers in the here and now." *(More info: www.evergreen.loyola.edu/~rpiedmont/STSR.htm)*

The second self-test, called the Index of Core Spiritual Experience (INSPIRIT), is the work of Dr. Jared Kass of Lesley College in Massachusetts. It measures your spiritual experience as well as your overall sense of well-being—and then assesses how the two intersect. For instance, when I took the test, I was told, "You have a healthy sense of well-being, but spirituality may not be a strong contributor." Again, this test isn't the be-all of self-understanding. But it can let you know how much spirituality plays a role in your overall happiness. *(More info: www.tinyurl.com/5sz7u)*

But Out.

Do you know what would make your life more meaningful, yet you find yourself stymied by the obstacles standing in your way? Break through those roadblocks with this simple exercise.

Compile a list of some of the important changes you'd like to make in your life and what's keeping you from realizing them.

I'd like to spend more time with my family, but I travel a lot for my job.

I'd like to eat better, but I'm surrounded at work by sugary snacks.

I'd like to read more, but I rarely have time when I can sit down with a book.

Now go back to each item and replace the word *but* with the word *and.*

I'd like to spend more time with my family, and I travel a lot for my job. So I need to find ways to bring my family along during some of my travels.

I'd like to eat better, and I'm surrounded at work by sugary snacks. So I need to pack my own supply of more healthful snacks to reduce my temptation to eat the bad stuff.

I'd like to read more, and I rarely have time when I can sit down with a book. So I need to get books on tape that I can listen to in the car or at the gym.

Exchanging *and* for *but* can move you out of excuse-making mode and into problem-solving mode. It's grammar's way of saying, "deal with this." And if this technique fails? You can always say, "I wanted to make changes in my life, but that exercise in Pink's book didn't help me enough."

Take a Sabbath.

Select one day a week and remove yourself from the maw. Stop working. Don't answer your email. Ignore your voice mail. Turn off your mobile phone. Most Western religions have established a Sabbath—the seventh day of the week—as a time of peace, reflection, and prayer. Whatever your faith, consider experimenting with this practice. (And this need not be religious at all. Secular Sabbaths can be equally re-energizing.) For guidance, check out Wayne Muller's book, *Sabbath: Finding Rest, Renewal, and Delight in Our Busy Lives.* If committing to this weekly ritual isn't right for you, consider Muller's alternative: "Choose one common act during your day to serve as a Sabbath pause." Whenever you, say, grasp a doorknob or reach for the telephone, "simply stop, take three mindful breaths, and then go through the door, or answer the phone." Sabbaths, however momentary, can be important punctuation marks in busy lives.

Read These Books.

Recommending books about meaning is difficult. Much of the world's great literature and religious texts tackle the topic of what meaning is and how to find it. So the following book recommendations don't trump great novels or sacred texts. Read the Sermon on the Mount, sections of the Torah, and parts of the Koran, too, if you'd like. But for more secular, contemporary, and prescriptive guides to meaning, consider any of these fine books.

Man's Search for Meaning *by Viktor Frankl*—Simply one of the most important books you'll ever read.

Authentic Happiness *by Martin E. P. Seligman*—It astonishes me that more people haven't read this book and absorbed its lessons. It's an ideal introduction to positive psychology and contains all sorts of exercises to help you put the findings into action in your own life. *(More info: www.authentichappiness.org.)*

Flow *by Mihalyi Csikszentmihalyi*—"Flow," when you're so absorbed and enthralled in an activity that you lose your sense of time and place, is an important component of the aptitude of Meaning. This book is your guide.

What Should I Do with My Life? *by Po Bronson*—That's a question all of us have asked ourselves—and it's one that Bronson got hundreds of people around the United States to ask themselves. He returned with a trove of moving, inspiring, and insightful stories.

***Mindfulness** by Ellen Langer*—Too many of us stumble through life mindlessly, says Harvard professor Langer. We're stuck in routines and unaware of our surroundings. Breaking out of that mindset, she says, can be the pathway to creativity and meaning.

***The Art of Happiness** by His Holiness the Dalai Lama and Howard C. Cutler, M.D.*—The Dalai Lama visits with physician Cutler—and in a series of interviews explains his philosophy of life and expands on his idea that "the very purpose of life is to seek happiness." Two related books are also excellent: *The Art of Happiness at Work*, another Dalai Lama–Cutler collaboration, extends Buddhist happiness principles into the office. *Destructive Emotions* is a fascinating "scientific dialogue" with the Dalai Lama that Daniel Goleman conducted during a Mind and Life conference in 2000.

Visit a Labyrinth.

I've tried meditating—and did a pretty bad job of it. I've considered yoga, but (physically at least) I'm not very flexible. However, I've found labyrinths to be surprisingly addicting—so much so that I'd consider installing one in some future backyard. The advantage to me—short attention span, inability to sit still—is that labyrinths require movement. And moving meditation can be calming and centering. To find a labyrinth, start with these Web sites:

The Worldwide Labyrinth Locator

wwll.veriditas.labyrinthsociety.org

Here you can type in your city and country—and find the labyrinths nearest to you.

The Labyrinth Society

www.labyrinthsociety.org

Known as TLS, this group operates a site with a wealth of information on labyrinths. The site also has its own, shorter list of labyrinths as well as a few nifty virtual labyrinths.

Labyrinthos

www.labyrinthos.net

A British resource center for all things labyrinthine and a good source for labyrinths in the United Kingdom.

To learn more about labyrinths, two books are worth perusing: *Walking a Sacred Path* by Lauren Artress and the photo-heavy *Labyrinths and Mazes* by German photographer Jurgen Hohmuth.

If you end up catching the labyrinth bug, you can find all sorts of portable labyrinths and labyrinth construction kits. One of the best Web sites for such products is the Labyrinth Company *(www.labyrinthcompany.com),* which designed the labyrinth I walked at Johns Hopkins. If you're not ready to plow a unicircular pathway into your lawn, consider a wooden "finger labyrinth"—a palm or lap-sized item in which you "walk" the labyrinth by tracing the grooved paths with your finger. They're oddly soothing and don't require leaving your home or office. *(More info: www.relax4life.com)*

Check Your Time.

Most of us can rattle off the things we consider most important. But does the reality of our daily lives match the rhetoric of our deepest aspirations? Find out with this exercise, a favorite of life coaches and time management gurus. First, make a short list of what is most important to you: the people, the activities, and the values. Pare the list to ten or fewer items. Next, take your PDA, day planner, or that free calendar from your insurance guy—and examine how you've spent your time in the past week and month. How many hours can you assign to each of the life priorities you identified? Where have you successfully aligned your values with your time? Where do you find gaps between what you preach and what you actually practice? This exercise can keep you honest and help you steer your days toward a more meaningful life.

Dedicate Your Work.

Look at the page immediately before the Table of Contents in this book. (Go on. I'll wait.) You'll find, as you will in many other books, a dedication. But why should authors have all the fun? Why can't everyone—managers, salespeople, nurses, even accountants—dedicate their work to someone else?

I got this idea from Naomi Epel's *The Observation Deck,* which was also the source of a Portfolio item in Chapter 7. Epel writes, "I once heard Danny Glover say that he dedicates every performance to someone—it might be Nelson Mandela or the old man who guards the stage door—but he is always working for someone other than himself. This focus gives his acting purpose and makes his work rich."

You can do the same. Dedicate your own work—a presentation, a sales call, a report—to someone you admire or who matters in your life. You can infuse your work with purpose and meaning when you think of it as a gift.

Picture Yourself at Ninety.

Longevity is increasing—and many of us will now live into our nineties. Set aside a half hour to picture yourself at age ninety and to put yourself in the mind of ninety-year-old you. What does your life look like when you view it from that vantage point? What have you accomplished? What have you contributed? What are your regrets? This isn't an easy exercise—neither intellectually nor emotionally. But it can be enormously valuable. And it can help you satisfy one of Viktor Frankl's most powerful imperatives: "Live as if you were living for the second time and had acted as wrongly the first time as you are about to act now."

AFTERWORD

We've covered a lot of ground together. And I hope your experience reading *A Whole New Mind* has been as enjoyable as mine writing it. As you prepare to step into the Conceptual Age, let me leave you with some parting thoughts.

As I explained in Chapter 3, your future will depend on your answers to three questions. In this new era each of us must look carefully at what we do and ask ourselves:

1. Can someone overseas do it cheaper?
2. Can a computer do it faster?
3. Am I offering something that satisfies the nonmaterial, transcendent desires of an abundant age?

These three questions will mark the fault line between who gets ahead and who gets left behind. Individuals and organizations that focus their efforts on doing what foreign knowledge workers can't do cheaper and computers can't do faster, as well as on meeting the aesthetic, emotional, and spiritual demands of a prosperous time, will thrive. Those who ignore these three questions will struggle.

In the time since I completed my manuscript, two sets of economists have produced studies that support this book's central idea. W. Michael Cox and Richard Alm, of the Federal Reserve Bank in Dallas, have examined ten years of employment data and discovered that the largest gains have been in jobs that require "people skills and emotional intelligence" (for example, registered nurses) and "imagination and creativity" (for example, designers). Frank Levy, of the Massachusetts Institute of Technology, and Richard Murnane, of Harvard University, have published an excellent book, *The New Division of Labor: How Computers Are Creating the Next Job Market*, in which they argue that computers are in the process of obliterating routine work. The arrival of desktop PCs and the automation of business processes, they say, have heightened the value of two categories of human skills. The first is what they call "expert thinking—solving new problems for which there are no routine solutions." The other is "complex communication—persuading, explaining, and in other ways conveying a particular interpretation of information."

It seems clear, then, that the Conceptual Age is dawning and that those who hope to survive in it must master the high-concept, high-touch abilities I've described. This situation presents both promise and peril. The promise is that Conceptual Age jobs are exceedingly democratic. You don't need to design the next cell phone or discover a new source of renewable energy. There will be plenty of work not just for inventors, artists, and entrepreneurs but also for an array of imaginative, emotionally intelligent, right-brain professionals, from counselors to massage therapists to schoolteachers to stylists to talented salespeople. What's more, as I've tried to make clear, the abilities you'll need—Design, Story, Symphony, Empathy, Play, and Meaning—are fundamentally human attributes. They are things we do out of a sense of intrinsic motivation. They reside in all of us, and need only be nurtured into being.

The peril is that our world moves at a furious pace. Computers and networks grow faster and more interconnected each day. China and India are becoming economic behemoths. Material abundance in the advanced world continues to grow. That means that the greatest rewards will go to those who move fast. The first group of people who develop a whole new mind, who master high-concept and high-touch abilities, will do extremely well. The rest—those who move slowly or not at all—may miss out or, worse, suffer.

The choice is yours. This new age fairly glitters with opportunity, but it is as unkind to the slow of foot as it is to the rigid of mind. I hope this book provides you with the inspiration and the tools you'll need to make your journey. I'd like to hear about your experiences. If you have a story to tell or an exercise to recommend, let me know. You can reach me at *dpp@danpink.com*.

Meantime, thanks for reading. Good luck in the age of art and heart.

DANIEL H. PINK

Washington, D.C., U.S.A.

NOTES

INTRODUCTION

1. To my knowledge, the originator of the term "high touch" is John Naisbitt, who first used it in his 1982 book, *Megatrends*, to describe the common historic reaction to technological advances. "Whenever new technology is introduced into society," Naisbitt wrote, "there must be a counterbalancing human response—that is, high touch—or the technology is rejected." Although I'm using the term in a different sense, I want to make clear that I did not coin the term and that I'm indebted to Naisbitt for adding it to the world's cultural vocabulary.

NOTES

CHAPTER 1: RIGHT BRAIN RISING

1. As it turned out, the task of clicking the buttons and matching the expressions was not central to the actual research. Those exercises were designed mostly to ensure that subjects were paying attention to the photos.
2. Floyd E. Bloom, M.D., M. Flint Beal, M.D., David J. Kupfer, M.D., *The Dana Guide to Brain Health* (Free Press, 2003), 14, 28, 85; Susan Greenfield, *The Human Brain: A Guided Tour* (Weidenfeld & Nicholson, 1997), 28.
3. Nicholas Wade, "Roger Sperry, a Nobel Winner for Brain Studies, Dies at 80," *New York Times* (April 20, 1994).
4. Betty Edwards, *The New Drawing on the Right Side of the Brain* (Tarcher/Putnam, 1999), 4.
5. Robert Ornstein, *The Right Mind: Making Sense of the Hemispheres* (Harcourt Brace & Company, 1997), 2.
6. Bloom et al., 8.
7. Eric A. Havelock, *The Muse Learns to Write: Reflections on Orality and Literacy from Antiquity to the Present* (Yale University Press, 1988), 110–117.
8. Neil R. Carlson, *Physiology of Behavior*, Eighth Edition (Allyn and Bacon, 2004), 84–85.
9. Ibid., 48.
10. Chris McManus, *Right Hand Left Hand: The Origins of Asymmetry in Brains, Bodies, Atoms and Cultures* (Harvard University Press, 2002), 181.
11. See Ornstein, 37. Another example: "Japanese use both a phonetic script (kana) and a pictographic script (kanji). Research shows that kana is better processed in the left hemisphere, while kanji is better handled by the right." See Ornstein, 41.
12. Ornstein, 140.
13. Carlson, 84–85.

14. Jerre Levy-Agresti and R. W. Sperry, "Differential Perceptual Capacities in Major and Minor Hemispheres," *Proceedings of the National Academy of Sciences* (vol. 61, 1968).
15. This metaphor is not mine. I've heard it from neuroscientists but none of them seems to know who came up with this delicious phrase.
16. Ahmad Hariri et al., "The Amygdala Response to Emotional Stimuli: A Comparison of Faces and Scenes," *NeuroImage* 17 (2002), 217–223. See also Elizabeth A. Phelps et al., "Activation of the Left Amygdala to a Cognitive Representation of Fear," *Nature Neuroscience* (April 2001).
17. Paul Ekman, *Emotions Revealed: Recognizing Faces and Feelings to Improve Communication and Emotional Life* (Times Books, 2003), 13.
18. McManus, 183–84.

CHAPTER 2: ABUNDANCE, ASIA, AND AUTOMATION

1. Drucker first discusses the broad concept of "knowledge work" in his 1959 book, *The Landmarks of Tomorrow*, though his first apparent use of the term is in Peter Drucker, "The Next Decade in Management," *Dun's Review and Modern Industry* 74 (December 1959). For the paragraph's first quotation, I've relied on the always excellent work of Richard Donkin and his October 30, 2002, *Financial Times* article, "Employees as Investors." The second and third quotations come from Peter Drucker, "The Age of Social Transformation," *Atlantic Monthly* (November 1994). For some of Drucker's latest thoughts on the subject, see Peter Drucker, "The Next Society," *The Economist* (November 1, 2003), in which he defines knowledge workers as "people with considerable theoretical knowledge and learning: doctors, lawyers, accountants, chemical engineers."
2. *Staples 2003 Annual Report*; Staples Corporate Overview (available at *www.corporate-ir.net/ireye/ir_site.zhtml?ticker=PR_96244&script=2100*); "PETsMART Reports Second Quarter 2003 Results," *PetSmart 2003 Annual Report* (August 28, 2003).

3. Gregg Easterbrook, *The Progress Paradox: How Life Gets Better While People Feel Worse* (Random House, 2003), 6. Easterbrook's smart book also contains a collection of other statistics that confirm the shift from scarcity to abundance.
4. Data are from the U.S. Bureau of Transportation Statistics' *2001 National Household Travel Survey*, available at *www.bts.gov.*
5. John De Graaf, David Wann, and Thomas H. Naylor, *Affluenza: The All-Consuming Epidemic* (Berrett-Koehler Publishers, Inc., 2002), 32. See also data at *www.selfstorage.org.*
6. Polly LaBarre, "How to Lead a Rich Life," *Fast Company* (March 2003).
7. Virginia Postrel, *The Substance of Style: How the Rise of Aesthetic Value Is Remaking Culture, Commerce, and Consciousness* (HarperCollins, 2003). More Postrel: "But, more important, aesthetics is also becoming more prominent relative to other goods. When we decide how next to spend our time or money, considering what we already have and the costs and benefits of various alternatives, 'look and feel' is likely to top our list. We don't want more food, or even more restaurant meals—we're already maxed out. Instead, we want tastier, more interesting food in an appealing environment. It's a move from physical quantity to intangible, emotional quality."
8. Andrew Delbanco, *The Real American Dream: A Meditation on Hope* (Harvard University Press, 1999), 113.
9. Robert William Fogel, *The Fourth Great Awakening and the Future of Egalitarianism* (University of Chicago Press, 2000), 3.
10. "Wax Buildup," *American Demographics* (March 2002).
11. Rachel Konrad, "Job Exports May Imperil U.S. Programmers," Associated Press (July 13, 2003).
12. Pankaj Mishra, "India: On the Downswing of Software Outsourcing," *Asia Computer Weekly* (January 13, 2003).
13. Khozem Merchant, "GE Champions India's World Class Services," *Financial Times* (June 3, 2003).

14. Amy Waldman, "More 'Can I Help You?' Jobs Migrate from U.S. to India," *New York Times* (May 11, 2003); Joanna Slater, "Calling India . . . Why Wall Street Is Dialing Overseas for Research," *Wall Street Journal* (October 2, 2003).
15. Pete Engardio, Aaron Bernstein, and Manjeet Kriplani, "Is Your Job Next?" *Business Week* (February 3, 2003); Merchant, "GE Champions"; "Sun Chief to Woo India in Software War," *Reuters* (March 4, 2003); Eric Auchard, "One in 10 Tech Jobs May Move Overseas, Report Says," *Reuters* (July 30, 2003); Steven Greenhouse, "I.B.M. Explores Shift of White-Collar Jobs Overseas," *New York Times* (July 22, 2003); Bruce Einhorn, "High Tech in China," *Business Week* (October 28, 2002).
16. Engardio et al., "Is Your Job Next?".
17. Auchard, "One in 10 Tech Jobs"; "Outsourcing to Usurp More U.S. Jobs," CNET News.com (August 31, 2003); Paul Taylor, "Outsourcing of IT Jobs Predicted to Continue," *Financial Times* (March 17, 2004).
18. John C. McCarthy, with Amy Dash, Heather Liddell, Christine Ferrusi Ross, and Bruce D. Temkin, "3.3 Million U.S. Services Jobs to Go Offshore," *Forrester Research Brief* (November 11, 2002); Mark Gongloff, "U.S. Jobs Jumping Ship," *CNN/Money* (March 13, 2003).
19. George Monbiot, "The Flight to India," *Guardian* (October 21, 2003); Moumita Bakshi, "Over 1 Million Jobs in Europe Moving Out," *The Hindu* (Sept. 3, 2004).
20. "Not So Smart," *Economist* (January 30, 2003).
21. Rudy Chelminski, "This Time It's Personal," *Wired* (October 2001).
22. Robert Rizzo, "Deep Junior and Kasparov Play to a Draw," *Chess Life* (June 2003).
23. Steven Levy, "Man vs. Machine: Checkmate," *Newsweek* (July 21, 2003).
24. A similar pattern occurred the year before when another chess champion, Vladimir Kramnik, played another computer, Deep Fritz, in a Persian Gulf contest that promoters dubbed "Brains in Bahrain."

Kramnik went into the sixth game with a lead, but at a critical juncture, instead of playing a conventional move, Kramnik attempted one that he felt was more creative and aesthetic. The fool. It cost him the game—and ultimately the match. Said Kramnik of his loss, "At least I played like a man." Daniel King, "Kramnik and Fritz Play to a Standoff," *Chess Life* (February 2003).

25. Chelminski, "This Time It's Personal."
26. Paul Hoffman, "Who's Best at Chess? For Now, It's Neither Man Nor Machine," *New York Times* (February 8, 2003).
27. "The Best and the Brightest," *Esquire* (December 2002).
28. "Software That Writes Software," *Futurist Update* (March 2003).
29. Laura Landro, "Going Online to Make Life-and-Death Decisions," *Wall Street Journal* (October 10, 2002).
30. Laura Landro, "Please Get the Doctor Online Now," *Wall Street Journal* (May 22, 2003); "Patient, Heal Thyself," *Wired* (April 2001).
31. Jennifer 8. Lee, "Dot-Com, Esquire: Legal Guidance, Lawyer Optional," *New York Times* (February 22, 2001).

CHAPTER 3: HIGH CONCEPT, HIGH TOUCH

1. As I explained in the Introduction, I believe John Naisbitt coined the term "high touch," though he used it to describe a different phenomenon.
2. Hilary Waldman, "Art & Arteries: Examining Paintings, Medical Students Learn to Be More Observant Doctors," *Hartford Courant* (March 1, 2000); Mike Anton, "Adding a Dose of Fine Arts," *Los Angeles Times* (May 24, 2003).
3. Yumiko Ono, "Rethinking How Japanese Should Think," *Wall Street Journal* (March 25, 2002); Anthony Faiola, "Japan's Empire of Cool," *Washington Post* (December 27, 2003); Geoffrey A. Fowler, "AstroBoy Flies Again," *Wall Street Journal* (January 15, 2004).

4. Danny Hakim, "An Artiste Invades Stodgy G.M.; Detroit Wonders if the 'Ultimate Car Guy' Can Fit In" *New York Times* (October 19, 2001); Danny Hakim, "G.M. Executive Preaches: Sweat the Smallest Details," *New York Times* (January 5, 2004)
5. John Hawkins, *The Creative Economy: How People Make Money from Ideas* (Allen Lane/The Penguin Press, 2001), 86. Virginia Postrel, *The Substance of Style: How the Rise of Aesthetic Value Is Remaking Culture, Commerce, and Consciousness* (HarperCollins, 2003), 17.
6. "2002 National Cross-Industry Estimates of Employment and Mean Annual Wage for SOC Major Occupational Groups," Occupational Employment Statistics Program, Bureau of Labor Statistics, available at *www.bls.gov/oes/home.htm.*
7. Richard Florida, *The Rise of the Creative Class: And How It's Transforming Work, Leisure, Community, and Everyday Life* (Basic Books, 2002), 328. To his credit, Florida has reinvigorated the debate about urban planning in America. However, his appealing vision of economic development through brewpubs and loft apartments has also been roundly criticized. Some commentators score him for excluding large population segments, most notably racial minorities and couples with children. Others claim his data don't support his arguments. My view is that he's performed a valuable public service merely by sparking discussion on this topic.
8. Hawkins, *Creative Economy*, 116; Justin Parkinson, "The Dawn of Creativity?" *BBC News Online* (June 24, 2003).
9. Remarks of Daniel Goleman, Human Resource Planning Society Annual Meeting, Miami Beach, Florida (March 27, 2002).
10. Adam D. Duthie, "Future SAT May Test Creativity," *Badger Herald* via University Wire (March 3, 2003); Rebecca Winters, "Testing That Je Ne Sais Quoi," *Time* (October 27, 2003); Robert J. Sternberg, "The Other Three R's: Part Two, Reasoning," *American Pyschological Association Monitor* (April 2003).

11. Arlene Weintraub, "Nursing: On the Critical List," *Business Week* (June 3, 2002).
12. Joel Stein, "Just Say Om," *Time* (August 4, 2003); Richard Corliss, "The Power of Yoga," *Time* (April 21, 2001); Mark Nollinger, "TV Goes with God," *TV Guide* (January 24, 2004)
13. Sandra Timmerman, "The Elusive Baby Boomer Market: In Search of the Magic Formula," *Journal of Financial Service Professionals* (September 2003).
14. Paul H. Ray and Sherry Ruth Anderson, *The Cultural Creatives: How 50 Million People Are Changing the World* (Three Rivers Press, 2000), 5, 11, 12.

CHAPTER 4: DESIGN

1. John Heskett, *Toothpicks and Logos: Design in Everyday Life* (Oxford University Press, 2002), 1.
2. Virginia Postrel, *The Substance of Style* (HarperCollins, 2003), 16.
3. "Pricing Beauty: Reflections on Aesthetics and Value, An Interview with Virginia Postrel," *Gain 2.0*, AIGA Business and Design Conference, American Institute of Graphic Arts (September 2002).
4. Heskett, 89.
5. "U.S. Bans Time-Honoured Typeface," Agence France-Presse (January 30, 2004).
6. Jason Tanz, "From Drab to Fab," *Fortune* (December 8, 2003).
7. Quoted in *Re-imagine! Business Excellence in a Disruptive Age* (Dorling Kindersley Limited, 2003), 134.
8. John Howkins, *The Creative Economy: How People Make Money from Ideas* (Allen Lane/The Penguin Press, 2003), 95.
9. Design Council UK, "Design in Britain 2003–04," 9. Available at *www.design-council.org.uk.*
10. Jean-Leon Bouchenaire, "Steering the Brand in the Auto Industry," *Design Management Journal* (Winter 2003).

11. Chris Bangle, "The Ultimate Creativity Machine: How BMW Turns Art into Profit," *Harvard Business Review* (January 2001).
12. Kevin Naughton, "Detroit's Hot Buttons," *Newsweek* (January 12, 2004).
13. Ibid.
14. Charles C. Mann, "Why 14-Year-Old Japanese Girls Rule the World," *Yahoo! Internet Life* (April 2001). The terms come from Iizuka. The material inside the parentheses is from Mann's excellent article.
15. Carolina A. Miranda, "Wow! Love Your Ring!" *Time* (January 21, 2004).
16. Marilyn Elias, "Sunlight Reduces Need for Pain Medication," *USA Today* (March 2, 2004).
17. "The Value of Good Design," report from the Commission for Architecture and the Built Environment (2002), available at *www.cabe.org.uk.*
18. Chee Pearlman, "How Green Is My Architecture," *Newsweek* (October 27, 2003); John Ritter, "Buildings Designed in a Cool Shade of 'Green,'" *USA Today* (March 31, 2004).
19. Peter Orszag and Jonathan Orszag, "Statistical Analysis of Palm Beach Vote" (November 8, 2000), available at *www.sbgo.com*.
20. Dennis Cauchon and Jim Drinkard, "Florida Voter Errors Cost Gore the Election," *USA Today* (May 11, 2003).

CHAPTER 5: STORY

1. Mark Turner, *The Literary Mind: The Origins of Thought and Language* (Oxford University Press, 1996), 4–5.
2. Don Norman, *Things That Make Us Smart: Defending Human Attributes in the Age of the Machine* (Perseus, 1994), 146.
3. "Storytelling That Moves People: A Conversation with Screenwriting Coach Robert McKee," *Harvard Business Review* (June 2003).

4. See Steve Denning's Web site, *www.stevedenning.com/index.htm;* D. McCloskey and A. Klamer (1995). One quarter of GDP is persuasion. *American Economic Review* 85, 191–195.
5. Stephen Denning, *The Springboard: How Storytelling Ignites Action in Knowledge-Era Organizations* (Butterworth Heiman, 2001), xvii.
6. "Interview with Richard Olivier," *Fast Company* (October 2000).
7. Jamie Talan, "Storytelling for Doctors; Medical Schools Try Teaching Compassion by Having Students Write About Patients," *Newsday* (May 27, 2003).
8. Rita Charon, "Narrative Medicine: A Model for Empathy, Reflection, Profession, and Trust," *Journal of the American Medical Association* (October 17, 2001).
9. Ibid.
10. Mike Anton, "Adding a Dose of Fine Arts," *Los Angeles Times* (May 24, 2003).
11. Christine Haughney, "Creative Writing: Old Balm in a New Forum," *Washington Post* (August 3, 2003); Michael Bond, "The Word Doctor," *New Scientist* (January 14, 2003).
12. Katherine S. Mangan, "Behind Every Symptom, a Story," *Chronicle of Higher Education* (February 13, 2004).

CHAPTER 6: SYMPHONY

1. Thanks to Bill Taylor and Ron Lieber for pointing me to these examples.
2. Mihalyi Csikszentmihalyi, *Creativity: Flow and the Psychology of Discovery and Invention* (HarperCollins, 1996), 9.
3. "Interview with Clement Mok," *Fast Company* (January 2003).
4. Nicholas Negroponte, "Creating a Culture of Ideas," *Technology Review* (February 2003).
5. Csikszentmihalyi, 71.

6. M. Jung-Beemna, E. M. Bowden, J. Haberman, et al., "Neural Activity When People Solve Verbal Problems with Insight," *PloS Biology* (April 2004).
7. George Lakoff and Mark Turner, *More Than Cool Reason: A Field Guide to Poetic Metaphor* (University of Chicago Press, 1989), 214–15; George Lakoff and Mark Johnson, *Metaphors We Live By* (University of Chicago Press, 1980), 6.
8. Keith J. Holyoak, *Mental Leaps: Analogy in Creative Thought* (MIT Press, 1996), 6.
9. Twyla Tharp, *The Creative Habit: Learn It and Use it for Life* (Simon and Schuster, 2003), 157.
10. See Gerald Zaltman, *How Customers Think* (Harvard Business School Press, 2003); Daniel H. Pink, "Metaphor Marketing," *Fast Company* (April 1998).
11. Lakoff and Johnson, 233.
12. Charlotte Gill, "Dyslexics Bank of Disability," *Courier Mail* (Queensland, Australia) (October 7, 2003).
13. Sally Shaywitz, *Overcoming Dyslexia* (Knopf, 2003), 366.
14. Michael Gerber, "The Entrepreneur as a Systems Thinker: A Revolution in the Making," *Entreworld* (August 17, 2003). See also the work of Peter Senge, who helped bring "systems thinking" into the business vocabulary.
15. Daniel Goleman, *Working with Emotional Intelligence* (Bantam, 1998), 33.
16. Sidney Harman, *Mind Your Own Business: A Maverick's Guide to Business, Leadership and Life* (Currency Doubleday, 2003), 10.
17. From the mission statement of the American Holistic Medical Association, available at *www.holisticmedicine.org*.

CHAPTER 7: EMPATHY

1. Steven M. Platek et al., "Contagious Yawning: The Role of Self-Awareness and Mental State Attribution," *Cognitive Brain Research*, vol. 17 (2003), 223–27.
2. Daniel Goleman, *Emotional Intelligence: Why It Can Matter More Than IQ* (Bantam, 1995), 96–97.
3. Richard Restak, M.D., *Mozart's Brain and the Fighter Pilot: Unleashing Your Brain's Potential* (Harmony Books, 2001).
4. Rowan Hooper, "Reading the Mind Through the Face," *Japan Times* (May 22, 2003).
5. Akiko Busch, ed., *Design Is . . .* (Metropolis Books, 2001), 105.
6. Paul Ekman, *Emotions Revealed: Recognizing Faces and Feelings to Improve Communication and Emotional Life* (Times Books, 2003), 220.
7. Ibid., 205–206.
8. Ibid., 220.
9. Jodi Halpern, *From Detached Concern to Empathy: Humanizing Medical Practice* (Oxford University Press, 2001).
10. Susan Okie, "An Act of Empathy," *Washington Post* (October 21, 2003). Rachel Zimmerman, "Doctors' New Tool to Fight Lawsuits: Saying 'I'm Sorry,'" *Wall Street Journal* (May 18, 2004)
11. M. Hojat et al., "Empathy in Medical Students as Related to Academic Performance, Clinical Competence and Gender," *Medical Education* (June 2002).
12. S. K. Fields et al., "Comparisons of Nurses and Physicians on an Operational Measure of Empathy," *Evaluation and the Health Professions* (March 2004).
13. Sandra Yin, "Wanted: One Million Nurses," *American Demographics* (September 2002); Julie Appleby, "Professionals Sick of Old Routine Find Healthy Rewards in Nursing," *USA Today* (August 16, 2004).
14. "Public Rates Nursing as Most Honest and Ethical Profession," Gallup press release (December 1, 2003).

15. Fran Foo, "Survey: Outsourcing May Hit IT Careers," *CNET News* (July 9, 2003).
16. David G. Myers, *Intuition: Its Powers and Perils* (Yale University Press, 2002), 46.
17. Simon Baron-Cohen, *The Essential Difference: The Truth About the Male and Female Brain* (Basic Books, 2003), 31.
18. Myers, 46.
19. Baron-Cohen, 1.
20. Ibid., 8.
21. Ibid., 5.
22. Ibid., 176.

CHAPTER 8: PLAY

1. David L. Collinson, "Managing Humour," *Journal of Management Studies* (May 2002).
2. For more on the term "play ethic," see Pat Kane, *The Play Ethic: A Manifesto for a Different Way of Living* (Macmillan, 2004).
3. Diya Gullapalli, "To Do: Schedule Meeting, Play with Legos," *Wall Street Journal* (August 16, 2002).
4. Collinson, "Managing Humour."
5. For excellent longer accounts of the genesis of this game, see "Tap into What's Hot," *Business 2.0* (April 2003) and Brian Kennedy, "Uncle Sam Wants You (To Play This Game)," *New York Times* (July 11, 2002).
6. T. Trent Gegax, "Full Metal Joystick," *Newsweek* (October 14, 2002).
7. *Essential Facts About the Computer and Video Game Industry: 2003 Sales, Demographics and Usage Data (2003)*, published by the Interactive Digital Software Association, available at *www.idsa.com.*
8. Ellen Edwards, "Plug (the Product) and Play," *Washington Post* (January 26, 2003); David Brooks, "Oversimulated Suburbia," *New York Times Magazine* (November 24, 2002); Peter Lewis, "The Biggest Game in Town," *Fortune* (September 15, 2003).

9. David Kushner, "The Wrinkled Future of Online Gaming," *Wired* (June 2004); Zev Borow, "The Godfather," *Wired* (January 2003).
10. James Sullivan, "Digital Art Finds More Than Joy in Joysticks," *San Francisco Chronicle* (January 22, 2004).
11. Don Marinelli and Randy Pausch, "Edutainment for the College Classroom," *Chronicle of Higher Education* (March 19, 2004).
12. James Paul Gee, *What Video Games Have to Teach Us About Learning and Literacy* (Palgrave Macmillan, 2003), 205.
13. Scott Carlson, "Can Grand Theft Auto Inspire Professors?" *Chronicle of Higher Education* (August 15, 2003).
14. Gee, 91.
15. Shawn Greene and Daphne Bavelier, "Action Video Game Modifies Visual Selective Attention," *Nature* (May 2003).
16. "Study: Gamers Make Good Surgeons," *CBSNews.com* (April 7, 2004).
17. "Games at Work May Be Good For You," *BBC News* (November 10, 2003).
18. "Study Finds Video Games Good for Treating Phobias," Reuters (October 17, 2003); Fred Guterl, "Bionic Youth: Too Much Information?," *Newsweek International* (September 1, 2003).
19. Kenneth Aaron, "Where Play Is Serious Business," Albany, NY, *Times Union* (December 10, 2002).
20. Tom Loftus, "Gaming Tries to Shed Boys' Club Image," *MSNBC.com* (June 17, 2004).
21. Marc Krantz, "Video Game College Is 'Boot Camp' for Designers," *USA Today* (December 3, 2002).
22. Alex Pham, "Action Morphs into Art," *Los Angeles Times* (March 26, 2004).
23. P. Shammi and D. T. Stuss, "Humour Appreciation: A Role of the Right Frontal Lobe," *Brain* (1999), vol. 122, 663.
24. Fabio Sala, "Laughing All the Way to the Bank," *Harvard Business Review* (September 2003).
25. Sala, "Laughing All the Way to the Bank."

26. Collinson, "Managing Humour."
27. Ibid.
28. Ibid.
29. Thomas A. Stewart, "Laughter, the Best Consultant," *Harvard Business Review* (February 2004).
30. The headline took its name from the popular *Reader's Digest* column. And the piece followed in the tradition of Norman Cousins, an American who overcame a life-threatening degenerative disease with a self-prescribed regimen of vitamin C, Marx Brothers movies, and back episodes of *Candid Camera*, an experience he chronicled in a 1976 *New England Journal of Medicine* article and a 1979 book, *Anatomy of an Illness.*
31. L. Berk, S. Tan, W. Fry, et al., "Neuroendocrine and Stress Hormone Changes During Mirthful Laughter," *American Journal of the Medical Sciences*, vol. 298, no. 6 (1989), 390–396. L. Berk and S. Tan, "A Positive Emotion: The Eustress Metaphor. Mirthful Laughter Modulates Immune System Immunocytes," *Annals of Behavioral Medicine,* vol. 19, no. D009 (1997 Supplement).
32. Robert R. Provine, *Laughter: A Scientific Investigation* (Penguin Books, 2001), 202.
33. Ibid., 193.

CHAPTER 9: MEANING

1. In 1991, when the Library of Congress and the Book-of-the-Month Club asked readers about the books that had most influenced their lives, *Man's Search for Meaning* ranked ninth—on a top-ten list that included the Bible and the Book of Mormon. See Esther B. Fein, "Book Notes," *New York Times* (November 20, 1991).
2. Viktor Frankl, *Man's Search for Meaning* (Washington Square Press, 1984), 136.

3. Robert William Fogel, *The Fourth Great Awakening and the Future of Egalitarianism* (University of Chicago Press, 2000), 1 (parentheses in the original).
4. Frankl, 165.
5. "In America, the Meaning of Life Is on Most People's Minds," *Spirituality & Health* (March/April 2004).
6. Ronald Inglehart, *Modernization and Postmodernization: Culture, Economic and Political Change in 43 Societies* (Princeton University Press, 1997), 4 (parentheses in the original).
7. Gregg Easterbrook, *The Progress Paradox: How Life Gets Better While People Feel Worse* (Random House, 2003), 317.
8. Anne McIlroy, "Hard-Wired for God," *Globe and Mail* (December 6, 2003). However, it should be noted that most of the meditating monks showed a leftward shift in brain function. Their thought processes were R-Directed but in a neurological sense dominated by the left hemisphere.
9. See *www.edge.org/q2003/*.
10. See Harold G. Koenig et al., *Handbook of Religion and Health* (Oxford University Press, 2000); Jeff Levin, PhD, *God, Faith, and Health: Exploring the Spirituality-Healing Conncetion* (John Wiley and Sons, 2001); Harold G. Koenig, *Spirituality in Patient Care: Why, How, When, and What* (Templeton Foundation Press, 2001); Claudia Kalb, "Faith & Healing," *Newsweek* (November 10, 2003); Richard Morin, "Calling Dr. God," *Washington Post* (July 8, 2001); Bridget Coila, "Finding Meaning in Life Means Greater Immunity," *Spirituality & Health* (January/February 2004).
11. Kalb, "Faith & Healing."
12. Mary Jacobs, "Treating the Body and Spirit," *Washington Post* (September 6, 2003).
13. Rich Karlgaard, "The Age of Meaning," *Forbes* (April 26, 2004).

14. Martin E. P. Seligman, *Authentic Happiness* (Free Press, 2003), 166.
15. Laurie Goodstein, "Reviving Labyrinths, Paths to Inner Peace," *New York Times* (May 10, 1998).
16. For an excellent account of the popularity and design of modern labyrinths, see Juanita Dugdale, "Paths of Least Resistance," *I.D.* (March/April 2004).
17. "The Labyrinth: A Medieval Tool for the Postmodern Age: An Interview with Dr. Lauren Artress," available at *www. gracecathedral. org/enrichment/interviews/int_19961206.shtml.*

ACKNOWLEDGMENTS

A Whole New Mind is the product of a whole lot of minds. A few hundred people answered questions large and small and sat for interviews long and short to help me sort through a welter of ideas and information. Thanks, everyone. A few folks, however, deserve special mention:

Rafe Sagalyn is simply the finest literary agent, canniest adviser, and greatest friend an author can have. He was helpful in every aspect of this book. He also had the good sense to hire Jennifer Graham and Amy Rosenthal.

Many thanks to my editor at Riverhead Books, Cindy Spiegel, for countenancing my anal-retentive tendencies—and to her assistants, Susan Ambler and Charlotte Douglas, for their boundless patience.

Marc Tetel, a neuroscientist at Wellesley College, checked and rechecked every sentence I wrote about the brain. Little did I know a quarter century ago that the skinny kid from North Carolina who lived down the hall in my freshman dorm would turn out to be a top-notch scientist, a terrific editor, and a lifelong friend. (If any mistakes remain, they're mine—not his.) A tip of the hat as well to Jon Auerbach, another freshman-dormmate-turned-neuroscientist, who suggested I get my brain scanned at NIH.

Tom Peters, Seth Godin, and Po Bronson offered a bevy of excellent editorial and marketing advice. Dan Charles, Jack Donahue, Lesley Pink, Alan Webber, and Renee Zuckerbrot read portions of the manuscript and made valuable suggestions. Jeff O'Brien and Bob Cohn deftly sharpened my arguments about outsourcing and the Conceptual Age. Jim Coudal and Susan Everett of Coudal Partners gave this parcel of ideas the striking visual identity you see on the book jacket and, I hope, lots of other places. Claire Vaccaro and her team did a sensational job designing the look and feel of the book's interior. Mark Hill drew a great cartoon.

For this paperback edition, Jeffrey Cufaude did a brilliant job of helping me expand the Portfolios. His insights, feedback, and good humor were invaluable. Readers around the world also offered their suggestions for the paperback. I'm grateful for their contributions and extend special thanks to: Keri Alleton, Robert Ballard, Arnold Beekes, Glen Bell, Rasmus Bertelsen, Adam Blatner, Sarah Brophy, Kevin Buck, Anand Chhatpar, Patrick Clough, Ed Daniel, Patti Digh, Mike Doherty, Indra Dosanjh, Carl Garant, Jerry Gasche, Richard Gerson, Sean Heath, Helen Hegener, Jim Hurd, Bill Jeffrey, Jan Jopson, Victor Lombardi, Glenn Main, Phillip Marzella, Steve McCrea, Mary Migliorelli, Kenji Mori, Brian Mullins, Ziv Navoth, Steve Neiderhauser, Jimmy Neil, Roger Parker, Michael Pokocky, Stefani Quane, Peter Ralston, Basil Rouskas, Charlie Russell, John

Seiffer, Mark Selleck, Phil Shapiro, Dipankar Subba, Tina Tecce, Nerio Vakil, Dan Ward, Colin Warick, Lena West, Bill Wittland, Simon Young, and David Yorka.

As always, my deepest gratitude is on the home front. The Pink kids—Sophia, Eliza, and Saul—are an endless source of wonder, pride, and humility. Although they're still young, I'm happy to say that they all seem headed for high concept, high touch careers—Sophia as a novelist, Eliza as an art teacher, and Saul as the operator of a digger truck. Then there's their mom, Jessica Anne Lerner, who contributed more to this book than she knows. Without her, my mind, my heart, and my life would not be whole.

INDEX

Page numbers in *italic* indicate illustrations.

Abundance, era of, 2, 30–36, 46, 49–50, 247; and arts, 55; and Design, 70; and Meaning, 218; and metaphor, 139; and Play, 187; and Story, 104
Achievement, R-Directed Thinking and, 50
Acting classes, 182–83
Aesthetic imperative, 33
Aesthetics, 76, 252–7. *See also* Design
Affective computing, 164
Agarawal, Kiri, 200
Aggressive behavior, video games and, 194
Aging of populations, 60
Agricultural Age, 49
Allen, Barbara Chandler, 73, 86
Allen, Woody, 13
Alm, Richard, 246
Alphabetic mind, 18–19
Alvarez, Christina, 74
Amateur status, 157
Ambidextrous magazine, 90
America's Army (video game), 188–91, *189*
Amygdalas, 23–25
Analogy, 134
Analysis, left hemisphere and, 22–23, 24, 25
Analytical thinking, storytelling and, 108
Anderson, Sherry Ruth, 60–61
Androgynous minds, 136, 174
Animators at Law, 55
Antonelli, Paola, 72, 81
Appligenics, 44
Aptitude tests, 29, 57–58
Aptitudes, essential, 2, 4, 65–67; Design, 68–97; Empathy, 158–84; Meaning, 216–44; Play, 185–215; Story, 100–128; Symphony, 129–57
Architecture, and environment, 83
Art of Happiness, The, Dalai Lama and Cutler, 241
Artist-in-residence programs, 56
Artists, 55; children as, 68–69
Artress, Lauren, 230
Asenio, Anne, 79
Asia: design schools in, 74; knowledge work in, 36–40, 46, 50, 247; and MBAs, 54; and synthesis, 130
ATG (affluence, technological progress, globalization), 49–50

INDEX

Atkinson, Cliff, *Beyond Bullet Points: Using Microsoft PowerPoint to Create Presentations That Inform, Motivate, and Inspire,* 127
Authentic Happiness, Seligman, 240
Autism, 163, 173
Automation, 40–47, 50, 246; and synthesis, 130
Automobile design, 79
Ayres, Ian, *Why Not?: How to Use Everyday Ingenuity to Solve Problems Big and Small,* 153–54

Baby boomers, 60; and Meaning, 218
Bangle, Chris, 79
Barnes, Jhane, 135
Baron-Cohen, Simon, *The Essential Difference,* 172–73
Batcha, Maribeth, 123–24
Baylis, Trevor, 137, 138
Beauty, creation of, 2, 33, 51
Beethoven's Anvil: Music in Mind and Culture, Benzon, 154
Bellevue Literary Review, 113–14
Benzon, William, *Beethoven's Anvil,* 154
Berk, Lee, 203
Berlin, Isaiah, "The Hedgehog and the Fox," 22
Beyond Bullet Points: Using Microsoft PowerPoint to Create Presentations That Inform, Motivate, and Inspire, Atkinson, 127
Bibliography: Meaning, 240–41; Story, 126–28; Symphony, 154–55
Big-picture thinking, 140–44; Cultural Creatives and, 61; right-brain hemisphere and, 25
Body control, brain hemispheres and, 17–18
Bomeisler, Brian, 131–34, 144–45, 151
Bonnet, James, *Stealing Fire from the Gods: A Dynamic New Story Model for Writers and Filmmakers,* 127
Boundary crossers, 134–36
Brain hemispheres, 3, 13; differences, 17–25; misconceptions about, 15–17. *See also* Left hemisphere of brain; Right hemisphere of brain
Brain imaging project, NIMH, 7–13
Brain journal, 197
Brainstorming, 156–57
Branson, Richard, 141–42
Braverman, Louise, Chelsea Court, 82, *83*
Broca, Paul, 14
Brody, Howard, 112
Bronson, Po, *What Should I Do with My Life?,* 240–41
Buchner, Dan, 98–99
Buck, Kevin, 182
Business: big-picture thinking, 142–43; and Design, 70, 77–81; and laughter, 204; and Play, 187–88; and spirituality, 223–25; and Story, 106–10; video games as, 194–95
"But" out, 238–39
Butterfly ballots, *84,* 84–86

Caesar, Sid, 142
Calling, work as, 226
Campbell, Joseph, 108; *The Hero with a Thousand Faces,* 104–5, 127–28
Canty, Sean, 72
Cards, personal vs. mass-produced, 183–84
Caring professions, 59
Cars, design of, 79
Cartoon captions, 210
Cell phones, 80–81
CHAD (Charter High School for Architecture and Design), 71–74, *73*
Change: Design and, 81–86; Story and, 105
Charon, Rita, 112–14
Chelsea Court, New York City, 82, *83*
Chess competition, man-machine, 42–43, 253–54n24
Children, laughter of, 203
China, engineers, 38
Clinton, Bill, 160
Cole, Megan, 170
Coleridge, Samuel Taylor, xi, 136
College students, and video games, 192
Collins, Jim, 237
Collinson, David, 187, 199
Comedic aptitude test, 58–59
Computer games. *See* Video games
Computer industry, Symphony and, 135–36
Computer programmers, 44, 56; Asian, 36–38
Computer services, outsourced to Asia, 38–39
Computers, 19, 43–44, 246–47; and Empathy, 161, 164; and medical practice, 168–69
Conceptual Age, 2, 49–51, 246–47; Design, 68–97; education for, 74; Empathy, 158–84; essential aptitudes, 65–67; Meaning, 216–44; personal changes, 60; Play, 185–215; Story, 100–128; Symphony, 129–57
Conceptual blending, 137, 150–51
Contextuality, 21–23, 25; Story and, 103–4
Contralateralism, 18
Corpus callosum, 14
Coulehan, Jack, 112
Cousins, Norman, 263n30
Coworkers, empathy with, 181–82
Cox, W. Michael, 246
C-R-A-P-ify (contrast, repetition, alignment, proximity), 97–98
Creative class, 56
Creativity, 2; boundary crossing and, 135; and gender roles, 136
Creators, 49, 50
Csikszentmihalyi, Mihaly, 135, 136, 198; *Flow,* 240

INDEX

Cultural Creatives, 60–61
Customization of consumer products, 94
Cutler, Howard C., *The Art of Happiness,* 241

Dalai Lama (Tenzin Gayatso), 220–21; *The Art of Happiness,* 241
Darwin, Charles, *The Expression of the Emotions in Man and Animals,* 161–62
Davidson, Richard, 220
de Mestral, Georges, 139
Dedicating your work, 243–44
Deep Blue (IBM supercomputer), 42–43
Deep Junior (computer), 42
Delbanco, Andrew, 35
Democracy of Design, 74–77
Denning, Steve, 107–8
Denton, Elizabeth, 223–24
Design, 33–34, 65, 68–97; Empathy and, 168
Design detective, becoming a, 93
Design Within Reach (DWR), 76
Dialogue: The Art of Thinking Together, Isaacs, 155
Differentiator, Story as, 109–11
Digital storytelling, 125
Dissecting a joke, 214
Drawing on the Right Side of the Brain, Edwards, 15, 131, 151
Drawing skills, 131–34, 144–45, 151
Drucker, Peter, 29, 251n1
Duchenne smile, 157–67, *167*
Dwell magazine, 91
DWR (Design Within Reach), 76
Dyslexia, 141

Eames, Charles and Ray, *Powers of Ten,* 154–55
Earnings of international knowledge workers, 38
Easterbrook, Gregg, 219
Eastland Mall, Ohio, 30–31
Eavesdropping, 179–80
Economist, 54
Economy, 1–2; Japanese, 52–53; L-Directed Thinking and, 30, 32–33; Story and, 107; video games and, 195–96
Education: in Design, 71–74; in Empathy, 164–65; in game art and Design, 195–96; in Japan, 53; medical schools and, 170
Edwards, Betty, 15, 129–30, 151; *Drawing on the Right Side of the Brain,* 15, 131, 151
Einstein, Albert, 191
Ekman, Paul, 24–25, 162, 163, 165–66, 178–79
Ellis, Quincy, 73
Emerson, Ralph Waldo, 80
Emotion: Empathy and, 162; facial signals, 165–67; Story and, 103–4
Emotional devices, 81
Emotional expression, right hemisphere and, 25
Emotional intelligence, 246; humor and, 199
Emotional Intelligence, Goleman, 57–58, 161, 162
Emotions Revealed, Ekman, 178–79
Empathizers, 49, 50
Empathy, 3, 52, 66, 158–84; Cultural Creatives and, 61; laughter and, 204; medical practice and, 52, 168, 182; medical students and, 113–14; video games and, 194
Entertainment industry, 55; and spirituality, 60; video games, 195–96
Environment, Design and, 82–83
Epel, Naomi, *The Observation Deck,* 179–80, 243–44
Essential Difference, The, Baron-Cohen, 172–73
Etcoff, Nancy, 163
Eureka (Xerox database), 108
Europe, jobs outsourced to Asia, 39
Evaluation of design, 98–99
Experiences, design of, 89–90
Expression of the Emotions in Man and Animals, The, Darwin, 161–62

Fabel, John, 137
Facial Action Coding System, 24–25
Facial expressions, 162, 165–67; right-brain hemisphere and, 19, 24–25, 163
Facial matching exercise, *10,* 10–11, *11*
Facts, and story, 102–3
Faith, 221
Fear, amygdalas and, 23–24
Ferrieri, Anna Castelli, 81
Financial services, outsourcing of, 38, 54
Firestone, Robert, 225
Fitzgerald, F. Scott, 180
Flawed designs, record of, 89
Florida, Richard, 55–56, 255n7
Flow, Csikszentmihalyi, 240
fMRI (functional magnetic resonance imaging), 9–13; and facial expressions, 163
Fogel, Robert William, 35, 218
Ford, Henry, 187
Ford Motor Company, 186–87
Forrester Research, 39
Forster, E. M., 103
Fortune, 108
Fouconnier, Gilles, 137
"Fourth Great Awakening," 218
Frankl, Viktor, 225, 244; *Man's Search for Meaning,* 216–18, 240, 263n1
Fry, William, 203
Functional magnetic resonance imaging (fMRI), 9–13
Future, 245–47; Design and, 81–86; Empathy and, 161–65

Gallagher, Claire, 72
Gallo, John, 187
Games, 66, 188–96, 204. *See also* Video games
Gee, James Paul, 192–94

INDEX

Gender: and brain function, 198n; and creativity, 136; and Empathy, 172–73
Genealogy studies, 115
General Motors, 53
Gerber, Michael, 142
Giangregorio, Helen, 202
Globalization, 2, 50
Glover, Danny, 243–44
Goleman, Daniel, 142; *Emotional Intelligence,* 57–58, 161, 162
Good to Great, Collins, 237
Government, U.S., and Design, 77
Graphic design, 55, 75–76; C-R-A-P-ify (contrast, repetition, alignment, proximity), 97–98
Gratitude, 235–36
Graves, Michael, 34, 76
Green design movement, 82–83
Greeting cards, personal vs. mass-produced, 183–84

Halpern, Jodi, 168–69
Happiness, 225–27; joyfulness and, 202; prosperity and, 35
Hariri, Ahmad, 24
Harman, Sidney, 142–43
Havelock, Eric, 18
Health, spirituality and, 222–23
Health care: automation and, 45; and big-picture thinking, 143; Design and, 81–82; Empathy and, 168–71
"Hedgehog and the Fox, The" Berlin, 22
Henry, John, *40,* 40–41, 103
Hero with a Thousand Faces, The, Campbell, 104–5, 127–28
Hero's journey, 104–6, 107
Heskett, John, 69–70
High-concept aptitudes, 2–3, 51–53, 61, 65–67; Design, 86; and economy, 56; narrative medicine and, 113; Story, 103; Symphony, 129–57
High-touch aptitudes, 3, 52–53, 59, 61, 65–67, 249n1; narrative medicine and, 113; Story, 103
Holistic medicine, 143
Holistic thinking, design and, 72
Hospital Overnight Program, 52
Hospitals: Design in, 82; labyrinths at, 227–31
How magazine, 91
How to See: A Guide to Reading Our Man-made Environment, Nelson, 155
Howkins, John, 56
Human interactions, 3, 52
Humanity, 67; Empathy and, 165; left-brain hemisphere and, 14
Humor, 66, 188, 196–99, 204; and laughter, 202; measurement of, 211; right hemisphere and, 58

IAPS (International Affective Picture System), 12n
iD magazine, 91
IDEO (design firm), 180–81
Iizuka, Toshiro, 81
Illness, spirituality and, 222–23
Imagination, 58, 130; metaphorical, 140
Imaginative rationality, 139
Immune system, laughter and, 203
Improvements, design of, 90
Incongruity, humor and, 197
India, knowledge workers, 36–38
Industrial Age, 48–49
Information, interpretation of, 22
Information Age, 2, 26, 48–49, 67; brain hemispheres and, 3; and Empathy, 160–61; and Story, 102–3
Information economy, 32–33
Inglehart, Ronald, 218–19
Initiation of hero, 105
Inside Chess, 42
Inspiration board, 154
Integrative medicine, 143
International Affective Picture System (IAPS), 12n
Internet: Empathy evaluations, 177–78; and health care, 45; and law practice, 46; online storytelling, 125
Internet links, following, 152–53
Invention, 51, 211
Inventors, 130, 137–38
"Investigating the Mind" conference, 220–21
IQ (intelligence quotient), 57–59
Isaacs, William, *Dialogue: The Art of Thinking Together,* 155
Isay, David, 120

Japan, economy of, 52–53
Jefferson Scale of Physician Empathy (JSPE), 170–71
Job, empathy on the, 181–82
Jobs, lost to outsourcing, 39
John, Henry, *40,* 40–41, 103
Johnson, Mark, *Metaphors We Live By,* 155
Joke, dissecting a, 214
Journal of the American Medical Association, 113
Joyfulness, 52, 58, 188, 200–205
JSPE (Jefferson Scale of Physician Empathy), 170–71

Kane, Pat, 193
Karlgaard, Rich, 224–25
Kasparov, Garry, *41,* 42–44, 101, 103
Kass, Jared, 238
Kataria, Madan, *185,* 185–86, 200–203, 204, 205, *205,* 209
Kay, Alan, 109
Kearney, A. T., 54

INDEX

Kelley, Tom, *The Ten Faces of Innovation,* 156
Kitchen design, 80
Klamer, Arjo, 107
Knowledge management, 107–8
Knowledge work, 50
Knowledge workers, 2, 29, 46, 48, 141, 251n1; Asian, *36,* 36–39; and economy, 32–33; hero's journey, 105
Koenig, Harold, 223
Koshalek, Richard, 70
Kramnik, Vladimir, 253–54n24

LaBarre, Polly, 33
Labyrinths, 227–31, *229,* 241–42
Lakoff, George, 139, 140; *Metaphors We Live By,* 155
Lander, Eric, 221
Lang, Peter J., 12n
Langer, Ellen, *Mindfulness,* 241
Language, brain hemispheres and, 14, 18, 20–22, 250n11
Laugh for No Reason, Kataria, 209
Laughter, 66, 185–86, 188; benefits of, 203
Laughter: A Scientific Investigation, Provine, 203
Laughter clubs, 186, 200–202, *201,* 204, *205,* 209–10
L-Directed Thinking, 26–27, 48, 50, 61; and abundance, 32–33; IQ tests and, 57; knowledge workers and, 29; male brain and, 173; utility and, 70
Le Guin, Ursula K., 105
Leadership qualities, 58; humor, 198–99
Learned responses, left brain and, 24
Left hemisphere of brain, 3, 13–15, 25, 26–27; and analysis, 22–23, 24; and body control, 17–18; damage to, and facial expressions, 163; dominance of, written language and, 18; and language, 20–21; sequentiality of, 18–19
Legal practice, 45–46; and Empathy, 165
Legal services, outsourced to India, 38
Levy, Frank, 246
Levy-Agresti, Jerre, 22–23
Lies, detection of, 163
Links (Internet), following, 152–53
Literary journals, at medical schools, 113
Literary Mind, The, Turner, 101
Logic, 66; left hemisphere and, 25; Story and, 103
Logical devices, 81
Logotherapy, 217
London Financial Times, 37–38
Longevity, 244
Lopez, Barry, 114
Lutz, Robert, 53, 79

Machover, Todd, 135
MacKenzie, Gordon, 68–69
Magazines, design, 90–91
Magikist sign, *132*
Magnetic resonance imaging (MRI) machines, 8–9
Mankoff, Robert, *The Naked Cartoonist,* 210
Man's Search for Meaning, Frankl, 216–18, 240, 263n1
Markets, new, created by design, 81
Martin, Roger, 78
Master of fine arts (MFA) programs, 54
Mazes, 227–28
MBA programs, 54
McCloskey, Deirdre, 107
McCloud, Scott, *Understanding Comics: The Invisible Art,* 127
McKee, Robert, 106; *Story, Style, and the Principles of Screenwriting,* 126–27
McManus, Chris, *Right Hand Left Hand,* 21, 25–26
Meaning, 66–67, 216–44; makers of, 50; metaphor and, 140; search for, 3, 35, 52, 60, 61; Story and, 104
Medical practice, 45; and big-picture thinking, 143; Design and, 82; Empathy and, 52, 168, 182; and spirituality, 223; Story and, 111–15; video games and, 193–194
Medical schools, 52; and Empathy, 170; and spirituality, 223; and Story, 113–14
Medical services, outsourced to Asia, 38
Meditation, 60, 202, 264n8; labyrinths and, 228
Megatrends, Naisbitt, 249n1
MET (Master of Entertainment Technology) degree, 196
Metaphors, 138–40; log of, 152; right-brain hemisphere and, 21–22
Metaphors We Live By, Lakoff and Johnson, 155
Metropolis magazine, 91
MFA (master of fine arts) programs, 54
Michaels, James, 171
Millionaires, dyslexic, 141
Mimicry, empathy and, 159–60
Mind Reading (CD-ROM), 183
Mindfulness, Langer, 241
Mini-sagas, 119–20
Mitroff, Ian, 223–24
Mok, Clement, 135
Morris, Marney, 99
Moyers, Bill, interviews with, 128
MRI (magnetic resonance imaging) machines, 8–9
Muller, Wayne, *Sabbath: Finding Rest, Renewal, and Delight in Our Busy Lives,* 239–40
Murname, Richard, 246
Museums of design, 94–97
Music, symphonic, listening to, 149–50
Myers, David G., 172
Myth, 108
Mythodrama, 108

INDEX

Naisbitt, John, *Megatrends,* 249n1
Naked Cartoonist, The, Mankoff, 210
Nalebuff, Barry, *Why Not?: How to Use Everyday Ingenuity to Solve Problems Big and Small,* 153–54
"Namaste laugh," 200
Narrative, 2, 51, 66. *See also* Story
Narrative imagining, 101
Narrative medicine, 52, 113–14
National Institute of Mental Health, brain imaging project, 7–13
Nature magazine, and video games, 193
Needleman, Jacob, 218
Negative humor, 199
Negative space, 133, 157
Negroponte, Nicholas, 136
Nelson, George, *How to See: A Guide to Reading Our Man-made Environment,* 155
Neurotheology, 222
New Division of Labor: How Computers Are Creating the Next Job Market, The, Levy and Murname, 246
New York Times, 46, 228; and Lutz, 53; Sperry obituary, 15
Newberg, Andrew, 221–22
Newsstand roundup, 150–51
Newsweek, 43, 223; and automobile design, 79
Ninety years old, 244
No Waste project, 155
Non-Designer's Design Book: Design and Typographic Principles for the Visual Novice, The, Williams, 97–98
Nonverbal communication, laughter as, 204
Nonverbal expression of emotions, 162–63
Norman, Don, 76; *Things That Make Us Smart,* 103
Not So Big House, The, Susanka, 93
Notebooks: for design, 89–90; metaphor log, 152
Nuovo, Franke, 74–75
Nurses, shortage of, 59
Nursing profession, 171

O magazine, 91
Observation Deck, The, Epel, 179–80, 243–44
Ofri, Danielle, 114
Ohga, Norio, 78
Olivier, Richard, 108
One Story, 123–24
Opening line, Story from, 124
Organizational storytelling movement, 107
Organizations, and humor, 199
Ornstein, Robert, 21–22; *The Right Mind,* 16
Outsourcing, 37–40, 46
Outsourcing empathy, 183–84

Pattern recognition, 2, 50, 51, 130, 142; video games and, 194
Pay, of international knowledge workers, 38
People skills, 246
Perception, tests of, 11–12
Persinger, Michael, 221
Personal narrative, 115
Personal satisfaction, R-Directed Thinking and, 50
Persuasion, 66; Story and, 107
Pesce, Gaetano, 94
Peters, Tom, 44, 78
Philadelphia, public schools, 73–74
Photo, Story from, 125
Physicians, 45; and video games, 193. *See also* Medical practice
Picard, Rosalind, 164
Piedmont, Ralph, 237–38
Pink, Daniel H., *167;* self-portrait, *129,* 129–33, 144–45, *145*
Platek, Steven, 160
Play, 66, 185–215
Playground, going back to, 213–14
Poets, as systems thinkers, 143
Pollard, Cayce, 135
Portfolios, 4, 67; Design, 87–99; Empathy, 175–84; Meaning, 233–44; Play, 207–15; Story, 117–28; Symphony, 147–57
Positive psychology movement, 225
Postmaterialism, 219
Postrel, Virginia, 33, 76, 252n7
Potomac Yards Mall, Virginia, 31–32
Powers of Ten, Eames and Eames, 154–55
Prayer, 222
Presidential election, 2000, 83–85
Print magazine, 91
Problems and solutions, 153–54
Problem-solving, video games and, 194
Professions: IQ and, 58; L-Directed, 44–47
Provine, Robert, *Laughter: A Scientific Investigation,* 203
Psychology, and happiness, 225
Public, Story from, 126
Public housing, Design in, 82
Public schools: Design in, 82; design studies, 73–74
Publications, Design magazines, 90–91. *See also* Reading material

Quane, Stefani, 142
Quartz, Steven, 222

Rainbow Project, 58–59, 210
Rashid, Karim, 33, 92
Ray, Paul, 60–61
R-Directed Thinking, 26–27, 30, 39–40, 46, 49, 50–51, 61; abundance and, 33–35; and creativity, 137–38; Cultural Creatives and, 60–61; female brain and, 173; games for, 215; in medical practice, 113–14; and significance in Design, 70; synthesis, 130

INDEX

Reading material: Design, 90–91; Meaning, 240–41; Story, 126–28; Symphony, 154–55
Real estate sales, and Story, 109–10
Real Simple magazine, 91
Reasoning modes, 14, 26
Recorded stories, 120–21
Reese's Peanut Butter Cups, 137
Reingold, Mike, 71
Relationships: big picture and, 140–44; in drawing, 131, 133–34, 151; laughter and, 203–4; Symphony and, 134
Religion, and health, 222–23
Restak, Richard, 163
Return of hero, 105
Ricard, Mathieu, 221
Right Hand Left Hand, McManus, 21, 25–26
Right hemisphere of brain, 3, 13, 14–15; and body control, 17–18; and contextuality, 21–23; and facial expressions, 163; and humor, 197–98; ideas of, 15–17; and language, 20–21; simultaneity of, 19; specialties, 25; and synthesis, 22; thinking mode, 26–27
Right Mind, The, Ornstein, 16
Right Side of the Brain, 15, 131, 151
Role-playing games, 194
Rules-based medicine, 168–69

Sabbath: Finding Rest, Renewal, and Delight in Our Busy Lives, Muller, 239–40
Saboteur, right brain as, 16–17
Sagmeister, Stefan, 90
Sala, Fabio, 198–99
SAT (Scholastic Aptitude Test): alternative test, 58–59; revision, 59
Satisfaction, personal, R-Directed Thinking and, 50
SAT-ocracy, 29–30, 57
Savior, right brain as, 15–16
Schank, Roger C., 102
School, going back to, 213–14
Schools, public, design in, 82
Schwab, Charles, 141–42
Scrapbooking movement, 115
Self-assessments, 177–78, 237–38
Self-portrait, *129,* 129–33, 144–45, *145;* five-line, 151, *151*
Self-understanding, 66; metaphor and, 140; Story and, 115
Seligman, Martin E. P., 225–27, 235–36; *Authentic Happiness,* 240
Sequentiality of left brain hemisphere, 18–19, 25
"Serious Play" technique, 188
Shammi, Prabitha, 197–98
Shaywitz, Sally, 141
Shopping malls, 30–32
Significance of design, 70
Simon, Paul, 168
Simultaneity of right-brain hemisphere, 19
Six senses, 2, 4, 61, 65–67; Design, 68–97; Empathy, 158–84; Meaning, 216–44; Play, 185–215; Story, 100–128; Symphony, 129–57
Small, David, 94
Smiles, interpretation of, 166–67, *167*
Smith, Paul, 79
Social dexterity, 58
Society, 1–2; L-Directed Thinking and, 29–30
Software, 56; to write software, 44
Solutions and problems, 153–54
Sperry, Roger W., 14–15, 17, 22–23
Spiritual Audit of Corporate America, A, Mitroff and Denton, 223–24
Spiritual fulfillment, 67
Spirituality, 219–25; medical schools and, 52
Stealing Fire from the Gods: A Dynamic New Story Model for Writers and Filmmakers, Bonnet, 127
Sternberg, Robert, 210; Rainbow Project, 58–59
Stewart, Thomas A., 199
Story, 65–66, 100–128; Empathy and, 168
Story: Substance, Structure, Style, and the Principles of Screenwriting, McKee, 106, 126–27
StoryCorps, 120–21
StoryQuest, 108
Storytelling festivals, 121–23
Streep, Meryl, 173
Stress hormones, laughter and, 203
Stuss, Donald, 197–98
Success, prediction of, 57–59
Success, thinking modes and, 29–30
Suffering, and Meaning, 217
Susanka, Sarah, *The Not So Big House,* 93
Sustainability principles in design, 82–83
Sutton-Smith, Brian, 187
Swain, Chris, 195
Sympathy, and empathy, 159
Symphonic music, 149–50
Symphony, 66, 129–57; Empathy and, 168; and video games, 194
Synthesis, 66, 130; Cultural Creatives and, 61; right-brain hemisphere and, 22, 24, 25
Systematizing, 173
Systems thinkers, entrepreneurs as, 142

Target (store), 31, 76
Teaching of design, 71–74
Technology, 2; and Design, 70
Telling Lies, Ekman, 179
Ten Faces of Innovation, The, Kelley, 156
Tenzin Gayatso, Dalai Lama, 220–21; *The Art of Happiness,* 241
Terkel, Studs, 226
Tharp, Twyla, 139

INDEX

Things That Make Us Smart, Norman, 103
Third Industrial Revolution, 94
Thompson, Paul, 78
Thorson, James, 211
Thought-free laughter, 202
Time management, 243
Tinti, Hannah, 123–24
Toilet brush, *34*
Tolzman, David, 229
Transcendence, 67; quest for, 35, 60
Tuck, Andy, 135
Turner, Mark, 137; *The Literary Mind,* 101
TV Guide, 60
20-10 Test, 237

Understanding Comics: The Invisible Art, McCloud, 127
United Kingdom: creative sector, 56; design students, 74; job loss, 39; Story in, 108
Urban planning, 244n7
USA Today, 195
Utility of design, 70

Velcro, 139
Verditas, 230
Video games, 188–96, 212–13
Vinge, Vernor, 44
Volunteering, 184

Wall Street Journal, 45, 169, 188
Wanders, Marcel, 157
Wardynski, Casey, 189–90
Wasow, Omar, 136
Watson, James, 13
Web sites: gaming, 212–13; labyrinths, 241–42; legal, 46; medical, 45
Wernicke, Carl, 14
What Should I Do with My Life?, Bronson, 240–41
What Video Games Have to Teach Us About Learning and Literacy, Gee, 193
White-collar jobs, outsourced, 39
White-Hammond, Gloria, 135
Who Moved My Cheese?, 227
Why Not?: How to Use Everyday Ingenuity to Solve Problems Big and Small, Nalebuff and Ayres, 153–54
Williams, Robin, *The Non-Designer's Design Book: Design and Typographic Principles for the Visual Novice,* 97–98
Wilson, Charlie, 55
Wilson, Steve, 204
Winfrey, Oprah, 160
Wolfe, David, 60
Women, and Empathy, 172
Work, 164; as calling, 226; dedicating your, 243–44
Workplace: empathy in, 181–82; humor in, 199; laughter clubs, 186; laughter in, 204; spirituality in, 223–24
World, change of, Design and, 81–86
World Bank, and knowledge management, 107–8
World Laughter Day, 209–10
World Values Survey, 219
Writing, mini-sagas, 119
Written language, and left-brain dominance, 18

Yawning, contagious, 159–60
Yeats, William Butler, 164
Yoga, 60

Zaltman, Gerald, 140

A SPECIAL EXCERPT FROM

To Sell Is Human:
The Surprising Truth About Moving Others

BY DANIEL H. PINK

WE'RE ALL IN SALES NOW

Norman Hall shouldn't exist. But here he is—flesh, blood, and bow tie—on a Tuesday afternoon, sitting in a downtown San Francisco law office explaining to two attorneys why they could really use a few things to spruce up their place.

With a magician's flourish, Hall begins by removing from his bag what looks like a black wand. He snaps his wrist and—voilà!—out bursts a plume of dark feathers. And not just any feathers, he reveals.

"These are . . . Male. Ostrich. Feathers."

This $21.99 feather duster is the best on the market, he tells them in a soft-spoken but sonorous voice. It's perfect for cleaning picture frames, blinds, and any other item whose crevices accumulate dust.

Penelope Chronis, who runs the small immigration firm with her partner in law and in life, Elizabeth Kreher, peers up from her desk and shakes her head. Not interested.

Hall shows her Kitchen Brush #300, a sturdy white and green scrub brush.

They already have one.

Onto Chronis's desk he tosses some "microfiber cloths" and an "anti-fog cloth for car windows and bathroom mirrors."

No thanks.

Hall is seventy-five years old with patches of white hair on the sides of his head and not much in between. He sports conservative eyeglasses and a mustache in which the white hairs have finally overtaken the brown ones after what looks like years of struggle. He wears dark brown pants, a dress shirt with thin blue stripes, a chestnut-colored V-neck sweater, and a red paisley bow tie. He looks like a dapper and mildly eccentric professor. He is indefatigable.

On his lap is a leather three-ring binder with about two dozen pages of product pictures he's clipped and inserted into clear plastic sheets. "This is a straightforward spot remover," he tells Chronis and Kreher when he gets to the laundry page. "These you spray on before throwing something into the washing machine." The lawyers are unmoved. So Hall goes big: moth deodorant blocks. "I sell more of these than anything in my catalog combined," he says. "They kill moths, mold, mildew, and odor." Only $7.49.

Nope.

Then, turning the page to a collection of toilet brushes and bowl cleaners, he smiles, pauses for a perfect beat, and says, "And these are my romantic items."

Still nothing.

But when he gets to the stainless-steel sponges, he elicits a crackle of interest that soon becomes a ripple of desire. "These are wonderful, very unusual. They're scrubber pads, but with a great difference," he says. Each offers eight thousand inches of continuous stainless steel coiled forty thousand times. You can stick them in the dishwasher. A box of three is just $15.

Sold.

Soon he reaches one of his pricier products, an electrostatic carpet sweeper. "It has four terminal brushes made out of natural bristle and nylon. As it goes along the floor, it develops a static current so it can pick up sugar and salt from a bare wood floor," he explains. "It's my favorite wedding gift." Another exquisitely timed pause. "It beats the hell out of a toaster."

Chronis and Kreher go for that, too.

When about twenty minutes have elapsed, and Hall has reached the final sheet in his homemade catalog, he scribbles the $149.96 sale in his order book. He hands a carbon copy of the order to Chronis, saying, "I hope we're still friends after you read this."

He chats for a few moments, then gathers his binder and his bags, and rises to leave. "Thank you very much indeed," he says. "I'll bring everything forthwith tomorrow."

Norman Hall is a Fuller Brush salesman. And not just any Fuller Brush salesman.

He is . . . The. Last. One.

IF YOU'RE YOUNGER than forty or never spent much time in the United States, you might not recognize the Fuller Brush Man. But if you're an American of a certain age, you know that once you couldn't avoid him. Brigades of salesmen, their sample cases stuffed with brushes, roamed middle-class neighborhoods, climbed the front steps, and announced, "I'm your Fuller Brush Man." Then, offering a free vegetable scrubber known as a Handy Brush as a gift, they tried to get what quickly became known as "a foot in the door."

It all began in 1903, when an eighteen-year-old Nova Scotia farm boy named Alfred Fuller arrived in Boston to begin his career. He was, by his own admission, "a country bumpkin, overgrown and awkward, unsophisticated and virtually unschooled"*—and he was promptly fired from his first three jobs. But one of his brothers landed him a sales position at the Somerville Brush and Mop Company—and days before he turned twenty, young Alfred found his calling. "I began without much preparation and I had no special qualifications, as far as I knew," he told a journalist years later, "but I discovered I could sell those brushes."†

After a year of trudging door-to-door peddling Somerville products, Fuller began, er, bristling at working for someone else. So he set up a small workshop to manufacture brushes of his own. At night, he oversaw the mini-factory. By day he walked the streets selling what he'd produced. To his amazement, the small enterprise grew. When he needed a few more salespeople to expand to additional products and new territories, he placed an ad in a publication called *Everybody's Magazine.* Within a few weeks, the Nova Scotia bumpkin had 260 new salespeople, a nationwide business, and the makings of a cultural icon.

By the late 1930s, Fuller's sales force had swelled to more than five thousand people. In 1937 alone, door-to-door Fuller dealers gave away some 12.5 million Handy Brushes. By 1948, eighty-three hundred North American salesmen were selling cleaning and hair "brushes to 20 million families in the United States and Canada," according to *The New Yorker.* That same year, Fuller salesmen, all of them independent dealers working on straight commission, made nearly fifty million

*Alfred C. Fuller (as told to Hartzell Spence), *A Foot in the Door: The Life Appraisal of the Original Fuller Brush Man* (New York: McGraw-Hill, 1960), 2.

†John Bainbridge, "May I Just Step Inside?" *The New Yorker,* November 13, 1948.

house-to-house sales calls in the United States—a country that at the time had fewer than forty-three million households. By the early 1960s, Fuller Brush was, in today's dollars, a billion-dollar company.*

What's more, the Fuller Man became a fixture in popular culture—Lady Gagaesque in his ubiquity. In the Disney animated version of "The Three Little Pigs," which won an Academy Award in 1933, how did the Big Bad Wolf try to gain entry into the pigs' houses? He disguised himself as a Fuller Brush Man. How did Donald Duck earn his living for a while? He sold Fuller Brushes. In 1948 Red Skelton, then one of Hollywood's biggest names, starred in *The Fuller Brush Man*, a screwball comedy in which a hapless salesman is framed for a crime—and must clear his name, find the culprit, win the girl, and sell a few Venetian blind brushes along the way. Just two years later, Hollywood made essentially the same movie with the same plot—this one called *The Fuller Brush Girl*, with the lead role going to Lucille Ball, an even bigger star. As time went on, you could find the Fuller Brush Man not only on your doorstep, but also in *New Yorker* cartoons, the jokes of TV talk-show hosts, and the lyrics of Dolly Parton songs.

What a Fuller Man did was virtuosic. "The Fuller art of opening doors was regarded by connoisseurs of cold-turkey peddling in somewhat the same way that balletomanes esteem a performance of the Bolshoi—as pure poetry," *American Heritage* wrote. "In the hands of a deft Fuller dealer, brushes became not homely commodities but specialized tools obtainable nowhere else."† Yet he‡ was also virtuous, his constant presence in neighborhoods turning him neighborly. "Fuller Brush Men pulled teeth, massaged headaches, delivered babies, gave

*"The Ups and Downs of the Fuller Brush Co.," *Fortune,* 1938, available at http://features.blogs.fortune.cnn.com/2012/02/26/the-fuller-brush-co-fortune-1938/; Gerald Caron, "The Fuller Brush Man," *American Heritage*, August–September 1986; Bainbridge, "May I Just Step Inside?"

†Carson, "The Fuller Brush Man."

‡A Fuller dealer was almost always a "he," although in the 1960s, when the company launched a line of cosmetics, it recruited a group of saleswomen it called Fullerettes.

emetics for poison, prevented suicides, discovered murders, helped arrange funerals, and drove patients to hospitals."*

And then, with the suddenness of an unexpected knock on the door, the Fuller Brush Man—the very embodiment of twentieth-century selling—practically disappeared. Think about it. Wherever in the world you live, when was the last time a salesperson with a sample case rang your doorbell? In February 2012, the Fuller Brush Company filed for reorganization under the U.S. bankruptcy law's Chapter 11. But what surprised people most wasn't so much that Fuller had declared bankruptcy, but that it was still around to declare anything.

Norman Hall, however, remains at it. In the mornings, he boards an early bus near his home in Rohnert Park, California, and rides ninety minutes to downtown San Francisco. He begins his rounds at about 9:30 a.m. and walks five to six miles each day, up and down the sharply inclined streets of San Francisco. "Believe me," he said during one of the days I accompanied him, "I know all the level areas and the best bathrooms."

When Hall began in the 1970s, several dozen other Fuller Brush Men were also working in San Francisco. Over time, that number dwindled. And now Hall is the only one who remains. These days when he encounters a new customer and identifies himself as a Fuller Man, he's often met with surprise. "No kidding!" people will say. One afternoon when I was with him, Hall introduced himself to the fifty-something head of maintenance at a clothing store. "Really?" the man cried. "My father was a Fuller Brush salesman in Oklahoma!" (Alas, this prospect didn't buy anything, even though Hall pointed out that the mop propped in the corner of the store came from Fuller.)

After forty years, Hall has a garage full of Fuller items, but his

---

*Fuller, *A Foot in the Door*, 197–98.

connection to the struggling parent company is minimal. He's on his own. In recent years, he's seen his customers fade, his orders decline, and his profits shrink. People don't have time for a salesman. They want to order things online. And besides, brushes? Who cares? As an accommodation to reality, Hall has cut back the time he devotes to chasing customers. He now spends only two days a week toting his leather binder through San Francisco's retail and business district. And when he unloads his last boar bristle brush and hangs up his bow tie, he knows he won't be replaced. "I don't think people want to do this kind of work anymore," he told me.

Two months after Fuller's bankruptcy announcement, *Encyclopædia Britannica*, which rose to prominence because of its door- to-door salesmen, shut down production of its print books. A month later, Avon—whose salesladies once pressed doorbells from Birmingham to Bangkok—fired its CEO and sought survival in the arms of a corporate suitor. These collapses seemed less startling than inevitable, the final movement in the chorus of doom that, for many years, has been forecasting selling's demise.

The song, almost always invoking Arthur Miller's 1949 play *Death of a Salesman*, goes something like this: In a world where anybody can find anything with just a few keystrokes, intermediaries like salespeople are superfluous. They merely muck up the gears of commerce and make transactions slower and more expensive. Individual consumers can do their own research and get buying advice from their social networks. Large companies can streamline their procurement processes with sophisticated software that pits vendors against one another and secures the lowest price. In the same way that cash machines thinned the ranks of bank tellers and digital switches made telephone operators all but obsolete, today's technologies have rendered salesmen and saleswomen irrelevant. As we rely ever more on websites and smartphones to locate and purchase what we need, salespeople themselves—not to mention the very act of selling—will be swept into history's dustbin.*

Norman Hall is, no doubt, the last of his kind. And the Fuller Brush Company itself could be gone for good before you reach the last page of this book. But we should hold off making any wider funeral preparations. All those death notices for sales and those who do it are off the mark. Indeed, if one were to write anything about selling in the second decade of the twenty-first century, it ought to be a birth announcement.

---

*See, for instance, James Ledbetter, "Death of a Salesman. Of Lots of Them, Actually," *Slate*, September 21, 2010. Available at http://www.slate.com/articles/business/moneybox/2010/09/death_of_a_salesman_of_lots_of_them_actually.html.

Daniel H. Pink is the author of *A Whole New Mind*, the long running *New York Times* bestseller that has been translated into twenty-four languages. The author of two other bestselling books, *The Adventures of Johnny Bunko* and *Free Agent Nation*, Pink has contributed to the *New York Times*, *Harvard Business Review*, *Fast Company*, and *Wired*. He also lectures to corporations, associations, and universities around the world on economic transformation and the workplace. Pink lives in Washington, D.C., with his family. He invites readers to e-mail him at dhp@danpink.com.

Daniel H. Pink has been thinking about you.

About how you can be more creative.

How you can motivate yourself and the people in your life.

And how to sell your product, your idea, or yourself more effectively—and more ethically.

He's pulled together some cutting-edge scientific research and translated it into practical, human terms.

Because Pink understands that as the world changes, you must, too. So he writes books that give you the world—along with the tools and tips you need to work smarter and live better.

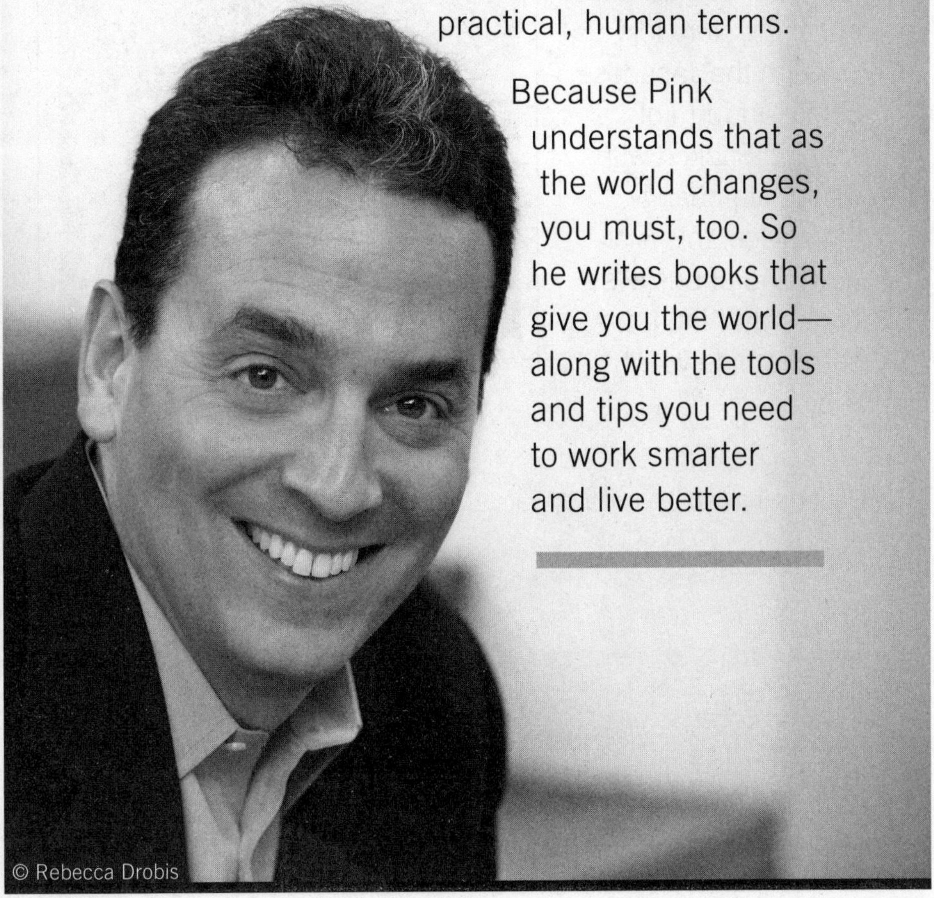

© Rebecca Drobis

The power of selling: It's in all of us.

Today 1 in 9 people are in sales. But dig deeper and a startling truth emerges: So are the other eight. That's right. No matter what we do for a living, we're all in sales now. But thanks to a cluster of economic forces, sales isn't what it used to be. The sooner you understand this, the better prepared you'll be for the challenges ahead.

AUTHOR OF THE *NEW YORK TIMES*–BESTSELLING
DRIVE AND *A WHOLE NEW MIND*

DANIEL H. PINK

TO SELL IS HUMAN

THE SURPRISING TRUTH ABOUT MOVING OTHERS

In *To Sell Is Human*, Daniel H. Pink shows how everyone who expends effort moving others—convincing clients, colleagues, students and family members—is in sales. He explores the new science of selling, details the essential qualities we need to master to sell effectively, and lays out the key abilities for thriving in this new environment.

"Artfully blend(s) anecdotes, insights, and studies from the social sciences into a frothy blend of utility and entertainment."

—***Bloomberg***

"A fresh look at the art and science of sales" —**Forbes.com**

T323-0613